D1615339

Refugees and expellees in post-war Germany

Manchester University Press

Refugees and expellees in post-war Germany

Ian Connor

Manchester University Press
Manchester and New York
distributed exclusively in the USA by Palgrave

Published by Manchester University Press
Oxford Road, Manchester M13 9NR, UK
and Room 400, 175 Fifth Avenue, New York, NY 10010, USA
www.manchesteruniversitypress.co.uk

Distributed exclusively in the USA by
Palgrave, 175 Fifth Avenue, New York,
NY 10010, USA

Distributed exclusively in Canada by
UBC Press, University of British Columbia, 2029 West Mall,
Vancouver, BC, Canada V6T 1Z2

British Library Cataloguing-in-Publication Data
A catalogue record for this book is available from the British Library

Library of Congress Cataloging-in-Publication Data applied for

ISBN 978 0 7190 6886 7 *hardback*

First published 2007

16 15 14 13 12 11 10 09 08 07 10 9 8 7 6 5 4 3 2 1

Typeset in Sabon by
Koinonia, Manchester
Printed in Great Britain by
Biddles Ltd, King's Lynn, Norfolk

Contents

List of tables

List of plates

Acknowledgements

I would like to express my thanks to the staff at the many archives where I carried out research in connection with this book. I owe a particular debt of thanks to the supervisor of my doctoral thesis, Professor Volker Berghahn, who first stimulated my interest in the issue of German refugees and expellees. I would also like to thank Professor Friedrich Kahlenberg for his support during my research visits to the *Bundesarchiv* in Koblenz. I am grateful to my colleagues in the German Section at the University of Ulster, Professor Pól Ó Dochartaigh and Dr Nicholas Railton, and a former colleague, Michael Jones, for their encouragement. I am also indebted to Professor John Gillespie for supporting my application for a period of research leave to complete this book. I would also like to express my gratitude to the anonymous referees appointed by Manchester University Press for their constructive observations and criticisms. I also want to take this opportunity to thank the staff at Manchester University Press for their excellent support and advice.

I am very grateful for the generous financial support I have received in connection with this book, in particular a Research Leave Award from the Arts and Humanities Research Board in 2001–02. I would also like to acknowledge the grants I was awarded by the Elisabeth Barker Fund of the British Academy and the German Academic Exchange Service.

I would like to thank the *Bundesarchiv* in Koblenz for permission to reproduce a number of copyright photographs. I am also very grateful to Sage Publications Ltd for permission to reprint short passages from my article 'German Refugees and the SPD in Schleswig-Holstein, 1945–1950', *European History Quarterly*, Vol. 36 (2), pp. 173–99. I am also grateful to Berg Publishers for giving me permission to reproduce short extracts from my chapter entitled 'The Refugees and the Currency Reform', in I. Turner (ed.), *Reconstruction in Post-War Germany: British Occupation Policy and the Western Zones, 1945–1955* (Oxford 1989), pp. 301–24. I would also like to thank Oldenbourg Verlag in Munich for granting me permission to reproduce Table 2.2 from S. Schraut, *Flüchtlingsaufnahme in Württemberg-Baden 1945–1949*, and the *Bundesarchiv* in Berlin for allowing me to reproduce Tables 7.1 and 7.2, originally published in M. Wille, 'Compelling the Assimilation of Expellees in the Soviet Zone of Occupation and the GDR', in P. Ther and A. Siljak (eds), *Redrawing Nations: Ethnic Cleansing in East-Central Europe, 1944–1948* (Lanham, Boulder, New York and Oxford 2001). In one instance I have been unable to trace the copyright owner and anyone claiming copyright should contact the author.

Finally, I owe a special debt of gratitude to my parents, Graham and Margaret Connor, my wife Cheryl and our children, David and Jenny.

List of abbreviations

Abt.	Abteilung (Department)
ACDP	Archiv für Christlich-Demokratische Politik, Sankt-Augustin
ACSP	Archiv für Christlich-Soziale Politik der Hanns-Seidel Stiftung, Munich
ADL	Archiv des Deutschen Liberalismus der Friedrich-Naumann-Stiftung, Gummersbach
AdsD	Archiv der sozialen Demokratie der Friedrich-Ebert-Stiftung, Bonn
ADW	Archiv des Diakonischen Werkes der Evangelischen Kirche in Deutschland, Berlin
AHL	Archiv der Hansestadt Lübeck
AHR	American Historical Review
APZ	Aus Politik und Zeitgeschichte
BA	Bundesarchiv, Koblenz
BHE	Block der Heimatvertriebenen und Entrechteten (Bloc of Expellees and Dispossessed Persons)
BHStA	Bayerisches Hauptstaatsarchiv, Munich
BLA	Bayerisches Landtagsarchiv, Munich
BSL	Bayerisches Statistisches Landesamt
BvD	Bund der vertriebenen Deutschen (League of German Expellees)
CDU	Christlich-Demokratische Union (Christian Democratic Union)
CSU	Christlich-Soziale Union (Christian Social Union)
DA	Deutschland Archiv
DCV	Archiv des Deutschen Caritasverbandes, Freiburg im Breisgau
DCSVP	Deutsche Christlich-Soziale Volkspartei (German Christian Social People's Party)
DG	Deutsche Gemeinschaft (German Association)
DP	Deutsche Partei (German Party)
DRP	Deutsche Rechtspartei (German Right-Wing Party)
DSAP	Deutsche Sozialdemokratische Arbeiterpartei in der Tschechoslowakei (German Social Democratic Workers' Party in Czechoslovakia)

DVP	Demokratische Volkspartei (Democratic People's Party)
DZP	Deutsche Zentrumspartei (German Centre Party)
EHQ	European History Quarterly
EHW	Das Hilfswerk der Evangelischen Kirche in Deutschland (Protestant Church Welfare Organisation in Germany)
EZA	Evangelisches Zentralarchiv, Berlin
FDJ	Freie Deutsche Jugend (Free German Youth)
FDP	Freie Demokratische Partei (Free Democratic Party)
FO	Foreign Office
FRG	German Federal Republic
GB	Gesamtdeutscher Block (All German Bloc)
GDP	Gesamtdeutsche Partei (All German Party)
GDR	German Democratic Republic
GH	German History
GNP	Gross National Product
GP	German Politics
GStA	Geheimes Staatarchiv, Munich
HstA	Nordrhein-Westfälisches Hauptstaatsarchiv, Düsseldorf
IfZ	Institut für Zeitgeschichte, Munich
JCH	Journal of Contemporary History
KA	Kriegsarchiv, Munich
KH	Kirchliche Hilfsstelle
KPD	Kommunistische Partei Deutschlands (Communist Party of Germany)
KRO	Kreis Resident Officer
LDP	Liberal-Demokratische Partei (Liberal Democratic Party)
LDPD	Liberal-Demokratische Partei Deutschlands (Liberal Democratic Party of Germany)
LKA	Landeskirchliches Archiv, Nuremberg
LRA	Landratsamt
LS	Landsmannschaft Schlesien
LSH	Landesarchiv Schleswig-Holstein, Schleswig
LV	Landesverband
NB	Neubürgerbund (New Citizens' Alliance)
NG	Notgemeinschaft (Emergency Association)
NHStA	Niedersächsisches Hauptstaatsarchiv, Hanover
NL	Nachlaß
NLP	Niedersächsische Landespartei (Regional Party of Lower Saxony)
NPD	Nationaldemokratische Partei Deutschlands (National Democratic Party of Germany)
NSDAP	Nationalsozialistische Deutsche Arbeiterpartei (National Socialist Workers' Party of Germany)
OA	Oberbayerisches Archiv

OMGB	Office of Military Government for Bavaria, United States
OMGUS	Office of Military Government for Germany, United States
PRO	National Archives (formerly known as Public Record Office), Kew
PSQ	Political Science Quarterly
PV	Politische Vierteljahresschrift
SBZ	Sowjetische Besatzungszone (Soviet Occupation Zone)
SdP	Sudetendeutsche Partei (Sudeten German Party)
SED	Sozialistische Einheitspartei Deutschlands (Socialist Unity Party of Germany)
S-H	Schleswig-Holstein
SMAD	Sowjetische Militäradministration in Deutschland (Soviet Military Administration in Germany)
SPD	Sozialdemokratische Partei Deutschlands (Social Democratic Party of Germany)
SR	Slavic Review
SRP	Sozialistische Reichspartei (Socialist Reich Party)
SSW	Südschleswigscher Wählerverband (South Schleswig Voters' League)
StA	Staatsarchiv München
StD	Stadtarchiv München
VdgB	Vereinigung der gegenseitigen Bauernhilfe (Association for Mutual Farmers' Assistance)
VdL	Verband der Landsmannschaften (Association of Homeland Societies)
VfZ	Vierteljahrshefte für Zeitgeschichte
WAV	Wirtschaftliche Aufbau-Vereiningung (Economic Reconstruction Union)
WEU	Western Economic Union
ZfS	Zeitschrift für Soziologie
ZvD	Zentralverband vertriebener Deutschen (Central Association of German Expellees)
ZVU	Zentralverwaltung für deutsche Umsiedler (Central Agency for German Resettlers)

Introduction

The conclusion of the Second World War in May 1945 did not bring an end to the suffering of the civilian population in Germany or the other European countries involved in the conflict. This was particularly true of the German refugees and expellees who fled or were expelled from their homelands in Eastern and Central Europe from the autumn of 1944 onwards. They flooded into the remains of the former Reich, now divided into four occupation zones, each administered by one of the wartime Allies – the United States, Soviet Union, United Kingdom and France. By April 1949 no fewer than 12 million German refugees and expellees were resident in the four Occupation Zones. They had arrived in a country devastated by the effects of the war and the task of integrating them was one of the most daunting facing the Allied and German authorities. In fact, both the Western Allies and the Soviet Union harboured deep fears that the poverty stricken refugees and expellees would become a source of political radicalisation in post-war German society. For example, a British Military Government official predicted in the autumn of 1948 that 'unless action is taken to improve the conditions of refugees ... there will be a large body of discontented persons ... who will either rise in revolt or become facile tools in the hands of political agitators'.[1]

The early post-war years witnessed the publication of many works on the refugee problem in the German Federal Republic (FRG). Some focused on the economic integration of the newcomers in the individual federal states (*Bundesländer*),[2] while a number of sociological studies of the refugee question were also undertaken.[3] Several major research projects were financed by the West German Government. One study, edited by Theodor Schieder and published in five volumes between 1953 and 1961,[4] documented the harrowing experiences of the refugees and expellees during their flight or expulsion from their homelands, while the other, edited by Eugen Lemberg and Friedrich Edding and entitled *Die Vertriebenen in Westdeutschland,* appeared in three volumes in 1959.[5]

During the 1960s and 1970s interest in the refugee problem dwindled in West Germany. This can be partly attributed to an assumption that the economic and political integration of the refugees and expellees had been largely achieved. However, it was also a product of a change in the political climate, both domestically and internationally. Against the background of the efforts of Federal Chancellor Willy Brandt to reach an accommodation with the Communist regimes in Eastern Europe, public debate concentrated on German responsibility for the Holocaust and it would have been politically unacceptable to depict German expellees as victims of the Second World War.

The release of archival material from the mid-1970s onwards led to an upsurge in interest in the refugee problem, especially among younger West German historians. This resulted in the publication of a large number of regional and local studies during the 1980s and 1990s such as Siegfried Schier's monograph on Lübeck,[6] Uwe Weiher's volume on Bremen,[7] Evelyn Glensk's book on Hamburg[8] and Angelika Hohenstein's work on Dannenberg (Lower Saxony).[9] The results of these and other studies indicated that the integration process was more problematic than had previously been acknowledged and this conclusion was confirmed by Paul Lüttinger's empirical study which showed that the economic position of the expellees in 1971 still lagged behind that of the indigenous inhabitants.[10] Research during the 1980s and 1990s also focused on relations between the native and refugee populations, notably Rainer Schulze's work on Celle[11] and Andreas Lüttig's volume on Wewelsburg.[12] Another feature of this period was the employment of new research methods, especially oral history, where pioneering work was undertaken by Lutz Niethammer and Alexander von Plato.[13]

The fall of the Berlin Wall in November 1989 and the collapse of the Communist regimes in Eastern Europe represented a major turning point in research perspectives on the refugee problem. Western scholars were for the first time able to gain unrestricted access to archival material located in the former German Democratic Republic (GDR). Even among East German historians, research on the expellees in the GDR was at an early stage since it had been politically unacceptable to discuss the role of the Red Army in their flight or expulsion from their homelands. However, since the mid-1990s a number of regional studies have appeared, including Torsten Mehlhase's monograph on Saxony-Anhalt[14] and two volumes on Saxony, one by Stefan Donth[15] and the other by Norbert Schrammek.[16] A number of other major works have been published focusing on the GDR as a whole, in particular a monumental study by Michael Schwartz.[17] There is also an important three-volume collection of documents edited by Manfred Wille.[18]

The opening of archives in Eastern Europe has also paved the way for comparative studies. One of the pioneering works was Philipp Ther's monograph comparing government policy towards the expellees in the GDR and Poland, as well as relations between the native and refugee populations in both countries.[19] Ther also published an article comparing the integration of expellees in Poland, the FRG and the GDR.[20] Meanwhile, Pertti Ahonen has argued that the existence of expellee associations in West Germany and Finland promoted the newcomers' integration into their new homeland, while the decision of the Socialist Unity Party of Germany (SED) to outlaw such organisations impeded this process in the GDR.[21] In addition, Paul Erker has edited a volume containing contributions on the issue of Equalisation of Burdens in both the German states.[22]

The fall of the Communist regimes in Eastern Europe has also stimulated debate about issues of national identity and collective memory. Robert Moeller has undertaken pioneering work in this field,[23] while Rainer Schulze,[24] Michael von Engelhardt[25] and Helga Hirsch[26] have addressed these issues on the basis of interviews conducted with former refugees. In addition, Michael Schwartz[27] has discussed problems of identity.

While a large number of works on the refugees and expellees have been published in German since the 1980s, there are very few English-language monographs on this topic. Two studies appeared during the 1970s. Hans Schoenberg's *Germans from the East* (1970),[28] based on secondary literature, concentrated primarily on the expellee organisations, while Bertram Lattimore made a case study of the expellee problem in Eutin (Schleswig-Holstein).[29] Several of the more recent publications in English have focused on the expulsion of the expellees from their homelands, including a controversial work by Alfred de Zayas[30] and a collection of essays edited by Philipp Ther and Ana Siljak.[31] In addition, *Coming Home to Germany?*, a volume edited by David Rock and Stefan Wolff, contains several contributions on the integration of expellees in post-war Germany.[32] Pertti Ahonen's excellent monograph, *After the Expulsion*, published in 2004, analyses the interaction between the expellee organisations and the political elites in the FRG up to 1990.[33] However, there is as yet no study in English of the economic, social and political integration of the refugees and expellees in post-war Germany, a gap that this book proposes to fill.

At the same time, it is important to point out that, while this book contains some coverage of the refugee problem in the Soviet Occupation Zone (SBZ)/GDR, its main focus is on the Western Occupation Zones of Germany/FRG. This reflects the fact that research on the expellee problem in the western part of Germany is at a more advanced stage. It should also be underlined that this book does not aim to give equal chronological coverage to the refugee problem throughout the post-war period. Its main focus is on the immediate post-war years (1945–50) when the economic, social and political problems arising from the influx of millions of German refugees and expellees were most acute. A particular feature of the book is its treatment of the political dimension of the refugee question. German historians and political scientists have so far paid little attention to the relationship between the refugees and political parties, an issue that this book will seek to address.

Chapter 1 explores the origins of the refugee problem and shows that the flight and expulsion of the refugees and expellees from their homelands from the autumn of 1944 onwards was a direct consequence of National Socialist policies. This chapter will also outline briefly the appalling conditions under which the expulsions were carried out. Chapter 2 examines the immensity of the refugee problem in the Western Occupation Zones in economic and social terms, demonstrating that the task of integrating the refugees and expellees was one of the most urgent facing the Allied Occupying authorities and German State Governments after the Second World War. Chapter 3 analyses the relations between the refugee and native populations in the Western Occupation Zones of Germany in the period 1945–50. Chapter 4 focuses on the attitude of the political parties towards the refugees and expellees in the early post-war years and also analyses the newcomers' voting behaviour up to 1950.

Chapter 5 explores the economic, social and political integration of the refugees and expellees in the FRG from 1950 onwards, arguing that while economic and political integration had been largely accomplished by the late 1960s, social integration turned out to be a more protracted process. Chapter 6 examines the issue of political radicalisation: despite disturbances in a number of refugee camps in 1948–49 and the emergence of expellee trek associations in 1951–52, the feared political radicalisation of the refugees did not occur on a wide scale and this chapter discusses the reasons for the absence of widespread unrest. The final chapter focuses on the refugee problem in the SBZ/GDR and seeks to draw parallels and contrasts with the situation in the Western Occupation Zones.

Notes

1 Public Record Office (PRO), FO 1013/368, Matheson (Regional Governmental Officer) to Chief Manpower Officer, 27 September 1948.

2 See for example, F. Edding, *Die wirtschaftliche Eingliederung der Vertriebenen und Flüchtlinge in Schleswig-Holstein* (Berlin 1955).

3 See for example, E. Pfeil, *Der Flüchtling: Gestalt einer Zeitenwende* (Hamburg 1948).

4 T. Schieder (ed.), *Dokumentation der Vertreibung der Deutschen aus Ost- und Mitteleuropa*, 5 vols (Wolfenbüttel 1953–61).

5 E. Lemberg and F. Edding (eds), *Die Vertriebenen in Westdeutschland: Ihre Eingliederung und ihr Einfluß auf Gesellschaft, Wirtschaft, Politik und Geistesleben*, 3 vols (Kiel 1959).

6 S. Schier, *Die Aufnahme und Eingliederung von Flüchtlingen und Vertriebenen in der Hansestadt Lübeck: Eine sozialgeschichtliche Untersuchung für die Zeit nach dem Zweiten Weltkrieg bis zum Ende der 50er Jahre* (Lübeck 1982).

7 U. Weiher, *Flüchtlingssituation und Flüchtlingspolitik: Untersuchungen zur Eingliederung der Flüchtlinge in Bremen 1945–1961* (Bremen 1998).

8 E. Glensk, *Die Aufnahme und Eingliederung der Vertriebenen und Flüchtlinge in Hamburg 1945–1953* (Hamburg 1994).

9 A. Hohenstein, 'Aufnahme und Eingliederung von Flüchtlingen im Landkreis Dannenberg 1945–1948', in D. Brosius and A. Hohenstein, *Flüchtlinge im nordöstlichen Niedersachsen 1945–1948* (Hildesheim 1985), pp. 87–181.

10 P. Lüttinger, 'Der Mythos der schnellen Integration: Eine empirische Untersuchung zur Integration der Vertriebenen und Flüchtlinge in der Bundesrepublik Deutschland bis 1971', *Zeitschrift für Soziologie*, Vol. 15(1) (1986), pp. 20–36.

11 R. Schulze, 'Growing Discontent: Relations between Native and Refugee Populations in a Rural District in Western Germany after the Second World War', *German History*, Vol. 7(3) (1989), pp. 332–49.

12 A. Lüttig, *Fremde im Dorf: Flüchtlingsintegration im westfälischen Wewelsburg 1945–1958* (Essen 1993).
13 L. Niethammer and A. von Plato, *'Wir kriegen jetzt andere Zeiten'* (Berlin 1985).
14 T. Mehlhase, *Flüchtlinge und Vertriebene nach dem Zweiten Weltkrieg in Sachsen-Anhalt. Ihre Aufnahme und Bestrebungen zur Eingliederung in die Gesellschaft* (Münster 1999).
15 S. Donth, *Vertriebene und Flüchtlinge in Sachsen 1945–1952: Die Politik der Sowjetischen Militäradministration und der SED* (Cologne 2000).
16 N. Schrammek, *Alltag und Selbstbild von Flüchtlingen und Vertriebenen in Sachsen 1945–1952* (Frankfurt a. M. 2004).
17 M. Schwartz, *Vertriebene und 'Umsiedlerpolitik': Integrationskonflikte in den deutschen Nachkriegs-Gesellschaften und die Assimilationsstrategien in der SBZ/DDR 1945–1961* (Munich 2004).
18 M. Wille (ed.), *Die Vertriebenen in der SBZ/DDR: Dokumente*, 3 vols (Wiesbaden 1996–2003).
19 P. Ther, *Deutsche und polnische Vertriebene: Gesellschaft und Vertriebenenpolitik in der SBZ/DDR und in Polen 1945–1956* (Göttingen 1998).
20 P. Ther, 'The Integration of Expellees in Germany and Poland after World War II: A Historical Reassessment', *Slavic Review*, Vol. 55(4) (1996), pp. 779–805.
21 P. Ahonen, 'Collective Action and Expellee Integration: West Germany, East Germany and Finland after the Second World War', *Annali dell' Istituto storico italo-germanico in Trento*, XXIX (2003), pp. 617–38.
22 P. Erker (ed.), *Rechnung für Hitlers Krieg: Aspekte und Probleme des Lastenausgleichs* (Heidelberg 2004).
23 R. G. Moeller, 'War Stories: The Search for a Usable Past in the Federal Republic of Germany', *American Historical Review*, 101 (1996), pp. 1008–48.
24 See for example, R. Schulze, '"Wir leben ja nun hier". Flüchtlinge und Vertriebene in Niedersachsen – Erinnerung und Identität', in K.J. Bade, and J. Oltmer (eds), *Zuwanderung und Integration in Niedersachsen seit dem Zweiten Weltkrieg* (Osnabrück 2002), pp. 69–100.
25 M. von Engelhardt, 'Biographieverläufe von Heimatvertriebenen des Zweiten Weltkriegs', in Bayerisches Staatsministerium für Arbeit und Sozialordnung, Familie, Frauen und Gesellschaft (ed.), *Die Entwicklung Bayerns durch die Integration der Vertriebenen und Flüchtlinge: Forschungsstand 1995* (Munich 1995), pp. 49–77.
26 H. Hirsch, *Schweres Gepäck: Flucht und Vertreibung als Lebensthema* (Hamburg 2004).
27 M. Schwartz, 'Vertreibung und Vergangenheitspolitik. Ein Versuch über geteilte deutsche Nachkriegsidentitäten', *Deutschland Archiv*, 30

(1997), pp. 177–95.
28 H. Schoenberg, *Germans from the East: A Study of their Migration, Resettlement and Subsequent Group History since 1945* (The Hague 1970).
29 B. Lattimore, Jr, *The Assimilation of German Expellees into the West German Polity and Society since 1945: A Case Study of Eutin, Schleswig-Holstein* (The Hague 1974).
30 A. de Zayas, *Nemesis at Potsdam: The Expulsion of the Germans from the East*, 3rd edn (London 1989).
31 P. Ther and A. Siljak (eds), *Redrawing Nations: Ethnic Cleansing in East-Central Europe, 1944–1948* (Lanham, Boulder, New York and Oxford 2001).
32 D. Rock and S. Wolff (eds), *Coming Home to Germany? The Integration of Ethnic Germans from Central and Eastern Europe in the Federal Republic* (New York and Oxford 2002).
33 P. Ahonen, *After the Expulsion: West Germany and Eastern Europe 1945–1990* (Oxford 2003).

1

The origins of the refugee problem

German settlements in Eastern and Central Europe

Even before the end of the Second World War, German refugees and expellees began to flood into Central Europe from the eastern territories of the Reich. Many of those who fled or were expelled from their homelands in Eastern Europe from 1944 onwards were the descendants of German settlers who had arrived as early as the twelfth century. Some of the earliest recorded settlements took place in Silesia and the Carpathian mountains where the political elites encouraged the migration of German coal miners around 1150;[1] as a result, a number of coal mining towns such as Goldberg and Löwenstein had been founded in Silesia by approximately 1250.[2] Similar developments occurred elsewhere. For example, the rulers of Bohemia and Moravia encouraged the settlement of economically valuable German colonists such as farmers and coal miners from the beginning of the thirteenth century.[3] While the colonisation of these areas was achieved by peaceful means to the mutual economic benefit of both the settlers and the ruling elites, this was not the case everywhere. The German Teutonic Order, founded in 1190, conquered the Baltic states of Estonia, Latvia and Lithuania during the twelfth and thirteenth centuries, as well as East and West Prussia.[4] As a result of these developments, some 120 towns had already been established by German colonists in Silesia by the beginning of the fourteenth century and a further 43 in Pomerania, while East Prussia had witnessed the foundation of 55 towns early in the fifteenth century.[5]

This first wave of German colonisation in Eastern and Central Europe slackened off in the fifteenth century due to the expansion of the Ottoman Empire. However, the eviction of the Ottomans from parts of Hungary and the Balkans after their unsuccessful siege of Vienna in 1683 prompted a new phase of colonisation by German settlers. Supported by the Habsburg Emperors, they settled in Croatia, Northern Bosnia, Hungary and the Banat, a geographical region which includes parts of Rumania and Serbia.[6] The first and most successful of the three so-called 'Swabian tracks' (*Schwabenzüge*) was initiated by Charles VI between 1723 and 1726. Most of these settlers, who came from Bavaria, Lorraine, the Palatinate and south-west Germany, had arrived by around 1750 but further migration took place in the period 1763–73 under Maria Theresa and between 1782 and 1787 under Joseph II.[7]

A third stage of German colonisation took place in Russia, where in 1763 Catherine the Great offered tax and other incentives to German farmers who were prepared to set up home in the Volga steppes, Crimea and Ukraine.[8] This attracted farmers from Hesse, the Rhineland and elsewhere and by 1769 over 23,000 German settlers had made their home in the areas surrounding the lower and central Volga river.[9] A decree issued by Alexander I in 1804 prompted farmers and artisans from southern Germany to migrate to the Crimean peninsula and the Caucasus. This influx of German colonists continued throughout the nineteenth century: the census of 1897 revealed that no fewer than 1.79 million Germans were resident in Russia.[10]

The privileges enjoyed by the Ethnic German minorities located in Eastern and Central Europe were generally eroded during the nineteenth century and their relations with other ethnic groups became increasingly strained. This was partly due to economic and religious factors, but the most important cause was the growth of nationalist sentiments. A feature of German nationalism was that it was more deeply rooted in linguistic and cultural factors than political principles and in Bohemia, for example, the tensions which developed between Germans and Czechs during the nineteenth century were largely based on cultural issues.[11] The underlying problem was that the geographical borders of the German 'nation-state' did not correspond with the German 'cultural nation' (*Kulturnation*). Therefore, as new homogeneous nation-states were established along ethnic lines their leaders sought to assimilate or exclude all ethnic groups other than their own. This was not a new idea, and the Prussian reformer Baron Karl von Stein had expressed the view as early as June 1814 that German-speaking people should 'cleanse the Rhineland of everything which has made ... and keeps it un-German'.[12] The first examples of population transfers in order to change the ethnic composition of a particular area took place in the late nineteenth century. In 1886 the Prussian Government authorised the settlement of German farmers in West Prussia in an attempt to increase the German population in rural areas with a Polish majority. An amendment passed in 1908 went even further, sanctioning the dispossession of Polish landowners.[13]

The Paris Peace Settlement and the rise of National Socialism

While the emergence of nationalism in nineteenth-century Europe formed the background to the large-scale population transfers and forced migration which took place in Eastern and Central Europe during the first half of the twentieth century, these events were by no means predetermined in 1900. After all, up until 1918 the majority of Germans were incorporated in either the German or Austro-Hungarian Empire, while the German minority groups outside these Empires – in Russia, Serbia and Rumania – generally co-existed amicably with the indigenous populations. In fact, at least 300,000 of the German ethnic minority living in Russia served with the Russian army against Germany between 1914 and 1918.[14] However, the territorial changes set out in the Treaties of Versailles and St Germain in 1919 transformed the situation. The dissolution of the Second German Empire (1871–1918) and the Austro-Hungarian Empire (1867–1918) led to the creation of new states such as Yugoslavia, Poland and Czechoslovakia, whose populations included Germans as well as other ethnic groups. Although the US President, Woodrow Wilson, promised that borders would be drawn according to the principle of national self-determination, this proved impossible to implement in practice. Ethnic Germans formed one of a number of different nationalities in a new Kingdom of Serbs, Croats and Slovenes. In addition, some 750,000 Germans from the Banat, Bessarabia, Bukovina and south Dobrudja found themselves part of an enlarged Rumanian state;[15] the new Czechoslovakian state included as many 3.2 million Ethnic Germans. In addition, approximately two-thirds of West Prussia was ceded to Poland, which also gained about a third of Upper Silesia following a plebiscite in April 1921.

All in all, the territorial settlement after the First World War left some 7 million Ethnic Germans outside the borders of Germany and Austria, and this formed the background to the flight and expulsion of the refugees and expellees from their homelands from 1944 onwards. In accordance with the Paris Peace Settlement, the League of Nations was responsible for protecting the rights of these minority groups, who were to be granted a degree of cultural autonomy and the same rights as the indigenous inhabitants. However, problems soon arose and in the period 1919–34 the League of Nations received thousands of petitions from Germans who claimed that they were suffering discrimination from the authorities in Poland.[16] Although the Czechoslovakian Government was more even-handed in its treatment of the Sudeten Germans than its Polish counterpart, it nonetheless gave financial incentives to its own citizens to resettle in areas which had a German majority and took steps to reduce the percentage of Germans employed by the state.[17]

For their part, the German minorities, unused to being ruled by a foreign power, invariably proved to be dissident and destabilising elements within the new states which had been established. This was particularly the case after Hitler's rise to power in January 1933. In Czechoslovakia, for example, the German population, hard hit by the economic crisis, became increasingly susceptible to the slogans of the radical right. In October 1933, Konrad Henlein, a former school teacher, founded the Sudeten German Home Front (*Sudetendeutsche Heimatfront*), which was later renamed Sudeten German Party (*Sudetendeutsche Partei,* SdP). At the national elections held in May 1935, it won a sensational victory, obtaining 68 per cent of the Sudeten German vote.[18] Although Henlein had given a declaration of loyalty to the Czechoslovakian state in 1933 he was courted by Hitler and his Carlsbad Programme, announced in April 1938, made a series of demands, including equal rights for the German and Czech people and self-government for German speaking districts. The Czechoslovakian President, Dr Eduard Beneš, rejected these demands and the crisis intensified when the SdP won 85 per cent of the votes cast by the Sudeten Germans in local elections held in the summer of 1938.[19] It was against this background that the British and French Prime Ministers gave in to Hitler's demand at the Munich Conference in September 1938 for the Sudetenland to be ceded to Germany. The outcome of the Munich Conference, and the destruction of the Czechoslovakian state following the invasion of Prague by the German army in March 1939, had a profound effect on the attitude of Beneš to the 'Sudeten German problem'. In fact, as early as December 1938 he privately advocated the expulsion of the Sudeten Germans [20] and in September 1941 publicly put forward this idea.

The expansionist policies of the National Socialists were not confined to Czechoslovakia. They aimed to establish a Greater Germany comprising not just the Sudetenland and Austria, which had been annexed in March 1938, but also the Warthegau, a large area in western Poland. Following Germany's conquest of Poland some 450,000 Poles and 550,000 Jews were removed from their homes in the Warthegau in 1939–40 and replaced by repatriated Ethnic Germans who had formerly lived in the Baltic States, Hungary, Bosnia, Bulgaria, Bessarabia and other areas.[21] The enormous scale of forced migration under the Nazis is shown by the fact that they deported no fewer than 5.5 million people to Germany during the war, including some 2.8 million forced labourers of Polish extraction.[22] The Nazi occupation of Eastern Europe was accompanied by numerous other acts of brutality: in retaliation for the murder of Reinhard Heydrich, Deputy Protector of Bohemia and Moravia, in June 1942, the Nazis shot every male in the mining village of Lidice from whence the assassins were thought to have originated.[23] Similar atrocities were committed in other parts of Eastern and Central Europe and the German minorities were regarded as willing instruments of the expansionist policies of the National Socialists. Thus, when the German offensive in the East failed, Soviet troops, as well as the indigenous inhabitants of countries such as Czechoslovakia, began to exact revenge on the German population for the appalling suffering they had experienced at the hands of the Nazis. The flight and expulsion of German refugees and expellees from Eastern and Central Europe in 1944–45 was therefore a direct consequence of National Socialist policies.

The flight and expulsion of Germans from the East

The German defeat at Stalingrad proved to be the turning-point in the war and in October 1944 Soviet troops entered the eastern territories of the Reich. One of the first villages they reached was Nemmersdorf (East Prussia) and the brutality with which they treated its German civilian population led to a huge exodus of terror-stricken refugees from the eastern parts of the Reich in the face of the advancing Red Army. Many women in Nemmersdorf were raped and almost the entire village was wiped out.[24] The Soviet offensive which began on 12 January 1945 prompted some 4 million refugees from Upper and Lower Silesia, Pomerania, Brandenburg and Danzig to flee westwards from their homelands.[25] These so-called 'treks', often undertaken in horse-drawn vehicles, proved to be extremely hazardous. The refugees had to cope with bitterly cold weather, food shortages and the constant threat of American and Soviet air attacks. Thousands died of starvation and the effects of the cold. Some 2.4 million of these refugees were evacuated by ship from the Baltic Sea ports and this generally turned out to be less perilous than the treks overland.[26] However, a number of vessels were sunk by Soviet submarines, including the *Wilhelm Gustloff* in January 1945 with the loss of more than 5,000 lives and the *Goya* in April 1945 in which some 6,600 refugees perished.[27]

The flight of Ethnic Germans from their homelands in South Eastern Europe also began in the autumn of 1944. After gaining control in Yugoslavia, Tito's partisans wreaked revenge on its German minority. By the end of 1944 some 340,000 Germans had fled, while as many as 67,000 had perished in extermination camps.[28] In Rumania some 100,000 fled in the wake of Soviet troops,[29] while in Hungary the figure was approximately 50,000.[30] Although the Red Army was more restrained in its treatment of Rumanian and Hungarian Germans than those from the eastern territories, some 60,000 Hungarian Germans and 80,000 Germans from the Schwabian Banat and Transylvania were deported to forced labour camps in the Soviet Union.[31]

The end of the war witnessed the beginning of the so-called 'wild' expulsions carried out by the native populations of Poland and Czechoslovakia against their German minorities. Polish military leaders ordered their troops 'to treat the Germans as they treated us'.[32] At least 230,000 and perhaps as many as 300,000 Germans were expelled from the border region east of the Oder–Neisse rivers and were sometimes given as little as ten minutes to collect their most precious belongings.[33] The conditions under which they were expelled were invariably appalling. During the train journeys to the West, which sometimes lasted several weeks, groups of Poles attacked the refugees and stole the few remaining valuables they still possessed; the station at Stettin-Scheune gained particular notoriety in this respect.[34] Even Germans who were not initially expelled were confined in terrible conditions in internment camps and over a thousand inmates died in Lamsdorf Camp in Upper Silesia.[35] At the same time, German refugees attempting to return to their former homes were prevented from crossing the Oder–Neisse rivers. In Czechoslovakia, meanwhile, Beneš urged his fellow countrymen on 12 May 1945 to assist him in 'liquidating the German question'.[36] During the Prague Uprising (4–9 May) hundreds of German civilians were murdered, while others were interned or sent to nearby concentration camps such as Theresienstadt.[37] In Brünn some 1,700 of its 30,000 German inhabitants were murdered on 30 May during their notorious 'death march' to camps on the Austrian frontier.[38] All in all, it is estimated that about 750,000 Sudeten Germans were expelled from Czechoslovakia between May and the beginning of August 1945.[39] Local reports indicate that the Poles and Czechs invariably treated the Germans with even greater brutality than the Soviet troops.[40]

The decisions taken at the Potsdam Conference (17 July–2 August 1945) marked the beginning of the third phase of the expulsion of the Germans from their homelands. Even prior to the conference, the political leaders of the United States, United Kingdom and Soviet Union had expressed their support for the resettlement of the German population from Poland and Czechoslovakia. Under pressure from Beneš, President of the Czechoslovakian Government-in-exile, the British Foreign Minister Anthony Eden had secured cabinet approval as early as 6 July 1942 'for the general principle of the transfer to Germany of German minorities in Central and South-Eastern Europe after the war',[41] while Prime Minister Winston Churchill maintained in a speech to the House of Commons on 15 December 1944 that 'expulsion is the method which ... will be the most satisfactory and lasting ... A clean sweep will be made'.[42] There is also evidence that the Soviet leadership supported the principle of expulsion in January 1944.[43] The American President Franklin Roosevelt concurred, urging that 'we should take measures so that the Prussians will be removed from East Prussia in the same manner as the Greeks were removed from Turkey after the last war'.[44] It is interesting to observe that Roosevelt and the other Allied leaders based their ideas on what they perceived to be the success of the Lausanne Treaty of 1923. This agreement, drawn up by the Greek and Turkish Governments, legitimised the forced transfer of Greeks from Turkish Anatolia and Turks from Greece. Up to 500,000 people are thought to have perished during these expulsions.[45]

When Churchill subsequently expressed reservations about the population transfers during negotiations with Stalin at Potsdam,[46] the Soviet leader dismissed his concerns, pointing out that the Poles and Czechs had already expelled a large number of Germans and claiming that he was powerless to halt this process. Confronted with this *fait accompli*, Churchill and the new US President, Harry Truman, attempted to moderate the brutal and chaotic way in which the expulsions were being carried out. Although Article 13 of the Potsdam Agreement affirmed that 'the Three Governments ... recognize that the transfer to Germany of German populations, or elements thereof, remaining in Poland, Czechoslovakia and Hungary, will have to be undertaken', it went on to stipulate that 'any transfers that take place should be effected in an orderly and humane manner'.[47] The Allies also requested that the expulsions be halted temporarily in order to allow them to make preparations for the new arrivals. In the short term the Potsdam Protocol did little to improve the situation. Despite repeated protests by the British and American Governments, Germans continued to be expelled from Poland during the autumn of 1945 under extremely harsh conditions.[48] Moreover, even when transfers were suspended it resulted in large numbers of Sudeten Germans being marooned on the German border at the mercy of the native Czechoslovakian population.[49] However, the plan for organised population transfers announced by the Allied Control Council on 20 November 1945 did bring about during the first half of 1946 a gradual improvement in the conditions under which the expulsions were carried out. During the course of that year some 4 million Germans were expelled, mainly from Poland and Czechoslovakia, and expulsions on a smaller scale continued until 1950.

While it is impossible to provide reliable figures about the number of refugees and expellees who perished during their flight or expulsion from their homelands in Eastern and Central Europe between 1944 and 1946, at least 600,000 and perhaps as many as 1.5 million died.[50] Those who survived bore the physical and mental scars of their experiences. Many were ravaged by disease and malnutrition and traumatised by the ill treatment they had suffered and the horrific events they had witnessed. The arrival of some 12 million refugees and expellees in occupied Germany posed immense difficulties for the Allied and German authorities and chapter 2 will examine the enormity of the refugee problem in the Western Occupation Zones of Germany.

Notes

1 S. Wolff, 'Introduction: From Colonists to Emigrants: Explaining the "Return-Migration" of Ethnic Germans from Central and Eastern Europe', in Rock and Wolff (eds), *Coming Home to Germany?*, p. 5.
2 M. Frantzioch, *Die Vertriebenen: Hemmnisse, Arbeitskräfte und Wege ihrer Integration in der Bundesrepublik Deutschland* (Berlin 1987), p. 25.
3 *Ibid.*, p. 31.
4 Wolff, 'Introduction', p. 5.
5 G. Ziemer, *Deutscher Exodus: Vertreibung und Eingliederung von 15 Millionen Ostdeutschen* (Stuttgart 1973), p. 51
6 Schoenberg, *Germans from the East*, p. 12.
7 W. Ziegler (ed.), *Die Vertriebenen vor der Vertreibung: Die Heimatländer der deutschen Vertriebenen im 19. und 20. Jahrhundert: Strukturen, Entwicklungen, Erfahrung*, Vol. 2 (Munich 1999), pp. 710–11.
8 Schoenberg, *Germans from the East*, p. 12.
9 Ziegler (ed.), *Die Vertriebenen vor der Vertreibung*, Vol. 2, p. 1001.
10 *Ibid.*, p. 1002.
11 *Ibid.*, Vol. 1, p. 24.
12 Quoted in P. Ther, 'A Century of Forced Migration: The Origins and Consequences of "Ethnic Cleansing"', in Ther and Siljak (eds), *Redrawing Nations*, p. 45. I have amended the author's translation.
13 *Ibid.*, p. 48.
14 Ziegler (ed.), *Die Vertriebenen vor der Vertreibung*, Vol. 2, p. 1006.
15 *Ibid.*, p. 768.
16 De Zayas, *Nemesis at Potsdam*, p. 5.
17 E. Glassheim, 'The Mechanics of Ethnic Cleansing: The Expulsion of Germans from Czechoslovakia, 1945–1947', in Ther and Siljak (eds), *Redrawing Nations*, p. 198.
18 R. Jaworski, 'Die Sudetendeutschen als Minderheit in der Tschechoslowakei 1918–1938', in W. Benz (ed.), *Die Vertreibung der Deutschen aus dem Osten: Ursachen, Ereignisse, Folgen* (Frankfurt a. M. 1985), p. 35.
19 Glassheim, 'The Mechanics of Ethnic Cleansing', p. 198.
20 Frantzioch, *Die Vertriebenen*, p. 50.
21 Ther, *Deutsche und polnische Vertriebene*, p. 35.
22 Ther, 'A Century of Forced Migration', p. 51.
23 Glassheim, 'The Mechanics of Ethnic Cleansing', pp. 199–200.
24 H. Hirsch, 'Flucht und Vertreibung: Kollektive Erinnerung im Wandel', *Aus Politik und Zeitgeschichte*, B 40–41 (2003), p. 17.
25 *Ibid.*
26 A. Theisen, 'Die Vertreibung der Deutschen – Ein unbewältigtes Kapitel europäischer Zeitgeschichte', *APZ*, B 7–8 (1995), p. 24.
27 *Ibid.*, p. 25.

28 Hirsch, 'Flucht und Vertreibung', p. 17.
29 *Ibid.*
30 Theisen, 'Die Vertreibung der Deutschen', p. 28.
31 *Ibid.*
32 Ther, *Deutsche und polnische Vertriebene*, p. 55.
33 *Ibid.*, p. 57.
34 Schieder (ed.), *Dokumentation der Vertreibung*, Vol. 1, p. 141.
35 Ahonen, *After the Expulsion*, p. 21.
36 Quoted in Hirsch, 'Flucht und Vertreibung', p. 18.
37 Glassheim, 'The Mechanics of Ethnic Cleansing', p. 206.
38 Hirsch, 'Flucht und Vertreibung', p. 18.
39 Glassheim, 'The Mechanics of Ethnic Cleansing', p. 209.
40 N. Naimark, *Fires of Hatred: Ethnic Cleansing in Twentieth-Century Europe*, 2nd edn (Cambridge, Mass. and London 2002), pp. 116–17 and 126–32.
41 Quoted in D. Brandes, *Der Weg zur Vertreibung 1938–1945: Pläne und Entscheidungen zum 'Transfer' der Deutschen aus der Tschechoslowakei und aus Polen* (Munich 2001), p. 149.
42 Quoted in Naimark, *Fires of Hatred*, p. 110.
43 *Ibid.*, p.109.
44 Quoted in *ibid.*, p. 110.
45 Ther, 'A Century of Forced Migration', p. 50.
46 For details, see Brandes, *Der Weg zur Vertreibung*, p. 406.
47 Quoted in Naimark, *Fires of Hatred*, p. 111.
48 For details, see de Zayas, *Nemesis at Potsdam*, pp. 103–24.
49 Naimark, *Fires of Hatred*, p. 117.
50 Estimates vary widely. Gerhard Reichling puts the number at 2,020,000, while Helga Hirsch states that 'about two million' died. However, these figures are too high. Pertti Ahonen suggests that the number is significantly lower, estimating that 'up to 1.5 million Germans may have died', while Rüdiger Overmans has argued persuasively that the figure may be as low as 600,000. See G. Reichling, 'Flucht und Vertreibung der Deutschen: Statistische Grundlagen und terminologische Probleme', in R. Schulze, D. von der Brelie-Lewien and H. Grebing (eds), *Flüchtlinge und Vertriebene in der westdeutschen Nachkriegsgeschichte: Bilanzierung der Forschung und Perspektiven für die künftige Forschungsarbeit* (Hildesheim 1987), p. 46; Hirsch, 'Flucht und Vertreibung', p. 18; Ahonen, *After the Expulsion*, p. 21; R. Overmans, 'Personelle Verluste der deutschen Bevölkerung durch Flucht und Vertreibung', *Dzieje Najnowsze*, Vol. 26(2) (1994), p. 61.

2

The influx of refugees into Germany and its problems, 1945–50

The immensity of the refugee problem

Of the 12 million German refugees and expellees who flooded into Central Europe from the eastern parts of the Reich from 1944 onwards, almost 7.9 million had settled in the newly established West German state by September 1950.[1] They included some 4.4 million 'National Germans' (*Reichsdeutsche*) – groups who had lived in those areas east of the Oder–Neisse line which had formed part of Germany on 31 December 1937. The most numerous groups of *Reichsdeutsche* were the Silesians (2,053,000), East Prussians (1,347,000), Pomeranians (891,000) and East Brandenburgers (131,000). Sudeten Germans (1,912,000) made up over half of the 3.5 million refugees of Ethnic German origin (*Volksdeutsche*) – Germans who had lived as minority groups in foreign countries. Smaller groups of *Volksdeutsche* had inhabited the Baltic states of Latvia, Estonia and Lithuania, the former free city of Danzig, the Soviet Union, Rumania, Hungary, Yugoslavia and Poland.[2]

The task of integrating these refugees and expellees into the Western Occupation Zones of Germany represented one of the most formidable problems facing the Allied and German authorities after the Second World War. In 1939, the population of the area which was to become the FRG totalled 39,350,000; despite heavy civilian and military losses during the war years, this figure had risen to almost 47,696,000 by September 1950. The arrival of some 7.9 million refugees and expellees was the most important reason for this huge population increase. In fact, the number of newcomers residing in West Germany in the autumn of 1950 exceeded the total population of Switzerland (4.6 million), Sweden (6.9 million) and Austria (7.1 million).[3]

As Table 2.1 shows, the refugees and expellees were unevenly

Table 2.1 Refugees in the West German states, 13 September 1950

Zone/State	*Total population*	*Total refugees*	*% of refugees in population*
American Occupation Zone			
Bavaria	9,184,466	1,937,297	21.1
Hesse	4,323,801	720,583	16.7
Württemberg-Baden	3,907,848	649,597	16.6
Bremen	558,619	48,183	8.6
French Occupation Zone			
Württemberg-Hohenzollern	1,183,748	113,554	9.6
Baden	1,338,629	98,375	7.3
Rhineland-Palatinate	3,004,752	152,267	5.0
British Occupation Zone			
North Rhine-Westphalia	13,196,176	1,331,959	10.1
Lower Saxony	6,797,379	1,851,472	27.2
Hamburg	1,605,606	115,981	7.2
Schleswig-Holstein	2,594,648	856,943	33.0
Totals	47,695,672	7,876,211	16.5

Source: Tabulated from Archiv für Christlich-Demokratische Politik (ACDP), Nachlaß Nahm, 1–518–008/2, *10 Millionen Binnenwanderer in Westdeutschland* and Statistisches Landesamt Baden-Württemberg (ed.), *Ergebnis der Volks- und Berufszählung vom 13. September 1950*, Vol. 2 (Stuttgart 1954), pp. 2, 5, 40, 46, 52, 58. Refugees resident in the western sectors of Berlin have been excluded from this table.

distributed among the eleven West German states (*Länder*). At the Potsdam Conference, the Allies gave a commitment to securing 'an equitable distribution' of refugees 'among the several zones of occupation'.[4] However, the French, who had not been invited to the conference, did not feel compelled to abide by this decision and at first refused to accept newcomers into their zone; consequently, Württemberg-Hohenzollern, Baden and Rhineland-Palatinate were still sparsely populated with refugees as late as 1950. As a result, it was the American and British Occupation Zones which had to cope with the brunt of the refugee influx (see Table 2.1). However, even within these zones there were enormous variations. The vast majority of newcomers had to be accommodated in country areas, where employment opportunities were scarce, because the Allied wartime bombing campaign had created grave housing shortages in the large towns and cities where job prospects would have been more favourable. As a result, the mainly rural states of Bavaria, Lower Saxony and Schleswig-Holstein had to accommodate the majority of the newcomers. Yet, even here the refugees were not evenly distributed; as a rule, Schleswig-Holstein and the eastern parts of Bavaria and Lower Saxony were most severely overburdened with newcomers because of their close geographical proximity to the SBZ and, in the case of Bavaria, Czechoslovakia as well. The state most seriously affected by the arrival of the refugees was Schleswig-Holstein, one of the most impoverished areas of Germany even before the Second World War. Between 1939 and September 1950 it registered a population increase of 63 per cent, three times the national average.[5]

The question of terminology

A large number of different terms are used to describe the Germans who fled or were expelled from their homelands in Eastern and Central Europe into the Western Occupation Zones of Germany from 1944 onwards. The indigenous inhabitants generally referred to these new population elements as 'refugees' (*Flüchtlinge*) or 'refugees from the east' (*Ostflüchtlinge*), as well as 'expellees' (*Vertriebene* or *Ausgewiesene*) and 'expellees from their homeland' (*Heimatvertriebene*). As time went on, the term 'newcomers' (*Neubürger*) also came into common usage. An analysis of the legislative measures introduced by the various State Governments to help the refugees and expellees between 1945 and 1949 also reveals an absence of uniform terminology.[6] In fact, neither the State Governments nor the Occupying Powers made any meaningful distinction between those who fled as the Red Army advanced westwards in the closing months of the war and those who were systematically expelled from their homes. On the contrary, the changes in nomenclature which took place over time tended to reflect changes in the attitudes of the 'political elites' to the integration of the new population elements in the West and were also influenced by global political developments, in particular the outbreak of the Cold War.

In the period directly following the fall of the Reich, the term 'refugee' was generally used to describe all Germans who fled or were expelled from Eastern and Central Europe as a result of the war and its aftermath. The first official reference to 'expellees' was contained in a report from the US Military Government in January 1946. It described an expellee as 'a member of a German minority whose normal place of residence [was] in a country outside Germany or in that portion of Germany east of the Oder and Neisse Rivers now under Polish administration'.[7] On the other hand, a refugee was 'a German civilian whose normal place of residence is in occupied Germany and who is homeless or at some distance from his home because of war'. According to these definitions, the key distinction was that the 'expellees' would not be able to return to their homelands, while 'refugees' were evacuees and other groups temporarily displaced from their habitual place of residence.

However, this change of nomenclature was viewed with disquiet by German ministers and officials who generally continued to speak of 'refugees' rather than 'expellees' and it was significant that a 'Refugee' rather than 'Expellee' Law was introduced in 1947 in the states of the American Occupation Zone. As Mathias Beer has shown with regard to the State Government in Württemberg-Baden, the reluctance of the German authorities to adopt the term 'expellee' was based on the connotations of the word as defined by the Americans. The term 'expellee' implied that these new population elements would remain permanently in the Western Occupation Zones of Germany, a situation neither they nor the indigenous inhabitants wanted.[8] Under pressure from the US Military Government, the German authorities introduced a new expression – 'newcomers' – from December 1946 onwards. This term, which was consistent with the American emphasis on the swift 'assimilation' of the new population groups into German society, was designed to underline that the new population elements enjoyed exactly the same rights as the indigenous inhabitants.

However, the 'newcomers' themselves exerted pressure on German politicians to employ terminology which more accurately reflected the circumstances under which they had arrived in the Western Occupation Zones of Germany. As a result, the Parliamentary Council in Bonn decided at a meeting on 6 January 1949 that the most appropriate term was '*Heimatvertriebene*' because 'the German people expelled from their homes cannot in any circumstances be classified as refugees – people who have left their place of residence of their own free will'.[9] As a result, a Bizonal Office for

Expellees (*Amt für Heimatvertriebene*) was established in Frankfurt in March 1949 under Dr Ottomar Schreiber. The Soviet Union and its satellite states emphatically rejected the word *Heimatvertriebene* because of its clear implication that the German population had been expelled from their homes by force. In fact, the Soviet representative to the United Nations argued in January 1952 that Germans who were living in their own country could not be classified as 'expellees'.[10] In keeping with this point of view, the authorities in East Berlin published a directive in October 1945 which euphemistically referred to the Germans who had fled or been expelled from their homelands into the SBZ as 'resettlers' (*Umsiedler*).[11] A law promulgated on 8 September 1950 which made reference to the 'former resettlers' indicated that, in the eyes of the East German authorities, the 'resettler problem' had been successfully solved. Thus, the terminology used to describe the new population elements was once again determined by political considerations.

However, official statistics in the FRG did make a distinction between refugees and expellees from the east and German refugees from the SBZ or, after October 1949, the GDR. A residence permit was granted to those who could provide evidence of political persecution or wanted to join family members in the West. But many other so-called *illegale Grenzgänger* – East Germans who managed to evade the border police and cross illegally into the West – were also accepted since there was no legal basis for sending them back. At the time of the census of 13 September 1950, some 1,555,000 refugees from the GDR were residing in the FRG.[12] After 1949, the Federal Government in Bonn incorporated into federal legislation a more precise criterion for identifying 'genuine' refugees – those who had suffered 'a direct threat to life and limb or their personal freedom'.[13] Although only a small proportion fulfilled this criterion, the Bonn Government nevertheless accepted the vast majority as 'genuine' refugees since it wanted to depict them in public as victims of political persecution. Once again, political factors rather than consistent 'objective' criteria determined its interpretation of the term 'genuine' refugee.

It is clear, then, that the terminology used by the Allied and German authorities in the period 1945–49 was neither consistent nor uniform. Although the all-embracing term 'refugee' tended to be replaced during the course of the Occupation by the word 'expellee', many government reports continued to refer to 'refugees' well into

1949. The Federal Expellee Law of 19 May 1953 at last established some clarity about the terminology employed to describe the Germans from the East. It differentiated between *Heimatvertriebene*, *Vertriebene* and *Sowjetzonenflüchtlinge. Heimatvertriebene* had been resident on 31 December 1937 in one of the areas from which the expulsions were subsequently carried out. *Vertriebene* moved to the 'expulsion areas' after 31 December 1937, while the term *Sowjetzonenflüchtlinge* referred to German nationals who had fled to the FRG from the SBZ.[14] However, the definitions set out in the Federal Expellee Law differed significantly from the usage of these terms in the period 1945–53. This study will therefore follow the normal administrative and academic practice and use the expressions 'refugees', 'expellees', 'newcomers' and 'new population groups' interchangeably.

The economic predicament of the refugees

Lack of material possessions

The economic prerequisites for integrating the refugees and expellees in post-war German society could scarcely have been less favourable. Although many had enjoyed a good standard of living prior to their expulsion, they arrived in the Western Occupation Zones of Germany without the financial means to begin a new life. They had lost their savings, as well as any monies they had contributed to pension schemes in their homelands.[15] More important still, they had all forfeited their homes and many had been able to salvage only their most precious personal possessions.

Refugees who fled or were expelled prior to March 1946 generally fared worst. Some of the *Reichsdeutsche* who fled from the advancing Soviet troops during the first half of 1945 managed to secure transportation by train or ship, but for many the only means of escape was on foot and few managed to carry their luggage to its destination. One witness from the port of Pillau in East Prussia reported that fatigue and cold sapped the refugees' strength 'until they could go no further and were forced to leave their luggage behind piece by piece'.[16] The plight of the *Volksdeutsche* was in many cases little better. Frequently they were permitted only half an hour to vacate their homes and even those who, anticipating their expulsion, had packed bags in readiness, were often unable to take them.

Of course, the ill-treatment the refugees received must be seen in perspective. The Poles, Czechs and Russians were exacting revenge for their appalling suffering at the hands of the Nazis. Moreover, the conditions under which the refugees were expelled gradually improved after the Potsdam Conference. According to an agreement reached by the American Military Government and the authorities in Prague, the Sudeten Germans were to be permitted to bring 1,000 reichsmarks and 50 kg of luggage. The luggage allowance for the Hungarian German refugees was more generous, increasing to 100 kg from 1 September 1946.[17] However, the Czechoslovakian and Hungarian authorities did not always adhere to these agreements and representatives of ecclesiastical welfare organisations reported that by no means all Sudeten Germans had either 1,000 reichmarks or luggage weighing 50 kg.[18] It is impossible to assess the precise value of the property the refugees had to leave behind; 75 Sudeten German experts calculated on the basis of price levels in 1938 that their fellow countrymen had lost possessions to the value of 32 billion reichmarks, but a less cautious estimate put the total as high as 100 billion.[19]

Whatever the exact figure, the pertinent fact was that when the refugees arrived in the Western Occupation Zones of Germany they lacked many of the basic necessities of daily life. Few newcomers had been able to retrieve any of their furniture and in August 1947 refugees living in private accommodation in North Rhine-Westphalia required 82,523 kitchen stoves, 215,201 beds, 200,469 chairs, 100,134 tables and 159,993 cupboards.[20] Household equipment was also in very short supply and, according to a survey carried out by the American Military Government, 90 per cent of refugees had no cooking or household utensils as late as September 1949.[21] Few newcomers had adequate clothing and, although sewing rooms were provided in many towns and villages, there were reports of refugee children being unable to attend school during the bitterly cold winter of 1946–47 because they had no warm clothes or adequate footwear.[22] In Oldenburg, for example, 12.3 per cent of refugee schoolboys did not possess a shirt, 19.3 per cent did not own a pair of socks and 25 per cent had no waterproof shoes.[23] A lack of clothing or shoes also prevented some refugees from obtaining work and in June 1947 the owner of a vineyard in Würzburg requested the Bavarian Government to provide ninety refugees with shoes and clothing so that they could be employed to bring in the grape harvest.[24]

The task of integrating almost 8 million dispossessed refugees into an economy still recovering from the impact of the war was enormous and the acute material distress suffered by the newcomers in the early post-war years is illustrated graphically by examining the three main economic indicators – their food situation, housing conditions and employment prospects.

Food

After the Second World War, the Western Occupation Zones of Germany experienced a severe food shortage. In fact, the monthly public opinion polls conducted by the US Military Government revealed that, prior to the Currency Reform of June 1948, the food situation represented the most pressing concern of the German people.[25] The deterioration in food supplies which began during the last year of the war continued after the collapse of the Reich and reached crisis levels at the beginning of 1946. In parts of the British Occupation Zone, the daily rations for 'normal' consumers slumped to just over 1,000 calories in March 1946, fewer than half the minimum level prescribed by the United Nations for a working person.[26] In March 1947, following a bitterly cold winter, cuts in food rations led to demonstrations and unrest in towns and cities throughout the British Occupation Zone,[27] while in the Ruhr, the area most severely affected by food shortages, the situation in January 1948 was more critical than at any other time during the Occupation.[28] Although foodstuffs became more plentiful and varied from the middle of 1948 onwards, a significant section of the population still could not afford to buy them. In fact, the average daily calorie level for 'normal' consumers in Lower Saxony in 1948 totalled just 1,382, well below the figure of 2,435 in the first year of the war.[29]

Although the post-war food shortage in the Western Occupation Zones of Germany was to a large extent a legacy of the war, it should be borne in mind that, even in 1939, Germany had to import 17 per cent of its food supplies.[30] The loss of the eastern territories of the Reich as a result of the post-war territorial settlement was a serious problem since this area produced some 25 per cent of Germany's food before the Second World War.[31] In addition, it possessed the advantage of being sparsely populated so that much of its food could be consumed in other parts of Germany. In fact, a study carried out by the German Institute for Economic Research in 1934–35 concluded that the food surplus produced by the eastern territories was sufficient to feed 5.5 million people.[32] The loss of this area would have resulted in a scarcity of food even if Germany's pre-war population level had remained static but the additional burden of some 7.9 million refugees and expellees who arrived in 1945–46 exacerbated the crisis.

The chaotic economic conditions prevailing in post-war Germany increased the severity of the food shortage. The poor yield of the harvest in 1945 was mainly due to the inadequate supply of insecticides and fertilisers. The dislocation to the transportation system as a result of wartime bombing had an adverse effect on the distribution of foodstuffs during the winter of 1945–46, while the exceptionally harsh winter of 1946–47 once again disrupted the movement of food.[33] However, the main problem was the emergence of a barter economy. As the reichsmark lost its value, farmers were reluctant to sell all their produce to the government distribution agencies, preferring instead to barter it for greater profit on the flourishing black market. In fact, it was estimated in March 1947 that as much as 20 per cent of the harvest in the American Occupation Zone found its way on to the black market.[34] It was clear to Allied observers that substantial food imports would be required to prevent widespread hunger and starvation in the Western Occupation Zones of Germany. However, although food shipments were sent to Germany from both Britain and the United States, fears of a world food crisis prompted the Americans to reduce the quantity of aid in 1946 and large-scale imports of food did not begin until the second half of 1948.

The post-war food crisis affected the refugees more severely than the indigenous inhabitants. A public opinion poll of 2,839 people conducted in the American Occupation Zone in the autumn of 1947 concluded that 80 per cent of the refugees as opposed to 66 per cent of the native population believed that they were not getting enough to eat.[35] Generally speaking, newcomers who were billeted with farmers suffered least from the food crisis because, up until the middle of 1948, many of them worked or helped on the farm in return for potatoes, vegetables, milk, eggs and fruit. On the other hand, refugees living in rural parishes who did not have access to farm produce were often hit extremely hard by the food crisis[36] and deeply resented the allocation of extra rations to Hamburg and the Ruhr during the crisis in the spring of 1947. Most of the refugees accommodated in camps at first took advantage of communal eating facilities and in October 1946 only 31,000 of Bavaria's 145,822 refugee camp occupants were cooking for themselves.[37] Reports compiled by government inspectors and ecclesiastical representatives who visited the camps concluded that the quality and quantity of the food varied considerably according to the availability of rations, the location of the camp and the attitude of the camp authorities.[38] However, the food in many camps was inadequate and lacked variety. For example, the refugees at Plassenburg Camp in the Upper Franconian town of Kulmbach complained in December 1945 that, for most of the week, their diet consisted exclusively of black coffee for breakfast, soup for lunch and, in the evening, potatoes and white cabbage.[39] In fact, the poor quality of the food was one of the grievances which prompted hunger strikes in several refugee camps in Bavaria in September 1948.[40]

Refugees living in urban areas suffered most from the post-war food shortage. This is illustrated by the situation in the Baltic port of Lübeck, where refugees comprised more than 40 per cent of the population in 1947. At the end of the extremely harsh winter of 1946–47, food deliveries were no fewer than six weeks in arrears and in April 1947 the daily rations never exceeded 1,200 calories, 350 below the promised allocation. In response to this crisis, 25,000 refugees and local people took part in a hunger demonstration in April 1947[41] and similar events occurred in other parts of the British Occupation Zone. In Hamburg, for example, the bread ration was cut by half in April 1947 and, when no meat appeared in the shops in the first week of May, 500,000 people supported the call for a general strike on 9 May.[42]

Although all sections of the urban population were affected by the food shortage, the newcomers were hit with particular severity since they lacked the 'connections' of the native inhabitants and, as a result of the expulsion, had fewer belongings that they could barter on the black market for additional food supplies. Many refugees and local people living in towns made regular weekend excursions into the surrounding countryside to exchange items such as cigarettes and clothes for potatoes or other farm produce. In fact, this became such a regular occurrence that some train services operating from towns or cities into the countryside became known as 'potato trains' or 'calorie expresses'.[43] Those with nothing to exchange had to rely on the compassion of the farming community and reports by the mayors of local parishes made frequent reference to 'refugees and expellees walking from one farmhouse to the next begging for potatoes and bread'.[44] The theft of fruit, vegetables and other farm produce was also commonplace in the early post-war years, prompting some farmers to employ security guards to protect their property.[45]

In the face of the post-war food crisis, the German Regional Governments took steps to help refugees supplement their diet by growing their own fruit and vegetables. To this end, Theodor Steltzer, the last *Oberpräsident* of Schleswig-Holstein, published a directive on 16 February 1946 ordering local parishes to provide allotments for the newcomers.[46] This project proved to be very successful and the number of allotments in Schleswig-Holstein increased from some 94,000 in May 1945 to 326,000 in July 1948.[47] A similar scheme operated in Lower Saxony, where the majority of the newcomers retained their allotments until at least the mid-1950s.[48]

A particular source of concern was the impact of the food crisis on schoolchildren and in parts of the British Occupation Zone, school-feeding projects, financed by foreign welfare organisations, were established as early as November 1945 to provide needy and undernourished children with a hot midday meal.[49] In February 1946, the British Military Government introduced its own school-feeding programme in towns and cities. After the visit to Germany of a fact-finding mission led by the former US President, Herbert Hoover, it was agreed to extend this project to the American and French Occupation Zones. This new programme, which began on 30 June 1947, targeted those most in need and proved to be of great benefit to the refugees since, unlike the British scheme, it included those located in rural areas.

From mid-1948 onwards the overall food situation in the British and American Occupation Zones eased, mainly due to higher grain imports.[50] Official ration levels increased [51] and a wider variety of foodstuffs became available. However, this did little to help the refugees because the sharp rise in prices after the Currency Reform of June 1948 meant that many could not afford to buy the extra rations to which their coupons entitled them. This applied particularly to unemployed, disabled or retired newcomers, and the head of the Refugee Office in Burgdorf (Lower Saxony) commented in November 1948 that, 'in view of the dizzy heights to which prices have risen, public welfare allowances are insufficient to purchase food'.[52] However, even refugees in gainful employment sometimes encountered this problem and reports from Schleswig-Holstein indicate that a substantial proportion of refugee families were unable to buy more than half of their potato rations in the autumn of 1948.[53] Indeed, it was common for them to have to sell their fat and sugar coupons to obtain basic necessities such as bread,[54] while the *Landrat* of Traunstein (Upper Bavaria) noted in June 1949 that refugee women were being 'forced to sell the few personal belongings they had managed to acquire in order to buy urgently needed foodstuffs'.[55] It is clear, then, that some refugees actually had less to eat in the second half of 1948 than in the six months before the introduction of the new currency.

The introduction of the deutschmark also had serious short-term effects on the diet of refugee schoolchildren. Even though the meals supplied by the school-feeding project were heavily subsidised, a survey conducted in Nuremberg concluded that, even before the adoption of the deutschmark, some 18 per cent of parents could not afford their nominal daily contribution of 15–25 pfennigs.[56] The Currency Reform exacerbated this problem and in some areas up to 60 per cent of children participating in the school-feeding scheme had to be withdrawn during July 1948.[57] As an especially impoverished group, refugee schoolchildren were worst affected and this represented a major concern since many of them were already seriously underweight. Even though the Regional Governments took steps to reduce the level of parental contributions, thousands of schoolchildren did not rejoin the school-feeding scheme until it became free in the spring of 1949.[58] The health of many young people remained a serious source of concern even after the establishment of the FRG and official figures indicate that some 60–70 per cent of children of school age in Schleswig-Holstein were still undernourished in July 1950.[59]

Housing

As well as suffering malnutrition, many refugees and expellees also had to endure deplorable housing conditions in the early post-war years. The housing situation in Germany had been a constant source of concern during the interwar period and, according to one estimate, 2.5 million new dwellings were required in 1939 to provide satisfactory housing for the German people.[60] The wartime bombing campaign against Germany greatly exacerbated the housing shortage and, according to Allied figures, 2,161,000 dwellings were destroyed in the British and American Occupation

Zones, more than 23 per cent of the pre-war housing stock (see Table 2.2). Germany's major cities and industrial centres bore the brunt of the air attacks mounted by British Bomber Command from the winter of 1943 onwards and many suffered extensive damage. In Kassel, 63.9 per cent of homes were completely destroyed, while in Dortmund (64.8 per cent), Cologne (70 per cent) and Würzburg (74.3 per cent) the situation was even worse.[61] The housing crisis in the large towns and cities was further aggravated by the confiscation of undamaged homes by the Western Allies to accommodate members of the occupation forces. In fact, by the spring of 1948, the British authorities had requisitioned 196,682 homes, while their American counterparts had taken over an additional 119,918 dwellings.[62]

Faced with this severe housing shortage, many urban and industrial centres were exempted from having to accept convoys of refugees. Even though the municipal authorities in heavily damaged towns and cities such as Munich, Mannheim, Kassel and Osnabrück did permit refugee construction workers and other occupational groups essential to post-war reconstruction to settle there, they represented a small minority of the newcomers. For example, in October 1948, refugees comprised 20 per cent of the population in Bavaria but only 8 per cent of those living in Augsburg, 6 per cent in Munich and Nuremberg and just 4 per cent in Würzburg.[63] On the other hand, towns such as Esslingen which had emerged relatively unscathed from the wartime bombing had to accept large numbers of newcomers.[64] However, the overwhelming majority of the refugees were accommodated in the rural areas where war damage was generally negligible. For instance, in October 1946, 74.7 per cent of the newcomers in Bavaria were residing in parishes with a population of fewer than 5,000.[65] It was, then, the availability of housing in the countryside which determined that the refugee problem was an essentially rural phenomenon.

How were the refugees and expellees to be accommodated? The housing policies of the British and American Military Governments were based on the fundamental principle that the newcomers were not to be located in refugee camps on a long-term basis because it was feared that the concentration of large numbers of economically impoverished people in a confined space might lead to outbreaks of political radicalisation.[66] The Occupying Powers therefore stipulated that the refugees were, as a rule, to be billeted with private house-

Table 2.2 War damage in the British and American Occupation Zones

Zone/State	*Housing stock 1939*	*Houses total*	*Destroyed as % of 1939*
American Occupation Zone			
Bavaria	1,762,000	225,000	12.8
Hesse	957,000	171,000	17.9
Württemberg-Baden	892,000	198,000	22.2
Bremen	166,000	69,000	41.6
British Occupation Zone			
North Rhine-Westphalia	3,356,000	1,024,000	30.5
Lower Saxony	1,160,000	150,000	12.9
Hamburg	556,000	277,000	50.0
Schleswig-Holstein	435,000	47,000	10.8
Totals	9,284,000	2,161,000	23.3

Source: S. Schraut, *Flüchtlingsaufnahme in Württemberg-Baden 1945–1949: Amerikanische Besatzungsziele und demokratischer Wiederaufbau im Konflikt* (Munich 1995), p. 229. The table has been reproduced by kind permission of Oldenbourg Wissenschaftsverlag.

holders. The number of newcomers to be allocated to individual rural districts was based on the amount of available housing space. The unenviable task of assigning the newcomers to individual householders at parish level had to be carried out by the local mayor in consultation with the housing boards. According to American guidelines, two people on average were to occupy a room (*Wohnraum*), a figure the German authorities considered far too high.[67] Mindful of the likely resistance to these instructions, the Americans insisted that 'physical discomfort or overcrowding' would not be regarded as sufficient reason for the indigenous inhabitants to refuse to accept refugees in their homes unless it could be shown this represented a threat to health.[68]

The Housing Law approved by the Allied Control Council on 8 March 1946 set out the legal basis for the accommodation of the newcomers in the homes of the native population. It confirmed the right of the state to confiscate occupied or unoccupied housing space and stipulated that a tenancy agreement should be drawn up between the householder and the tenant. It also laid down the penalties to be imposed on native householders who refused to share their homes with refugees – they could be sent to prison for up to a year and/or receive a fine of up to 10,000 reichmarks. Significantly, however, the Housing Law omitted to guarantee the refugees the same amount of space as the native householders and, as will be seen below, this contributed to the often strained relations between landlords and their refugee tenants.[69]

The housing conditions of the newcomers living in private lodgings varied enormously. Generally speaking, the refugees who arrived first obtained the best rooms, while those who did not set foot in the Western Occupation Zones until after the autumn of 1946 often had to accept small, cramped and sometimes damp accommodation. Housing conditions tended to be particularly bad in small towns and villages in Schleswig-Holstein and the eastern parts of Lower Saxony and Bavaria due to the constant influx of new refugees from the SBZ. However, there were instances of serious overcrowding throughout the British and American Occupation Zones. For example, the mayor of Söllingen, a parish in Württemberg-Baden, summed up the difficulties facing many rural communities in September 1946: 'We have 800 inhabitants, 200 of whom are refugees. No new housing has been built for ten years and we do not know where we are to accommodate the refugees. And, meanwhile, more refugees are flooding into our destroyed country ... We are supposed to fit 2–2.3 occupants into a room. That is possible in theory but not in practice.'[70]

Cooking facilities represented a major problem for newcomers living in private accommodation and in the parish of Oesede in the Rural District of Osnabrück only 400 of the 2,700 refugees and evacuees possessed their own kitchen in May 1946.[71] Although the situation improved during the next few years, the Housing Census of September 1950 revealed that, five years after the end of the war, fewer than a third of the newcomers had a kitchen of their own.[72] The census also showed that many refugees still had to endure very cramped living conditions. While 10.5 per cent of the West German population lived in accommodation where more than two people occupied a room, the figure in the states most heavily burdened with newcomers was significantly higher – 11.4 per cent in Bavaria, 12.2 per cent in Lower Saxony and 16.7 per cent in Schleswig-Holstein.[73]

The refugees' living conditions were significantly worse than those of the indigenous inhabitants. In fact, according to the census of September 1950, the 'occupant density' per room totalled 1.75 among the newcomers but only 1.18 among the native population.[74] The gulf in the quality of housing between the two groups was even greater than these figures suggest since the refugees were invariably allocated the smallest rooms in the house. This wide discrepancy between the housing conditions of the native and refugee populations can be partly attributed to the widespread opposition of local people to the billeting of refugees in their homes. Many native householders accepted the refugees only after the intervention of the police, others succeeded in gaining a temporary reprieve by mounting a legal challenge to the mayor's decision,[75] while independent surveys carried out by Allied and German officials indicated that influential members of society often managed to avoid sharing their homes with the newcomers. A commission set up by the Parliamentary Council of the *Länderrat* in the autumn of 1948 to investigate the housing situation in the American Occupation Zone concluded that, while poorer sections of the community and indigenous inhabitants from outside the locality were, as a rule, heavily burdened with refugees, the local elites often remained unaffected by the influx of newcomers.[76] US Military Government officials closely monitored the refugees' housing conditions and frequently intervened in the early post-war years. For example, the Director of the Military Government in Bavaria, General Walter Muller, pointed out to the Bavarian Minister-President, Hans Ehard, in October 1947 that, while the conditions in Freising's refugee camps were 'deplorable ..., former well known Nazis [were] being allowed to live in pure comfort'.[77] But, although, as noted above, the Housing Law laid down harsh penalties for declining to accept refugee tenants, the courts in Bavaria frequently refused to impose them.[78]

In spite of the misgivings of the British and American Governments, refugee camps had to be established in the early post-war years due to the shortage of private lodgings. However, even though these camps became symbols for the suffering and deprivation of the newcomers, it should be borne in mind that they accommodated only a small proportion of the refugees and expellees. In Bavaria, for example, the highest number of newcomers residing in camps (145,822) was recorded on 29 October 1946 but this represented only 9.4 per cent of its total refugee population;[79] moreover, the number of inmates decreased steadily up to the middle of 1948. The same pattern was discernible elsewhere and in Schleswig-Holstein the proportion of refugees accommodated in camps had fallen to 7.8 per cent by June 1948.[80]

In view of the acute shortage of undamaged housing in the towns and cities, refugees based in urban areas were more likely to be located in camps than their counterparts in the countryside. For example, as many as 48.4 per cent of the 21,000 refugees residing in Kiel in December 1946 lived in camps[81] and, even though this figure was reduced to 23.7 per cent by June 1948, it was still three times the average for Schleswig-Holstein as a whole.[82] Studies of Mannheim[83] and Munich[84] confirm this trend and also conclude that the closure of refugee camps located in urban areas proved far more difficult to achieve than in rural districts.

Some refugee camps had formerly been used as prisoner-of-war or forced labour camps during the Third Reich. In addition, schools, gymnasia, dance halls and even hospitals were requisitioned to provide shelter for the refugees and expellees. The existence of these camps represented a constant source of concern to the Allied and German authorities. Franz Bauer's observation that the conditions in Bavaria's refugee camps were 'occasionally tolerable, generally bad and in many cases atrocious'[85] was equally applicable to Lower Saxony and Schleswig-Holstein. Although some camps were in good repair, inspections by representatives of the State Governments and ecclesiastical welfare organisations revealed that many had serious structural defects. For example, a government official appointed in April 1949 by Heinrich Albertz, Refugee Minister in Lower Saxony, to examine conditions in a camp at Bomlitz-Benefeld (Rural District of Fallingbostel) discovered that it was in a dreadful state of disrepair: '200 people live in four wooden huts ... characterised by rotting floors and ceilings, doors and windows which ... do not close properly [and] roofs through which the rain pours straight in due to the absence of roofing felt.'[86] While the conditions in this camp were unusually bad, many similar examples could be found in each of the main refugee states. Most rooms were sparsely furnished; tables and chairs were in short supply and in some camps a single stove had to meet the needs of 40–50 occupants. Heating presented great difficulties in winter. Most camps had separate washing facilities for men and women but, as many of the bathrooms were not heated, the occupants often had to carry out their ablutions in public during cold weather.

Yet the most serious problem was overcrowding and an investigation carried out in October 1948 found that almost 25 per cent of Bavaria's Housing Camps and 15 per cent of its Mass Camps were filled beyond their capacity.[87] The discovery by a group of foreign students visiting the Munich-Allach camp in the autumn of 1948 of a room 16 m^2 which accommodated no fewer than 120 refugees attracted international attention.[88] The cramped conditions in camps often had adverse effects on the newcomers' health. Living in overcrowded, poorly ventilated and often inadequately heated rooms made camp occupants particularly vulnerable to tuberculosis and a study by the refugee committee of the *Länderrat* in May 1947 revealed that camp inmates in Bavaria were twice as likely to become infected as newcomers residing in private accommodation.[89] Significantly, tuberculosis figures were well below average among Ethnic German refugees from Austria, Hungary, Yugoslavia and Rumania, few of whom had spent much time in camps. The inadequate sanitary conditions in some camps, as well as the shortage of soap, posed additional health risks. This is illustrated by a report on the Kehlheim Refugee Camp (Lower Bavaria) drawn up by representatives of the Protestant Church Welfare Organisation (*Evangelisches Hilfswerk*) after visiting the camp in March 1946: 'Forty people are living in a room 42 metres square – one man, 10 women, two of whom are very old, and 29 children. There are 24 beds, placed three on top of each other because of the shortage of space. No proper washing facilitics are available ... A bucket is located in a dark corner ... which serves as the toilet facility for 40 (at first 50) people. The room is full of bugs. Some of the children have bug bites, while others are covered with a scabies rash.'[90] While conditions in Kehlheim were worse than average, it was by no means unrepresentative of many refugee camps throughout the Western Occupation Zones.

During 1947 and the first half of 1948, the number of refugees accommodated in camps fell steadily but the introduction of the new currency reversed any improvement in housing conditions.[91] The British Kreis Resident Officer (KRO) in Rendsburg (Schleswig-Holstein), where newcomers comprised some 40 per cent of the population, observed in July 1949 'that the housing situation ... during the past year has deteriorated to quite a marked extent'[92] and this view was shared by local officials in other parts of the Western Occupation Zones. Refugees billeted with private householders were the first to experience the adverse effects of the Currency Reform. Up until the middle of 1948, rents made up only a small proportion of the monthly outgoings of average families[93] and, even though landlords frequently overcharged refugee tenants, most newcomers were nonetheless able to pay the full rent even if this sometimes involved selling their cigarette ration or bartering private possessions on the black market. Refugees living on farms were in a more favourable position since they generally paid only a nominal rent or enjoyed free accommodation in return for working for the farmer. But the introduction of the deutschmark transformed the situation. Landlords simply converted the amount of the original rent from reichmarks into DM even though the purchasing power of the new currency was much greater than the old one. While unemployed refugees could reclaim this money from the state, those in gainful employment had to meet the new rent out of their own resources. As a result, many found themselves in debt and in Lower Saxony newcomers already owed more than a million DM in rent arrears in October 1948.[94]

Refugees who were occupying hotel rooms were hit with particular severity by the Currency Reform. Faced with the acute post-war housing shortage, State Governments compelled many hotel and guest house owners in tourist areas such as the Harz mountains, the East Friesian islands and the Bavarian alps to let their rooms to refugees and in October 1948 as many as 242,000 out of 363,000 hotel beds in the British and American Occupation Zones were occupied by newcomers.[95] This represented an enormous economic burden to regions heavily dependent on tourism. As a result, the Bizonal authorities in Frankfurt, under intense pressure from hotel owners, issued a directive on 8 October 1948 stipulating that rents for refugees accommodated in hotels were to be based on the amount the proprietor would have been able to charge a hotel guest for the room. This figure was, of course, significantly higher than the average rent for refugees living in private houses and sometimes amounted to more than half their total monthly income.[96] This caused enormous hardship for many newcomers and in Bad Pyrmont, one of Lower Saxony's best-known spa towns, 95 per cent of the refugee population had fallen behind with their rent by January 1949.[97]

The sharp increase in the cost of renting private quarters after the introduction of the deutschmark also led to an increase in the number of refugees living in camps. In Schleswig-Holstein, for example, the number of camps went up from 411 in June 1948 to 494 a year later, while the number of inmates rose from 90,582 to 100,469 in the same period.[98] Prior to the Currency Reform, most camp occupants had been anxious to move into private accommodation. However, since newcomers residing in camps either did not have to pay rent or contributed only a nominal sum,[99] the prospect of leaving them became much less attractive after the introduction of the deutschmark. Indeed, some refugees actually refused to move into private quarters on the grounds that they could not afford to pay the rent and one such incident in Düsseldorf in April 1949 resulted in rental charges being introduced for the inmates of all refugee camps in North Rhine-Westphalia.[100] Similar considerations prompted the Bavarian Government to bring in a rental charge for housing camp occupants in March 1949 and abolish communal eating facilities in all housing camps two months later.[101] The economic repercussions of the Currency Reform were so serious that some newcomers even sought refuge in the camps they had only recently left.[102]

The introduction of the deutschmark also led to a deterioration in the living conditions of refugee camp occupants. In Bavaria, for example, the number of beds, mattresses and blankets placed at the disposal of the camp authorities dropped sharply in the second half of 1948 due to the severe restrictions imposed on government expenditure.[103] The acute shortage of money after the Currency Reform also halted the implementation of urgent structural repairs to a number of refugee camps. In Schleswig-Holstein, plans to provide family accommodation by partitioning large barracks in some of the camps had to be postponed,[104] while in September 1949, fifteen months after the Monetary Reform, refugees in Springe (Lower Saxony) were still awaiting the resumption of a project to convert barracks into an old people's home.[105]

The only long-term solution to the post-war housing crisis was a large-scale building programme. In fact, it was estimated in 1949 that, in addition to repairing damaged housing, at least 1.8 million new dwellings would have to be constructed to accommodate the refugees and expellees residing in the FRG.[106] Allied and German politicians recognised the need to address this issue at the outset of the Occupation but, as Sylvia Schraut wryly observed, their efforts 'produced more paper than additional housing'.[107] Up until the middle of 1948, the major obstacle to house construction was the dearth of building materials such as lime, cement, glass and tiles. Refugee housing was, of course, only one of many projects competing for scarce resources and in Württemberg-Baden less than a third of the cement and no more than a quarter of the building tiles required to implement the refugee housing programme was actually available during the last three months of 1946.[108] Another important problem was that, despite the large population increase in the Western Occupation Zones of Germany after the Second World War, there was actually a shortage of construction workers in urban areas. The Labour Office in Munich, for example, was able to meet only 15 per cent of the demand for bricklayers at the end of 1945.[109] Some refugees who were qualified builders could not accept work in the heavily damaged and overcrowded towns and cities since they were unable to find anywhere to live.

Many newcomers had high hopes that the Currency Reform would bring about an improvement in their housing situation but, in actual fact, exactly the opposite occurred. While the introduction of the deutschmark made building materials more readily available, there was an acute shortage of public and private money for investment in housing projects. As a result, the construction of domestic houses practically came to a standstill and just 18,815 homes were built in North Rhine-Westphalia between June 1948 and June 1949.[110] Indeed, the scarcity of financial credit brought about by the Currency Reform continued to hamper federal and state house building programmes until the early 1950s.[111] The persistent influx of several thousand new refugees each week from the GDR aggravated the general housing shortage and, as will be seen in chapter 5, refugee camps continued to exist up to and even beyond the construction of the Berlin Wall on 13 August 1961.

Employment

As well as having to endure poor housing conditions, many refugees also encountered serious difficulties on the labour market. The geographical location of the newcomers was the most important factor influencing their job prospects. Although the severe housing shortages in the towns and cities left the Occupying Powers with no alternative but to distribute the majority of the refugees in the countryside, this decision undoubtedly had an adverse effect on their chances of securing suitable employment. The newcomers arrived in the Western Occupation Zones of Germany in such large numbers and at such short notice that the Allied authorities, despite pressure from German politicians, were unable to settle them according to their occupational structure. For example, in September 1950 the predominantly rural state of Bavaria, whose economy was heavily dependent on agriculture and tourism, accommodated as many as 1,026,000 Sudeten Germans, almost half of whom had been working in industrial concerns at the outbreak of the Second World War, and 461,000 Silesians, a significant proportion of whom also came from an industrial background.[112] After their arrival in the West, many of these refugees were directed to rural areas of Bavaria and in December 1949 no fewer than 40 per cent of the newcomers who in their homelands had lived in medium-sized or large towns were located in small communities with a population of fewer than 2,000 people where there was little or no opportunity of obtaining work in their chosen occupation.[113]

The problems arising from the inability of the Western Allies to distribute the refugees and expellees according to their occupational structure are illustrated by the fact that, despite high unemployment levels among the newcomers in Lower Saxony and Bavaria,[114] the number of job vacancies in the Western Occupation Zones of Germany in June 1946 (369,000) actually exceeded the number registered as out of work (329,000).[115] In fact, some large towns and cities experienced a serious shortage of labour and Hamburg had some 34,000 unfilled vacancies in November 1946.[116] During 1947 and the first half of 1948, the number of refugees without a job fell steadily. In Bavaria, for example, the unemployment rate among the newcomers fell from 23.3 per cent in March 1947 to 8 per cent in June 1948,[117] while in Württemberg-Baden only 4 per cent of refugees were out of work in September 1947.[118]

Although these figures might suggest that one aspect of the refugee problem had been largely solved by mid-1948, nothing was further from the truth. After all, the unemployment rate among the newcomers was much higher than that of the indigenous inhabitants.[119] Moreover, refugees tended to be overrepresented in what Mark Roseman has described as 'economically meaningless employment'[120] – jobs which had been created only due to the drastic fall in the value of the reichsmark. Furthermore, a significant number of refugees, unable to obtain employment in their chosen trade or profession, accepted work in an occupation for which they had not been trained (*berufsfremd*). The way in which official statistics were calculated makes it impossible to determine the true extent of this problem.[121] In Württemberg-Baden, for example, refugees who had been unable to resume their former profession were only classified as '*berufsfremd*' for the first six months after they had gained alternative employment.[122] Similarly, refugees who were able to pursue the same occupation as in their homelands, albeit at a lower level, were not identified in government statistics. In other words, an independent farmer (*Landwirt*) from East Prussia, who, after his arrival in the West, worked as an unskilled agricultural labourer was, according to official figures, engaged in the same occupation as before the expulsion.[123]

The employment prospects of the refugees and expellees up to the Currency Reform varied widely between the different occupational groups. There were generally good opportunities for refugee teachers because many of the original incumbents had been suspended pending the decisions of the denazification tribunals. In fact, 28 per cent of secondary school teachers in the British Occupation Zone in June 1948 were newcomers, well above their proportion of the total population.[124] Small businessmen such as bakers, butchers, hairdressers and electricians were usually able to establish themselves because there was an increased demand for these services due to the influx of new population. In addition, construction workers, bricklayers, carpenters and other groups essential to post-war reconstruction were in heavy demand in towns and cities which had suffered war damage. However, the prospects for many other occupational groups were bleak. Commercial, administrative and clerical employees were hit particularly hard and in Hesse they comprised 24 per cent of all unemployed refugees in September 1947.[125] In the long term, the plight of independent farmers was even worse. In Lower Saxony, just 7,720 of the 190,416 refugee *Landwirte* had managed to resume their former occupation by October 1948 [126] and it was a similar story elsewhere. For many refugees located in small rural communities, the only available work was on the land and in September 1947 almost 44 per cent of refugees in Württemberg-Baden were employed as agricultural labourers.[127] They invariably received very low wages and, due to the reichmark's loss of value, often preferred to work in return for food and accommodation rather than monetary payment.

The period 1945–48 also saw the establishment of a large number of commercial undertakings by the refugees and expellees in rural areas. In Lower Saxony, mining and manufacturing enterprises were set up, especially in the administrative districts of Brunswick, Hildesheim, Hanover and Lüneburg, while refugee clothing and textile firms were of particular importance in Schleswig-Holstein. Highly gifted refugee craftsmen who, prior to their expulsion, enjoyed a world-wide reputation for producing a variety of luxury goods were able to re-establish themselves in Bavaria after the Second World War. As a result, Bayreuth became a centre of the jewellery trade, while groups of Sudeten Germans from the Czechoslovakian town of Gablonz founded the parish of Neugablonz, which soon acquired a reputation for jewellery and glass making. In addition, Günzburg (Swabia) became known for its leather gloves industry, Cham (Upper Palatinate) for its shoes, while Neustadt a.d. Aisch and Erlangen (Middle Franconia) were noted for producing musical instruments. The early post-war period also witnessed a revival of cottage industries and in Bavaria alone over 150,000 refugees – mostly women – were engaged in weaving, knitting, cotton spinning, lace making and the production of children's toys and ornaments in their own homes.[128] This practice was especially common in economically impoverished areas such as the Bavarian Forest where there was little alternative employment. The wages were often pitifully low – the official rate of pay for domestic workers in the textile industry was 45 pfennigs an hour in 1948, but those paid by piece rate usually earned less.[129] In fact, their working conditions were in many respects reminiscent of a pre-industrial age.

To sum up, the refugees' employment situation in mid-1948 was less good than it appeared at first sight. Even though most newcomers had managed to find work of some description, only a small proportion had been able to gain employment commensurate with their qualifications. The majority had accepted unskilled jobs, often as agricultural or manual labourers. The social descent experienced by the refugees was reflected in the findings of a survey carried out by the Bavarian Statistical Office. Between 1939 and 1946, the proportion of 'workers' among the refugee population had increased from 40 to 79 per cent. During the same period, the number of self-employed newcomers had fallen from 31 to 7 per cent, while the proportion of 'civil servants' (*Beamte*) and 'employees' (*Angestellte*) had decreased from 29 to 15 per cent.[130] The fact that many refugees had taken unskilled jobs made them particularly susceptible to redundancy in the tough commercial climate prevailing after the introduction of the deutschmark on 20 June 1948 when the general shortage of money prompted employers to reduce the size of their work force.

In June 1948, just 3.2 per cent of the overall working population in the Western Occupation Zones of Germany was out of work (see Table 2.3).[131] Significantly, two of the states most heavily burdened with refugees, Lower Saxony and Schleswig-Holstein, actually recorded below-average unemployment levels at that time. However, as Table 2.3 shows, the proportion of the population without a job trebled in the eighteen months following the Currency Reform. This dramatic rise in unemployment affected the newcomers much

Table 2.3 Unemployment in the Western Occupation Zones of Germany after the Currency Reform

	30 June 1948		*30 June 1949*		*31 Dec. 1949*	
			Unemployed			
State	*Total*	*% of pop*	*Total*	*% of pop*	*Total*	*% of pop*
American Occupation Zone						
Bavaria	145,727	5.4	348,258	12.6	406,295	14.5
Hesse	41,895	3.4	104,909	7.9	132,977	9.9
Württemberg-Baden	29,972	2.6	57,338	4.7	68,298	5.4
Bremen	6,923	3.7	16,739	8.3	17,457	8.5
French Occupation Zone						
Württemberg-Hohenzollern	1,215	0.4	4,781	1.5	12,229	3.5
Baden	3,137	1.0	7,093	2.0	11,227	3.0
Rhineland-Palatinate	5,144	0.8	33,716	4.6	53,120	7.0
British Occupation Zone						
North Rhine-Westphalia	122,260	3.1	182,710	4.2	196,107	4.5
Lower Saxony	59,075	2.9	286,750	13.7	367,701	17.3
Hamburg	14,493	2.5	51,895	8.2	71,874	11.1
Schleswig-Holstein	21,250	2.7	189,113	22.6	221,184	26.3
Totals	451,091	3.2	1,283,302	8.7	1,558,469	10.3

Source: Bundesministerium für Arbeit (ed.), *Entwicklung und Ursachen der Arbeitslosigkeit in der Bundesrepublik Deutschland 1946–1950* (Bonn 1950), p. 6.

more acutely than the indigenous inhabitants. It was not just that the major refugee states – Bavaria, Lower Saxony and Schleswig-Holstein – recorded disproportionately high increases in the numbers out of work but that even within these states newcomers were much more likely to lose their jobs than the native population. In Schleswig-Holstein, for example, unemployment figures rose from some 21,000 at the time of the Currency Reform to more than 221,000 in December 1949; significantly, refugees comprised some 58 per cent of this total, even though they made up only 35 per cent of the population (see Table 2.4).

Table 2.4 Refugee unemployment in West Germany, 31 December 1949

State	*Total out of work*	*Refugees out of work*	*Out of work refugees as % of total*	*% of refugees in population*
American Occupation Zone				
Bavaria	406,295	162,129	39.9	21.0
Hesse	132,977	36,304	27.3	15.4
Württemberg-Baden	68,298	23,818	34.9	18.4
Bremen	17,457	1,448	8.3	6.9
French Occupation Zone				
Württemberg-Hohenzollern	12,229	5,426	44.4	8.0
Baden	11,227	1,691	15.1	5.6
British Occupation Zone				
North Rhine-Westphalia	196,107	25,527	13.0	9.1
Lower Saxony	367,701	159,514	43.4	26.8
Hamburg	71,874	1,441	2.0	5.9
Schleswig-Holstein	221,184	129,365	58.5	34.9
Totals	1,505,349	546,663	36.3	16.1

Source: Calculated from Statistisches Amt des Vereinigten Wirtschaftsgebietes (ed.), *Statistische Unterlagen zum Flüchtlingsproblem* No. 5 and Bundesministerium für Arbeit (ed.), *Entwicklung und Ursachen*, p. 6. No figures are available for Rhineland-Palatinate.

The deterioration in the employment situation after the introduction of the deutschmark was aggravated by the return of prisoners-of war and the continuing influx of *illegale Grenzgänger* – German refugees who entered the Western Occupation Zones illegally from the SBZ and Czechoslovakia. However, while these developments swelled the numbers looking for work, this cannot obscure the fact that in the period June 1948–December 1949 the main refugee states not only registered a sharp rise in the numbers out of work but also a marked decrease in the numbers in employment – as many as 136,000 in Bavaria, 157,000 in Schleswig-Holstein and 211,000 in Lower Saxony.[132] It seems clear, then, that the Currency Reform was the most important reason for the striking increase in refugee unemployment in the months prior to the establishment of the FRG.

The vulnerability of the newcomers to dismissal from mid-1948 onwards was due mainly to the fact that the majority of them were still living in rural areas. A regional analysis of unemployment trends suggests that the proportion of the population out of work in a particular district was determined less by the number of refugees it accommodated than the capacity of its economy to absorb surplus population. Thus, North Rhine-Westphalia, the most prosperous and industrialised state, recorded the smallest percentage increase in unemployment in the eighteen months following the adoption of the new currency, while Württemberg-Baden, a state with a mixed economy, registered only a moderate rise in the numbers out of work even though it was heavily burdened with refugees. By contrast, the unemployment crisis after the Currency Reform was especially acute in Bavaria, Lower Saxony and Schleswig-Holstein, predominantly rural states which also accommodated very large numbers of newcomers. The dichotomy between the employment situation in rural and urban areas is illustrated by the example of Hesse where, in 1950, 16 per cent of the population was out of work in the mainly agricultural districts in the north of the state but only 7.2 per cent in the more industrialised and urban south.[133]

At the same time, some rural districts which were heavily reliant on agriculture nonetheless had a low unemployment rate if they were situated within commuting distance of a major population centre. For example, the Rural District of Leonberg (Württemberg-Baden), where agriculture was the only major source of income, recorded virtually full employment in 1950 even though its population was 50 per cent above the pre-war level due to the arrival of the newcomers.[134] The explanation was its geographical proximity to the town of Stuttgart, to which some 17 per cent of its inhabitants commuted to work each day.[135] In fact, commuting became a common phenomenon in the early post-war years due to the acute housing shortage in the towns and cities,[136] and some refugees travelled considerable distances on a daily basis. On the other hand, newcomers who lived in outlying country districts which lacked adequate transportation links to larger centres of population were particularly susceptible to long-term unemployment. For example, Lower Bavaria, a geographically isolated region heavily dependent on agriculture, was a notorious unemployment black spot and in February 1951, 32.9 per cent of refugees were out of work in Pfarrkirchen, 33.9 per cent in Passau and 36.5 per cent in Deggendorf.[137] In fact, the Currency Reform accelerated the population movement from rural into urban areas,[138] a trend which was further reinforced in the first half of the 1950s by government resettlement programmes.

While no occupational group remained immune from the wave of dismissals in the aftermath of the Currency Reform, unskilled manual and agricultural labourers were among the worst affected. An American Military Government representative in Mannheim noted in February 1949 that, although 'there is still need for skilled building trades workers, ... unskilled help is ... difficult to place'[139] and similar observations were made throughout the Western Occupation Zones. The introduction of the deutschmark also had a catastrophic impact on the cottage industries and many small firms employing domestic workers collapsed during the summer of 1948. In Eiderstedt (Schleswig-Holstein), for example, the number of refugee women working in the hand-knitting industry fell from 300 to 30 in the first four months after the Monetary Reform.[140] The adoption of the new currency had equally disastrous effects on refugee firms. In Schleswig-Holstein just six of the 100 enterprises established in Lockstedt refugee camp survived[141] and a similar pattern was evident elsewhere. While the failure of some undertakings was inevitable since they had produced goods of inferior quality, many potentially viable businesses also went into liquidation and Fritz Schumacher, Economic Adviser to the British Control Commission in Germany, observed in February 1949 that the bankruptcies among the refugee concerns included 'productive and enterprising firms that could play a valuable part in recovery'.[142] Such was the fate of the world famous jewellery and glassmaking industries at Neugablonz. By the end of August 1948, 170 firms had been forced to close and by September 1949, 4,500 of the 5,892 workers employed in Neugablonz on the eve of the Currency Reform had been made redundant.[143] Although the firm began to recover in the early 1950s, others were not so fortunate.

While well-established native businesses were able to hoard their goods in the period leading up to the reform, and sell them for hard currency directly afterwards, the newly founded refugee firms rarely had sufficient capital to follow their example. They were forced to trade for inflationary reichsmarks which had to be exchanged at the unfavourable rate of ten to one on 20 June 1948. The sharp rise in the cost of renting business premises after the introduction of the deutschmark dealt a savage blow to many refugee firms.[144] The Currency Reform also brought to light the unsuitable geographical location of refugee industries established in isolated rural communities. In the unusual economic conditions prevailing until mid-1948 when a buyer could be found for almost every product, many of these enterprises had flourished but in the tough commercial climate which characterised the period after the reform they invariably proved uncompetitive.

However, the most intractable problem facing the refugee industries as a result of the Currency Reform was undoubtedly the shortage of medium- and long-term credit. The Refugee Commissioner in Hesse, Peter Paul Nahm, estimated in September 1949 that 750 million DM would be required to ensure the survival of the refugee firms,[145] but, in view of the drastic reductions in public expenditure necessitated by the Currency Reform, the State Governments were able to release no more than a fraction of this amount. For example, in October 1948, the Finance Ministry in Lower Saxony allocated to each of the state's 76 districts just 27,000 DM to help refugee firms finding themselves in financial difficulties.[146] This sum proved woefully inadequate and the Refugee Office in the Urban District of Celle was able to approve just 26 of the 151 requests for financial assistance.[147] The situation was no better in the other states heavily burdened with refugees and in the Rural District of Ansbach (Middle Franconia), where 396 refugee firms had applied for loans totalling 1,660,000 DM, the authorities were able to make available only 23 per cent of that amount.[148] Although government investment in the refugee industries increased in 1949–50, a study carried out in Bavaria shortly after the formation of the FRG concluded that the shortage of credit was responsible for the dismissal of some 30 per cent of newcomers made redundant since the Currency Reform.[149]

The overall impact of the Currency Reform on the employment situation of the refugees and expellees was summed up by Peter Paul Nahm in December 1948:

> Up until the Currency Reform, many refugees were able to make ends meet by doing odd jobs or taking advantage of other opportunities to earn a bit of extra money. They may also have been able to supplement their income by engaging in cottage industries. Others had saved their 'expulsion money' or put aside some money for a rainy day, while some tried to establish a modest livelihood and settle down. The Currency Reform removed this possibility with the result that, with a few exceptions, all [the refugees] are completely destitute.[150]

It should be borne in mind that the unemployment crisis in the main refugee states precipitated by the introduction of the deutschmark was not a transitory phenomenon and in Schleswig-Holstein, 25.6 per cent of the working population was without a job in March 1951.[151] Even though national unemployment figures fell steadily during the 1950s, refugees residing in Bavaria, Lower Saxony and Schleswig-Holstein continued to experience serious difficulties in obtaining a job, since not only was the unemployment rate in these states above the national average but newcomers were still less likely to be offered work than members of the indigenous population.[152] However, employment opportunities were available in other parts of the FRG, in particular the industrial conurbations of North Rhine-Westphalia, and one of the most important challenges facing the State and Federal Governments in the 1950s was to resettle the refugees in these areas. This issue will be explored in chapter 5.

Conclusion

It is clear, then, that many refugees and expellees suffered serious economic deprivation during the early post-war years. In fact, there was general agreement that the newcomers' economic position in the spring of 1949 was actually worse than in the period directly following the collapse of the Reich. At a meeting of Refugee Commissioners in the American Occupation Zone in April 1949, Nahm concluded that the refugees had not 'benefit[ed] from the economic progress in Western Germany. Only 5% ... have an income of 200 DM or over. An enormous number ... are dependent on welfare benefits'.[153] The Bavarian State Secretary for Refugees, Wolfgang Jaenicke, shared these sentiments, adding that 'the situation today is more difficult than ... [at] the beginning of 1946'.[154] This deterioration in the refugees' economic position can be attributed primarily to the introduction of the deutschmark in June 1948. While historians have justifiably drawn attention to the importance of the Currency Reform in bringing about West Germany's 'Economic Miracle', this chapter has shown that it undoubtedly caused great hardship to the weakest groups in society such as the refugees and expellees.

The adverse effects of the Monetary Reform on the newcomers also had wide-ranging implications for their relations with the native population. The refugees found it particularly difficult to accept the worsening of their own material position from mid-1948 onwards since it coincided with an improvement in the standard of living of large sections of the indigenous inhabitants. The normalisation of economic conditions after the Currency Reform underlined the wide gulf between the 'haves' and the 'have-nots'. While, as has been seen, many refugees could not afford to buy their full food rations in the period immediately after the Monetary Reform, the wealthy were once again able to eat luxurious meals in exclusive restaurants and consume expensive cream cakes and strawberries in cafes.[155] Developments in the building industry also focused attention on the social divisions created between the newcomers and the more affluent sections of the native population. For example, while plans to construct flats for the local refugee population in the holiday resort of Travemünde (near Lübeck) could not proceed during the first half of 1949 due to a shortage of money, private individuals had sufficient funds to build two new casinos.[156] This aroused deep resentment among the newcomers and both Allied and German observers feared that this would adversely affect relations between the refugee and native populations. How justified were these fears? To what extent can it be said that relations between the two groups were more harmonious in an urban as opposed to a rural environment? And what factors helped to determine refugee–native relations? These issues will be addressed in chapter 3.

Notes

1 Reichling, 'Flucht und Vertreibung der Deutschen', p. 46.
2 G. Reichling, *Die Heimatvertriebenen im Spiegel der Statistik* (Berlin 1958), pp. 22–3.
3 Figures compiled from the World Almanac of 1950. Bayerisches Hauptstaatsarchiv (BHStA), MArb, 27.
4 Quoted in Brandes, *Der Weg zur Vertreibung*, p. 416.
5 Statistisches Landesamt Schleswig-Holstein (ed.), *Das Flüchtlingsgeschehen in Schleswig-Holstein infolge des 2. Weltkriegs in der amtlichen Statistik* (Kiel 1974), p. 10.
6 M. Beer, 'Flüchtlinge – Ausgewiesene – Neubürger – Heimatvertriebene: Flüchtlingspolitik und Flüchtlingsintegration in Deutschland nach 1945, begriffsgeschichtlich betrachtet', in M. Beer, M. Kintzinger and M. Krauss (eds), *Migration und Integration: Aufnahme und Eingliederung im historischen Wandel* (Stuttgart 1997), p.147. For a detailed discussion of the issue of terminology, see also, V. Ackermann, *Der "echte" Flüchtling: Deutsche Vertriebene und Flüchtlinge aus der DDR 1945–1961* (Osnabrück 1995), pp. 65–95 and Reichling, 'Flucht und Vertreibung der Deutschen', pp. 46–56.
7 Quoted in Beer, 'Flüchtlinge – Ausgewiesene – Neubürger', p. 156.
8 *Ibid.*, p. 158.
9 Quoted in *ibid.*, p. 166.
10 P.P. Nahm, *... doch das Leben ging weiter: Skizzen zur Lage, Haltung und Leistung der Vertriebenen, Flüchtlinge und Eingesessenen nach der Stunde Null* (Cologne and Berlin 1971), pp. 26–7.
11 For a detailed study of this issue, see M. Schwartz, '"Vom Umsiedler zum Staatsbürger": Totalitäres und Subversives in der Sprachpolitik der SBZ/DDR', in D. Hoffmann, M. Krauss and M. Schwartz (eds), *Vertriebene in Deutschland: Interdisziplinäre Ergebnisse und Forschungsperspektiven* (Munich 2000), pp. 135–66.
12 Reichling, 'Flucht und Vertreibung der Deutschen', p. 52.
13 Ackermann, *Der 'echte' Flüchtling*, p. 13.
14 *Ibid.*, pp. 74–8. See also Ahonen, *After the Expulsion*, pp. 67–8. *Heimatvertriebene* received an identity card 'A' which entitled them to more generous financial allowances than *Vertriebene* who were granted an identity card 'B'.
15 Bundesarchiv (BA), NL Jaenicke, 103, Minutes of a Conference of German Minister-Presidents, 7 June 1947.
16 Schieder (ed.), *Dokumentation der Vertreibung*, Vol. 1, p. 148.
17 R. Messerschmidt, *Aufnahme und Integration der Vertriebenen und Flüchtlinge in Hessen 1945–1950: Zur Geschichte der hessischen Flüchtlingsverwaltung* (Wiesbaden 1994), pp. 62–3.
18 See for example, BA, Z18, 134, *Eindrücke von einer Besichtigungsfahrt*

durch die neuen Auffanglager an der Grenze, 9–22 February 1946.

19 *Das Flüchtlingsproblem in der amerikanischen Besatzungszone: Ein Bericht des Länderrates an General Clay* (Stuttgart 1948), p. 29, in Institut für Zeitgeschichte (IfZ), Fi.01.8.

20 G. Granicky, *Ergebnisse der Flüchtlingszählung des Jahres 1947 in Nordrhein-Westfalen*, p. 48, in BA, Z40, 468.

21 Y. R. Winkler, *Flüchtlingsorganisationen in Hessen 1945–1954: BHE – Flüchtlingsverbände – Landsmannschaften* (Wiesbaden 1998), pp. 15–16.

22 M. Skorvan, *Das Hilfswerk der Evangelischen Kirche und seine Flüchtlingsarbeit in Hessen 1945–1955* (Wiesbaden 1995), p. 129.

23 Nahm, *... doch das Leben ging weiter*, p. 7.

24 BHStA, MWi 9628, Bornheimer (State Secretariat for Refugees) to Pollack (Bavarian Economics Ministry), 26 June 1947.

25 Frantzioch, *Die Vertriebenen*, p. 91.

26 B. Marshall, 'German Attitudes to British Military Government 1945–47', *Journal of Contemporary History*, Vol. 15 (1980), p. 660.

27 Schier, *Die Aufnahme und Eingliederung*, p. 155.

28 J. Farquharson, 'The British Occupation of Germany 1945–6: A Badly Managed Disaster Area?', *GH*, Vol. 11(3) (1993), p. 337.

29 H. J. Malecki, *Die Heimatvertriebenen in Niedersachsen* (Hanover 1951), p. 17.

30 J. Farquharson, *The Western Allies and the Politics of Food: Agrarian Management in Postwar Germany* (Leamington Spa 1985), p. 16.

31 Bayerisches Statistisches Landesamt (ed.), *Bayern in Zahlen: Monatshefte des Bayerischen Statistischen Landesamtes*, No. 4 (April 1947), p. 79.

32 Frantzioch, *Die Vertriebenen*, p. 98.

33 I. Turner, 'British Occupation Policy and its Effects on the Town of Wolfsburg and the Volkswagenwerk 1945–49', PhD thesis, University of Manchester 1984, p. 134.

34 G. Trittel, 'Von der "Verwaltung des Mangels" zur "Verhinderung der Neuordnung". Ein Überblick über die Hauptprobleme der Wirtschaftspolitik in der Britischen Zone 1945–1949', in C. Scharf and H.-J. Schröder (eds), *Die Deutschlandpolitik Grossbritanniens und die Britische Zone 1945–1949* (Wiesbaden 1979), p. 135.

35 Quoted in Messerschmidt, *Aufnahme und Integration*, pp. 140–1.

36 G. Stüber, *Der Kampf gegen den Hunger 1945–1950: Die Ernährungslage in der britischen Zone Deutschlands, insbesondere in Schleswig-Holstein und Hamburg* (Neumünster 1984), p. 560. See also D. Brosius, 'Zur Lage der Flüchtlinge im Regierungsbezirk Lüneburg zwischen Kriegsende und Währungsreform', in D. Brosius and A. Hohenstein, *Flüchtlinge im nordöstlichen Niedersachsen 1945–1948* (Hildesheim 1985), p. 25.

37 F. J. Bauer, *Flüchtlinge und Flüchtlingspolitik in Bayern 1945–1950* (Stuttgart 1982), p. 183.

38 See for example, Archiv des Diakonischen Werkes der Evangelischen Kirche in Deutschland (ADW), ZB, 858, *Bericht über die V. Informationsfahrt durch Flüchtlingslager in Westfalen, Ostfriesland und Oldenburg* (30 August–12 September 1946), 18 September 1946. A total of 39 camps were visited. See also Archiv des Deutschen Caritasverbandes, Freiburg im Breisgau (DCV), 371 0, *Reisebericht über den Besuch im Flüchtlingsdurchgangslager Pöppendorf, im ständigen Flüchtlingslager Lübeck-Burgfeld* (13–14 November 1946), 15 November 1946.

39 T. Viewegh, 'Die Plassenburg – ein Vorzeigelager?', in R. Endres (ed.), *Bayerns vierter Stamm: Die Integration der Flüchtlinge und Heimatvertriebenen nach 1945* (Cologne 1998), p. 38.

40 The unrest began in Dachau and Munich-Allach camps on 4 September 1948 and soon spread to other camps in Rosenheim and Augsburg. See *Süddeutsche Zeitung*, 7 September 1948.

41 Schier, *Die Aufnahme und Eingliederung* , p. 155.

42 W. Tormin, *Die Geschichte der SPD in Hamburg 1945 bis 1950* (Hamburg 1994), p. 149.

43 Stüber, *Der Kampf gegen den Hunger*, pp. 578–9.

44 Staatsarchiv München (StA), Landratsamt (LRA), 30750, Weekly Report of the Mayor of Weissbach to the *Landrat* of Berchtesgaden, 27 June 1947.

45 See for example, P. Erker, 'Revolution des Dorfes? Ländliche Bevölkerung zwischen Flüchtlingszustrom und landwirtschaftlichem Strukturwandel', in M. Broszat, K.-D. Henke and H. Woller (eds), *Von Stalingrad zur Währungsreform: Zur Sozialgeschichte des Umbruchs in Deutschland* (Munich 1989), p. 393.

46 Stüber, *Der Kampf gegen den Hunger*, p. 265.

47 *Ibid.*, p. 267.

48 A. Wennemann, 'Flüchtlinge und Vertriebene in Niedersachsen: Vergangenheitsorientierung und Strukturwandel', in K.J. Bade (ed.), *Fremde im Land: Zuwanderung und Eingliederung im Raum Niedersachsen seit dem Zweiten Weltkrieg* (Osnabrück 1997), p. 104.

49 Stüber, *Der Kampf gegen den Hunger*, p. 535.

50 This section relies heavily on I. Connor, 'The Refugees and the Currency Reform', in I. Turner (ed.), *Reconstruction in Post-War Germany: British Occupation Policy and the Western Zones, 1945–55* (Oxford 1989), pp. 305–6.

51 For example, calorie rations in Kiel increased from 1,384 per day in May 1948 to 1,958 in August of the same year. See Stüber, *Der Kampf gegen den Hunger*, p. 379.

52 Niedersächsisches Hauptstaatsarchiv (NHStA) Hanover, Nds 120

Lüneburg, Acc. 31/67, 3, Refugee Office of Rural District of Burgdorf to *Regierungspräsident* of Lüneburg, 9 November 1948.

53 Landesarchiv Schleswig-Holstein (LSH), Abteilung (Abt.) 605, 1206, Hans Müthling to Hermann Lüdemann, 15 September 1948.

54 See for example, PRO, FO 1006/72, Monthly Report of the KRO of the Rural District of Norderdithmarschen to the Regional Commissioner of Schleswig-Holstein, 23 November 1948.

55 StA, LRA 29569, Labour Office (Traunstein) to Labour Office (Southern Bavaria), 27 June 1949.

56 W. Fuhrmann, *Die Bayerische Lagerversorgung 1948–1951: Ein ernährungswirtschaftlicher Beitrag zur Vesorgung von Gemeinschaftsverpflegungseinrichtungen und der Schulspeisung* (np, nd), p. 77.

57 Nordrhein-Westfälisches Hauptstaatsarchiv (HStA) Düsseldorf, Reg. Düs. 54328, *Oberkreisdirektor* of Rural District of Dinslaken to the *Regierungspräsident* of Düsseldorf, 18 July 1948; PRO, FO 1006/68, Monthly Report of the KRO of the Rural District of Plön to the Regional Commissioner of Schleswig-Holstein, 24 July 1948.

58 Fuhrmann, *Die Bayerische Lagerversorgung*, p. 77.

59 Stüber, *Der Kampf gegen den Hunger*, p. 576.

60 K.C. Führer, *Mieter, Hausbesitzer, Staat und Wohungsmarkt: Wohnungsmangel und Wohnungszwangwirtschaft in Deutschland 1914–1960* (Stuttgart 1995), p. 40.

61 *Ibid.*

62 *Ibid.*, p. 351.

63 BHStA, MArb 27, *Statistischer Informationsdienst*, No. 69.

64 In June 1947, there were 15,949 refugees in Esslingen, 24.7 per cent of the population. See S. Schraut, *Flüchtlingsaufnahme in Württemberg-Baden 1945–1949: Amerikanische Besatzungsziele und demokratischer Wiederaufbau im Konflikt* (Munich 1995), p. 280.

65 BSL (ed.), *Die Flüchtlinge in Bayern: Ergebnisse einer Sonderauszählung aus der Volks- und Berufszählung vom 29. Oktober 1946* (Munich 1948). Quoted in F.J. Bauer, 'Der Bayerische Bauernverband, die Bodenreform und das Flüchtlingsproblem 1945–1951', *Vierteljahrshefte für Zeitgeschichte*, Vol. 31(3) (1983), p. 444.

66 For example, in late 1946, a US Military Government representative, Major James Campbell, turned down a request to house 2,000 refugees in a former air-force base in the Rural District of Tauberbischofsheim in Württemberg-Baden on the grounds that 'the undesirable concentration of refugees' constituted 'a source of trouble and a state within a state'. See Schraut, *Flüchtlingsaufnahme in Württemberg-Baden*, p. 254.

67 Führer, *Mieter, Hausbesitzer*, p. 357.

68 Instructions of the Headquarters of the Seventh Army Western Division to the Military Government Directors of Hesse and Württemberg-Baden, 19 October 1945. Quoted in Schraut, *Flüchtlingsaufnahme in*

Württemberg-Baden, p. 226.

69 This paragraph is based on Schraut, *Flüchtlingsaufnahme in Württemberg-Baden*, pp. 89–90.

70 Quoted in *ibid.*, p. 239.

71 B. Parisius, 'Flüchtlinge und Vertriebene in Osnabrück und im Osnabrücker Land', in K.J. Bade, H.-B. Meier and B. Parisius (eds), *Zeitzeugen im Interview: Flüchtlinge und Vertriebene in Osnabrück nach 1945* (Osnabrück 1997), p. 41.

72 P. Waldmann, 'Die Eingliederung der ostdeutschen Vertriebenen in die westdeutsche Gesellschaft', in J. Becker, T. Stammen and P. Waldmann (eds), *Vorgeschichte der Bundesrepublik Deutschland: Zwischen Kapitulation und Grundgesetz* (Munich 1979), p. 177.

73 Calculated from Führer, *Mieter, Hausbesitzer*, p. 416.

74 Bauer, *Flüchtlinge und Flüchtlingspolitik*, p. 201.

75 For example, in the Rural District of Tauberbischofsheim, where the billeting of refugees in private accommodation was a particularly divisive issue, at least 90 per cent of native householders applied to the Administrative Court (*Verwaltungsgericht*) in Karlsruhe for a review of the decision requiring them to accept refugees in their home. See Schraut, *Flüchtlingsaufnahme in Württemberg-Baden*, p. 258.

76 Geheimes Staatsarchiv, Munich (GStA), MA 130674, *Bericht über die Prüfung der Wohnverhältnisse und der Unterbringung der Flüchtlinge in Bayern, Hessen und Württemberg*, p. 4.

77 Quoted in Bauer, *Flüchtlinge und Flüchtlingspolitik*, p. 191.

78 *Ibid.*, pp. 188–9.

79 I. Connor, 'The Attitude of the Ecclesiastical and Political Authorities in Bavaria to the Refugee Problem, *1945–50*', PhD thesis, University of East Anglia 1983, pp. 4, 37.

80 U. Carstens, *Die Flüchtlingslager der Stadt Kiel: Sammelunterkünfte als desintegrierender Faktor der Flüchtlingspolitik* (Marburg 1992), p. 25.

81 *Ibid.*, pp. 36–7.

82 *Ibid.*, pp. 24–5.

83 In Mannheim, 9.5 per cent of refugees lived in camps in September 1950 as opposed to 1.2 per cent in North Baden as a whole. See T. Grosser, '*Wir brauchten sie nicht zu nehmen, sind aber froh gewesen, daß sie hier gewesen sind*: Die Aufnahme der Heimatvertriebenen und SBZ-Flüchtlinge in Mannheim 1945–1960', in C. Grosser, T. Grosser, R. Müller and S. Schraut, *Flüchtlingsfrage – das Zeitproblem: Amerikanische Besatzungspolitik, deutsche Verwaltung und die Flüchtlinge in Württemberg-Baden 1945–1949* (Mannheim 1993), p. 76.

84 In Munich, 16.2 per cent of refugees were housed in camps, well above the state average. See S. Ellenrieder, 'Wohnverhältnisse von Flüchtlingen und Heimatvertriebenen in München in der Nachkriegszeit', *Oberbayerisches Archiv* (OA), Vol. 120 (1996), p. 351.

85 Bauer, *Flüchtlinge und Flüchtlingspolitik*, p. 185.
86 For further details, see D. von der Brelie-Lewien, *'Dann kamen die Flüchtlinge': Der Wandel des Landkreises Fallingbostel vom Rüstungszentrum im 'Dritten Reich' zur Flüchtlingshochburg nach dem Zweiten Weltkrieg* (Hildesheim 1990), p. 191.
87 BHStA, MArb 30, *Statistischer Informationsdienst*, No. 43.
88 BA, Z18, 113, Kirchliche Hilfsstelle (KH) Frankfurt (ed.), *Menschen im Hungerstreik*, 13 September 1948.
89 *Das Flüchtlingsproblem in der amerikanischen Besatzungszone*, p. 7.
90 Quoted in Bauer, *Flüchtlinge und Flüchtlingspolitik*, p. 186.
91 This section is heavily based on Connor, 'The Refugees and the Currency Reform', pp. 307–10.
92 PRO, FO 1006/71, Monthly report of the KRO of Rendsburg to the Regional Commissioner of Schleswig-Holstein, July 1949.
93 According to a survey carried out in March 1948, rent made up just 6.5 per cent of the outgoings of 'employee households' (*Angestelltenhaushalte*) and 6.6 per cent of households where the breadwinner was classified as a 'worker' (*Arbeiter*). See Führer, *Mieter, Hausbesitzer*, p. 252.
94 NHStA Hanover, Nds 380, Acc. 62/65, 555, Albertz to Kopf, 12 March 1949.
95 Führer, *Mieter, Hausbesitzer*, p. 257.
96 A family of six occupying two rooms in a holiday resort would be required to pay rent of 96 DM a month although its income often totalled no more than 130–150 DM.
97 NHStA Hanover, Nds 380, 62/65, 555, Bad Pyrmont Council to Mayor of Hameln, 17 January 1949.
98 H. Grieser, *Die ausgebliebene Radikalisierung: Zur Sozialgeschichte der Kieler Flüchtlingslager im Spannungsfeld von sozialdemokratischer Landespolitik und Stadtverwaltung 1945–1950* (Wiesbaden 1980), p. 101.
99 The occupants of refugee camps located in or on the outskirts of towns or cities were more likely to have to pay rent than their counterparts in the countryside. For example, the inmates of camps in Kiel and Hamburg had to pay rent as early as 1946. See Carstens, *Die Flüchtlingslager der Stadt Kiel*, pp. 65–70 and Führer, *Mieter, Hausbesitzer*, p. 259.
100 HStA Düsseldorf, *Regierungsbezirk* Düsseldorf, BR 1021/97, Monthly Report of *Regierungspräsiden*t to Military Government, 1 June 1949.
101 W. Jaenicke, *Vier Jahre Betreuung der Vertriebenen in Bayern 1945–1949. Ein Bericht über den Stand der bisherigen Eingliederung und über ungelöste Probleme, anläßlich des vierten Jahrestages der Errichtung der bayerischen Flüchtlingsverwaltung* (Munich 1950), pp. 29–30.
102 See for example, StA, LRA 31381, Freisehner to Extraordinary Meeting of Berchtesgaden District Council, 16 April 1949.

103 In 1948, the number of beds distributed in the camps was 16,000 (as opposed to 93,000 in 1947), while the number of mattresses totalled 14,000 (compared with 49,000 in 1947) and blankets 104,000 (as opposed to 181,000 in 1947).

104 See for example, PRO, FO 1006/70, Monthly Report of the KRO of the Rural District of Rendsburg to the Regional Commissioner of Schleswig-Holstein, 24 August 1948.

105 NHStA, Hanover, Nds 120, Acc 40/78, 61, *Oberkreisdirektor* of Springe to the Minister of Finance for Lower Saxony, 29 September 1949.

106 Bundesministerium für Vertriebene (ed.), *Vertriebene und Flüchtlinge volksdeutschen Ursprungs: Bericht eines Sonder-Unterkomitees des Rechtausschusses des Abgeordnetenhauses ...* (Bonn 1950), p. 83. (Hereafter known as *Der Walter-Bericht*).

107 Schraut, *Flüchtlingsaufnahme in Württemberg-Baden*, p. 241.

108 *Ibid.*, p. 244.

109 Ellenrieder, 'Wohnverhältnisse von Flüchtlingen', p. 328.

110 NHStA Hanover, Nds 380, Acc 62/65, 564, *Vierteljahresbericht über Wohnverhältnisse und Bautätigkeit im Lande Nordrhein-Westfalen*, p. 21.

111 See for example, Schier, *Die Aufnahme und Eingliederung*, p. 234.

112 BSL (ed.), *Volks- und Berufszählung am 13. September 1950 in Bayern: Volkszählung 1. Teil Gliederung der Wohnbevölkerung* (Munich 1953), p. 10 and Jaenicke, *Vier Jahre Betreuung der Vertriebenen in Bayern*, p. 13. In 1939, 21 per cent of the Sudeten Germans were engaged in agriculture and forestry, while 44 per cent had jobs in the industrial sector.

113 Erker, 'Revolution des Dorfes?', p. 380.

114 In Lower Saxony, for example, some 13 per cent of refugees were out of work in October 1946. See Malecki, *Die Heimatvertriebenen in Niedersachsen*, p. 16.

115 W. Carlin, 'Economic Reconstruction in Western Germany, 1945–55: The Displacement of "Vegetative Control"', in Turner (ed.), *Reconstruction in Post-War Germany*, p. 42.

116 E. Glensk, 'Großstädtischer Arbeitsmarkt und Vertriebenenintegration: Das Beispiel Hamburg', in Hoffmann, Krauss and Schwartz, (eds), *Vertriebenene in Deutschland* , p. 254.

117 Compiled from BHStA, MArb 27, *Statistischer Informationsdienst*, No. 67.

118 Schraut, *Flüchtlingsaufnahme in Württemberg-Baden*, pp. 339–40.

119 In Württemberg-Baden, for instance, the unemployment rate in September 1947 was 2.7 per cent among the native population (as opposed to 4 per cent among the newcomers) and in the states most severely affected by the refugee problem the discrepancy was even greater. See Schraut, *Flüchtlingsaufnahme in Württemberg-Baden*, p. 339.

120 M. Roseman, 'The Uncontrolled Economy: Ruhr Coal Production, 1945–8', in Turner (ed.), *Reconstruction in Post-War Germany*, p. 96.
121 According to one empirical study carried out in 1949, it affected some 20 per cent of the newcomers. See G. Reichling and F. H. Betz, *Die Heimatvertriebenen: Glied oder Außenseiter der deutschen Gemeinschaft?* (Frankfurt a. M. 1949), p. 20.
122 Schraut, *Flüchtlingsaufnahme in Württemberg-Baden*, p. 339.
123 Messerschmidt, *Aufnahme und Integration*, p. 230.
124 NHStA Hanover, Nds 380, Acc. 62/65, 566, Association of War Victims among Literature and Language Teachers to Refugee Minister of Lower Saxony, 23 March 1949.
125 Winkler, *Flüchtlingsorganisationen in Hessen*, p. 17.
126 Malecki, *Die Heimatvertriebenen in Niedersachsen*, p. 16.
127 Schraut, *Flüchtlingsaufnahme in Württemberg-Baden*, p. 339.
128 P. Erker, *Vom Heimatvertriebenen zum Neubürger: Sozialgeschichte der Flüchtlinge in einer agrarischen Region Mittelfrankens 1945–1955* (Wiesbaden 1988), p. 59.
129 *Ibid.*
130 BHStA, MArb 27, *Statistischer Informationsdienst*, No. 148.
131 This section draws heavily on Connor, 'The Refugees and the Currency Reform', pp. 310–16.
132 Bundesministerium für Arbeit (ed.), *Entwicklung und Ursachen der Arbeitslosigkeit in der Bundesrepublik Deutschland 1946–1950* (Bonn 1950), p. 13.
133 Messerschmidt, *Aufnahme und Integration*, p. 230.
134 T. Beckmann, '*Alle wollen in die Stadt*: Pendlertradition und Eingliederung der Vertriebenen im Altkreis Leonberg', in M. Beer (ed.), *Zur Integration der Flüchtlinge und Vertriebenen im deutschen Südwesten nach 1945: Ergebnisse der Tagung vom 11. und 12. November 1993 in Tübingen* (Sigmaringen 1994), p. 130.
135 *Ibid.*, p. 143.
136 For example, in 1950, some 20 per cent of the working population in the Westphalian village of Wewelsburg commuted to either Büren or Paderborn and in 1961 the figure was as high as 36.6 per cent. See Lüttig, *Fremde im Dorf*, p. 104.
137 Calculated from BHStA, MArb 27, *Statistischer Informationsdienst*, No. 95.
138 For example, the population of parishes in Bavaria accommodating less than 5,000 people fell by 254,500 in the period 1947–50. See Erker, 'Revolution des Dorfes?', p. 386.
139 Grosser, '*Wir brauchten sie nicht zu nehmen*', p. 88.
140 PRO, FO 1006/46, Monthly report of the KRO of the Rural District of Eiderstedt to the Regional Commissioner of Schleswig-Holstein, 26 October 1948.

141 Ziemer, *Deutscher Exodus*, p. 143.
142 PRO, FO 1036/94, 'Economic Trends in the Bizonal Economy: A Critical Analysis of Inflation and Deflation'. Paper by E.F. Schumacher, discussed at a conference of Regional Commissioners, 15 February 1949.
143 B. Dusik, 'Die Gablonzer Schmuckwarenindustrie', in F. Prinz (ed.), *Integration und Neubeginn: Dokumentation über die Leistungen des Freistaates Bayern und des Bundes zur Eingliederung der Wirtschaftsbetriebe der Vertriebenen und Flüchtlinge und deren Beitrag zur wirtschaftlichen Entwicklung des Landes*, Vol. 1 (Munich 1984), p. 496.
144 In January 1949, the *Landrat* of Mühldorf, fearful of the social and political implications of the collapse of the newly established refugee enterprises, reduced their rent by half in defiance of a ministerial directive. The fact that the Upper Bavarian Government did not formally overturn the *Landrat*'s decision until September 1950 suggests a certain degree of sympathy for his initiative. See E. Pscheidt, 'Die Ansiedlung der Graslitzer Musikinstrumentenhersteller auf dem Montan-Gelände in Kraiburg', in Prinz (ed.), *Integration und Neubeginn*, Vol. 1, pp. 581–3.
145 *Der Walter-Bericht*, p. 57.
146 Brosius, 'Zur Lage der Flüchtlinge im Regierungsbezirk Lüneburg', p. 43.
147 *Ibid.*
148 Erker, *Vom Heimatvertriebenen zum Neubürger*, pp. 80–1.
149 *Der Walter-Bericht*, p. 57.
150 Quoted in Winkler, *Flüchtlingsorganisationen in Hessen*, pp. 19–20.
151 *Die Umsiedlung der Heimatvertriebenen in der Bundesrepublik Deutschland: Gutachten des Instituts für Raumforschung Bonn in Verbindung mit dem Soziographischen Institut an der Universität Frankfurt am Main* (Bonn 1951), p. 12.
152 F. Neumann, *Der Block der Heimatvertriebenen und Entrechteten 1950–60: Ein Beitrag zur Geschichte und Struktur einer politischen Interessenpartei* (Meisenheim 1968), pp. 6–7.
153 Quoted in Schraut, *Flüchtlingsaufnahme in Württemberg-Baden*, p. 357.
154 *Ibid.*
155 For example, a leading restaurant in Hamburg sold more lobster in the month following the Currency Reform than in the whole of the previous year. See PRO, FO 1014/46, Monthly Report of the KRO of West Hamburg to the Regional Governmental Officer of Hamburg, 28 July 1948.
156 *Norddeutsche Zeitung*, 28 June 1949, in NHStA Hanover, Bestand 200, Acc. 53/83, 707.

3

Relations between the refugee and native populations, 1945–50

Introduction

German politicians have been apt to play down the difficulties involved in integrating the refugees and expellees into West German society since the Second World War. In particular, they have tended to portray the relations between the native and refugee populations in an excessively rosy light. For example, Hans Schütz, an influential CSU politician until the late 1960s who also played a leading role in the Sudeten German Homeland Society (*Sudetendeutsche Landsmannschaft*), asserted in 1975 that the 'acceptance of the ... expellees [in Bavaria] without any major incident must be regarded as proof of the generally positive attitude of the indigenous inhabitants [towards these new population groups]'.[1] However, numerous regional and local studies have demonstrated that this statement is unsustainable and it is clear that relations between the refugees and the native population in rural communities in the period 1945–50 were invariably characterised by tension and conflict.

Since 1990, a number of studies have been published about the integration of the refugees in large towns and cities, including Evelyn Glensk's volume on Hamburg,[2] Uwe Weiher's book on Bremen[3] and Thomas Grosser's chapter on Mannheim.[4] The towns of Lübeck, Osnabrück, Hameln and Oldenburg have also been the subject of case studies.[5] Several of these projects were based on interviews with former refugees, following the pioneering oral history project carried out by Alexander von Plato in the industrial Ruhr district in the 1980s.[6] There are also a large number of local studies of refugee–native relations in the rural parts of the Western Occupation Zones of Germany, where, of course, the majority of the newcomers were residing in the early post-war years. Much of this research has focused on Lower Saxony. Dieter Brosius has made a study of the

Regierungsbezirk of Lüneburg,[7] Angelika Hohenstein has investigated the integration of the newcomers in Dannenberg,[8] Martina Krug has analysed the refugee problem in the Rural Districts of Burgdorf, Hanover, Neustadt and Springe,[9] while Rainer Schulze has evaluated refugee–native relations in the Rural District of Celle.[10] Of particular interest is Doris von der Brelie-Lewien's book on Fallingbostel, a sparsely populated rural backwater in 1933 which, however, became an important armaments production centre during the Third Reich and, after 1945, had a large refugee population.[11]

In addition, several empirical studies have been undertaken of rural communities in Bavaria, most notably Paul Erker's work on Ansbach and the neighbouring agricultural region in Middle Franconia.[12] Several research projects on the integration of the refugees have been carried out in Westphalia. Peter Exner has made a comparative study of three rural communities,[13] while Andreas Lüttig has examined relations between the native inhabitants and newcomers in the village of Wewelsburg.[14] These local case studies make it possible to trace the course of refugee–native relations between 1945 and 1950 and also provide interesting evidence about the nature and causes of the friction which developed between the two population groups in both rural and urban areas.

There is general agreement that most of the native inhabitants initially responded sympathetically to the refugees and expellees. In fact, a public opinion poll conducted by the US Military Government in March 1946 revealed that some 75 per cent of the newcomers had received a better reception than they had anticipated.[15] Elisabeth Pfeil, a sociologist who had herself been expelled from East Prussia, observed that the attitude of the indigenous population was at first characterised 'by pity and ... a willingness to help'.[16] However, these feelings of compassion for the refugees soon began to disappear. While only 7 per cent of Ethnic Germans (*Volksdeutsche*) in the American Occupation Zone expressed dissatisfaction with their treatment by the native inhabitants in March 1946, this figure had soared to 50 per cent by June 1948.[17]

The deterioration in the relations between the two groups can be attributed partly to the refugees' greater willingness to challenge the interests of the native population as time went on. This was nicely summed up by an indigenous inhabitant living in the Rural District of Celle: 'Friction arose only later, as a result of living together over a longer period. The ... [refugees] were happy just to have somewhere to live at first; the demands didn't arise until later.'[18] These tensions were aggravated by the growing realisation that the refugees were not transient guests who would return home in the near future but were likely to settle permanently in the Western Occupation Zones of Germany. While many members of the native population were willing to accept disruption to their lives for a limited period, their attitude underwent a change as the growing conflict between the Western Allies and the Soviet Union in 1947–48 made it increasingly unlikely that the refugees would be able to return to their homelands.[19]

Many different factors helped to determine the relations between the refugee and native populations. Although the background, traditions and characteristics of the refugees – age, sex, religion, area of origin and mentality – influenced their capacity to establish good relationships in a new environment, the compatibility of these characteristics with those of the indigenous inhabitants in the community in which they found themselves was also important. For example, Doris von der Brelie-Lewien and Helga Grebing concluded that Pomeranians were more readily accepted in Lower Saxony than other groups of refugees since Lower Saxons and Pomeranians were both predominantly Protestant, came from farming backgrounds and had cultural links.[20] The age of the refugees also influenced their willingness to establish social contact with the native population. An empirical study carried out by the Bavarian Statistical Office in 1950 revealed that, while young newcomers were most likely to socialise with the native Bavarians, those over the age of sixty-five invariably remained isolated from the local community.[21] Peter Exner's study of rural Westphalia reached the same conclusion, noting that while younger refugees generally sought to involve themselves in village life, older newcomers were apt to think only of the time when they could return home.[22]

The refugees' willingness to establish social contact with the local people was adversely affected by the often traumatic impact on their psychological wellbeing of the expulsion from their homelands. Many mourned the death of loved ones, while others had become separated from their families and friends in the course of their flight or expulsion. The consequent loss of the refugees' support network was exacerbated by the Western Allies' decision to disperse groups of newcomers from the same area to prevent the creation of 'a state within a state'.[23] In other respects, the refugees all shared the same unhappy destiny. They had lost their homelands, including their houses, gardens and the possessions which they, their parents and grandparents had collected over generations.

Another important determinant of refugee–native relations was the economic and social structure of the community or municipality in which the newcomers settled. Social interaction between the two groups was influenced by the nature of the environment – rural or urban – as well as the size of the town or village. In rural areas, the response of the native inhabitants to the refugees also depended to some extent on their experiences with wartime evacuees or forced labourers during the Third Reich. In country districts, the attitude of the local political and religious leaders to the newcomers must also be taken into account and Rita Müller's study of Dossenheim (in the Rural District of Heidelberg) indicates that the 'village elites' could, on occasions, exert a decisive influence on relations between the native and refugee populations.[24] Economic issues also had a major impact on the lives of both population groups and local case studies confirm that the competition for food and employment, as well as mutual resentment over house-sharing arrangements, constituted a major obstacle to cordial relations between the refugees and indigenous inhabitants. However, as will be seen in the next section, the nature of the economic problems varied greatly between urban centres and rural areas.

Refugee-native relations in towns and cities

Paradoxically, the reception which awaited the refugees and expellees tended to be most friendly in the very areas which were least equipped to cope with them – the large towns and cities which had suffered severe bomb damage during the Second World War. Evelyn Glensk's study of Hamburg, where 61 per cent of the pre-war housing stock had been destroyed by the Allies' bombing campaign,[25] concluded that 'the integration process of the expellees and refugees did not lead to any significant social ... tensions'.[26] In his investigation of the newcomers in the industrial centre of Mannheim, where just 17 per cent of homes remained undamaged in May 1945,[27] Thomas Grosser concurred with the view expressed by a town councillor in April 1949 that 'the assimilation of the refugees will take place more quickly and more smoothly than in the countryside'.[28] Studies of Osnabrück[29] and industrial towns in the Ruhr[30] also support the conclusion that relations between the native and refugee populations were more harmonious in urban than rural areas.

This can be attributed partly to the fact that the newcomers represented only a small proportion of the overall population in large towns and cities and were therefore perceived by local people to be less of a threat than in villages, where they often made up more than a third of the inhabitants. Another factor promoting good relations with the native inhabitants of large towns was that the refugee population invariably comprised a variety of different ethnic groups (*Volksgruppen*) and therefore lacked a 'group identity'. It should also be borne in mind that town dwellers generally accept 'outsiders' more readily than the inhabitants of rural areas because they have had more contact with people from different backgrounds and cultures. It is clear, too, that the native Germans living in urban areas were better informed about the origins of the refugee problem than their compatriots in outlying villages and hamlets. In fact, an American survey carried out in July 1946 revealed that, while 45 per cent of the population in Munich, Frankfurt and Stuttgart admitted that the policies of the National Socialists were ultimately responsible for the expulsion of the refugees from their homelands, only 34 per cent of Germans resident in villages with a population of fewer than 10,000 took this view.[31] More important still, town and city dwellers were able to identify with the refugees' predicament because they, too, had experienced misery and hardship as a result of the Second World War. Alexander von Plato's study of the Ruhr found that almost 70 per cent of the native interviewees had suffered at least one family bereavement due to the war,[32] while others were separated from their loved ones. Just under half of the indigenous inhabitants had had their homes destroyed by Allied bombing,[33] and, like the refugees, the Ruhr population experienced severe food shortages in the years following the collapse of the Reich. These common experiences of deprivation and suffering by both natives and refugees created a basis for mutual understanding which was generally absent in rural areas which had escaped relatively unscathed from the war years.

Local studies point to another important reason for the relatively good relations between the native and refugee populations in large industrial centres. They suggest that the municipal authorities regarded the newcomers as an important economic asset in post-war reconstruction. Housing was in such short supply in industrial conurbations such as Hamburg, Bremen and Mannheim that they were not required to accept mass convoys of refugees in the early post-war years. In practice, however, the municipal authorities encouraged economically valuable groups to take up employment in these towns. For example, the Labour Exchange in Mannheim began a publicity campaign in the spring of 1947 to recruit 1,600 refugees to help rebuild its harbour.[34] Similarly, the authorities in Bremen announced in August 1947 that they were willing to issue residence permits to groups such as refugee bricklayers, carpenters and construction workers on the condition that they had the appropriate qualifications, were under the age of forty and signed a contract for two years.[35] Due to the accommodation shortage, the residence permit did not include the refugee's family. In fact, housing remained the most contentious issue in industrial centres well into the 1950s.[36] Wartime evacuees who had not been able to return home complained bitterly that the refugees received preferential treatment, claims which were sometimes justified. For example, the municipal authorities in Osnabrück, wary of upsetting the evacuees, claimed publicly that refugees were living in the town illegally whereas, in fact, local housing officials privately acquiesced in finding accommodation for those who had already obtained employment.[37] As a result of these restrictions, the newcomers who settled in large towns and cities tended to be young, single, well qualified and in employment – characteristics which made them more likely to enjoy good relations with the local people.

However, as Thomas Grosser has pointed out, refugee–native relations were generally less good in towns which had escaped heavy war damage and were therefore required to accommodate large numbers of newcomers.[38] One such example was the North German port of Lübeck. Although the town centre was badly damaged by incendiary bombs on 28–29 March 1942, the proportion of its houses totally destroyed during the war (8.5 per cent) was well below the average for towns and cities in the Western Occupation Zones.[39] As a result, refugees began to flood into Lübeck even before the collapse of the Reich and by 1948, some 97,000 were resident in the town, more than 40 per cent of its population.[40] Friction between the newcomers and the local population quickly developed and in the spring of 1946 a local government official described relations between them as 'very tense'.[41] Housing was a particular source of conflict and the relationship between refugees and the householders with whom they were billeted became so fraught in the second half of 1945 that a mediation office had to be opened.[42] Similarly, relations between the refugee and native populations were strained in the relatively undamaged city of Oldenburg which, as Andreas von Seggern has pointed out, became a 'large city against its own will' as a result of the enormous influx of newcomers in 1945–46.[43]

To sum up, relations between the refugees and indigenous inhabitants were generally less problematic in large industrial towns and cities than in smaller towns. This was mainly due to the small proportion of newcomers in these industrial conurbations and the fact that many of them were young, skilled workers who had in many cases been personally selected by the municipal authorities to promote post-war reconstruction. However, the vast majority of the refugees were initially based in rural areas where relations with the local population proved to be far less harmonious.

Refugee–native relations in rural areas

An article in the *Fränkische Zeitung* in the autumn of 1948 concluded that 'in the towns and most larger communities ... a fruitful relationship between the original population and the newcomers is, in spite of all the difficulties, gradually developing, whilst in small communities and outlying villages meanness and intolerance is still often making the hard existence of the expellees more difficult'.[44] This statement is borne out by local and regional studies. Elisabeth Pfeil showed that refugee–native relations in Bavaria were most strained in communities with a population of fewer than 2,000 people,[45] while Doris von der Brelie-Lewien's work on Lower Saxony revealed that newcomers encountered particular hostility in villages which were entirely dependent on farming.[46] This was partly the result of the huge economic and social gulf between the native and refugee populations. Many of the villages to which the refugees were sent in 1945–46 had emerged virtually unscathed from the war. There was little, if any, bomb damage, most local people had satisfactory housing, a secure job, access to adequate food supplies and a certain status within their community. On the other hand, the refugees had to rebuild their lives almost from scratch. They had lost their homelands and most of the possessions which they, their parents and grandparents had collected over generations. As Philip Raup, Head of the Food and Agriculture Branch in the American Occupation Zone, remarked: 'The people who have lost the most have come into very close contact with the farmers who have lost the least.'[47] In Bavaria, alone, some 852,000 refugees were living on farms in May 1949 and their relations with their hosts were invariably characterised by friction and conflict.[48]

One of the most frequent complaints among the farming community was that the refugees were idle and lazy. The Bavarian Government's Committee for Refugee Questions received numerous petitions deploring the reluctance of the newcomers to act as farmhands, collect wood for the farmers or give assistance at harvest time. This view was nicely summed up by a local landowner in the Rural District of Celle in 1947: 'Every farm is an organism, it does not have a healthy effect when one part works and gets up at 5.a.m. whilst the other part sleeps till 10 and then goes for a walk.'[49] Another common grievance of the native farmers was the alleged dishonesty of the refugees.[50] It was claimed that newcomers stole crops from the fields, stripped fruit trees and also helped themselves to the farmer's wood supplies. Typical of the complaints was that of a farmer in Schleswig-Holstein who asserted that the refugees' 'children steal so much fruit that I might as well cut down the trees'.[51] Thefts reached such a high level during the food crisis of 1946–47 that farmers in some areas appointed security guards to deter would-be thieves. Others took the law into their own hands and in a village in the Rural District of Deggendorf (Lower Bavaria) a local man murdered a newcomer he caught stealing fruit.[52] Some native farmers also regarded the refugees as dirty and unclean.[53] Moreover, there was a general feeling among the indigenous inhabitants that the newcomers did not appreciate the sacrifices local people had made for them and took their hospitality for granted.[54]

The native farming community reserved particular disdain for the refugee landowners (*Landwirte*) whom they regarded as arrogant and lazy. To quote one local farmer from Celle: 'The farmers from the East acted the gentleman in their homeland and did not contribute to the work. Here, if they help at all, they don't persist at the work. There is an otherwise very decent and reasonable farmer who cannot even plough a straight furrow ... In general ... [they] are not decent farmers ... They had most of their work done by the Poles.'[55] In spite of this lack of respect for the refugee landowners, the native farming community nevertheless saw them as a potential threat to their own livelihood, fearing in particular that they might have to give up some of their land to the newcomers.[56] For their part, many refugee farmers preferred to seek employment in the towns or cities rather than work as agricultural labourers.[57] Those who did accept jobs as farmhands often became frustrated at having to use farming methods they considered outmoded or impractical. Unlike refugees who held degrees or were able to gain social status through their titles, the large landowners had no proof of the high reputation they might have enjoyed in their homelands.[58]

Another group of refugees who experienced particular difficulties in rural areas were those from industrial conurbations and large towns. Rainer Schulze records that in Celle newcomers from an urban background were often viewed with hostility because, as one clergyman put it, 'they ... bring big city assumptions to the countryside as well as the unwillingness to help'.[59] Similar problems existed in Bavaria where large numbers of Silesians from towns and cities found themselves in small rural communities of fewer than 2,000 inhabitants. Paul Erker's study of an agricultural region in Middle Franconia concluded that the Silesians 'often encountered rejection because, with their urban attitudes and lifestyle, they seemed to represent a foreign way of life which destroyed the homogeneous character of the village'.[60] The reference to the refugees' 'foreign way of life' alludes to a wider issue which will be discussed later in the chapter.

The attitude of the indigenous political elites to the refugees

The response of the native population to the refugees was undoubtedly influenced by the example set by the political elites at both regional and local level. A number of leading political figures in the Western Occupation Zones of Germany were hostile to the newcomers and attempted to restrict their influence on government policy towards the refugees. In Bavaria, for example, the Minister of the Interior, Dr Willi Ankermüller, succeeded in reducing the powers and autonomy of the State Secretary for Refugees, Wolfgang Jaenicke, in November 1948 when the Refugee Administration was demoted to one of several departments within the Interior Ministry.[61] Similarly, the State Commissioner for Refugees in Lower Saxony was granted little 'power'.[62] Significantly, the Minister-President, Hinrich Wilhelm Kopf, justified his decision to appoint Martha Fuchs, a native of Bautzen, as the first Refugee Commissioner in January 1947 on the grounds that, as a respected member of the indigenous inhabitants, she was in a position to persuade leading native politicians to adopt a less antagonistic attitude to the newcomers.[63]

The 'political elites' at district (*Kreis*) and parish (*Gemeinde*) level frequently displayed antipathy towards the newcomers. The mayor of a parish in the Rural District of Feuchtwangen (Bavaria) described a refugee as 'foreign rabble',[64] while the *Landrat* of Griesbach stated publicly that refugees were culturally inferior to the Bavarian people.[65] It is clear that many local officials in Bavaria failed to implement the provisions of the Refugee Law which guaranteed the newcomers equality with the native population. For example, refugees comprised some 21 per cent of the population of Bavaria in 1948 but only 13 per cent of those employed in the Ministry of Agriculture.[66] Another instance of discrimination occurred in the Rural District of Osnabrück in March 1947 when the *Landrat* refused to publicise a ministerial directive inviting refugees to apply for financial help to purchase clothes and household utensils on the grounds that insufficient funds were available.[67]

However, the most contentious issue was housing. Local officials were expected to co-operate in billeting the refugees with native householders but in many parishes the mayor sought to safeguard the interests of the villagers against those of the refugees. The actions of the political elites in the parish of Dossenheim (Rural District of Heidelberg) illustrate the extreme measures some officials were prepared to take to protect the indigenous inhabitants from having to share their homes with refugees. The local elites in Dossenheim submitted false figures about the number of unoccupied rooms in the parish, refused to accept any further refugees in July 1947, even though they had no right to do so, and delayed plans to close the local refugee camp. Dossenheim's local government representatives considered themselves answerable not to the *Landrat* of Heidelberg or even the State Commissioner for Refugees but to the prominent families and local dignitaries in the parish. To quote Rita Müller: 'The political *leaders* of the parish refused to comply with instructions from "above" if they did not correspond with the wishes of the old-established citizens.'[68]

While the political elites in Dossenheim were unusually dependent on the eminent families in the parish, case studies of other rural districts indicate that local dignitaries were often able to exert considerable influence on their elected representatives. In fact, even *Landräte* and mayors who were personally well disposed towards the newcomers could not afford to be too sympathetic since they owed their positions to the native inhabitants who almost always outnumbered refugees on the electoral register.[69] Similarly, many local people who sat on the housing boards came under such pressure not to assign refugees to their friends and acquaintances that they resigned from their posts. In parts of southern Germany this practice became so widespread that the President of Baden announced in the autumn of 1946 that he would accept the resignation of local officials only if they could provide evidence of long-term illness or disability,[70] while in Bavaria some local authorities resorted to appointing representatives of the indigenous population from outside the village.[71]

It is clear, then, that during the early post-war years relations between the refugee and native populations in rural areas were generally characterised by tension and resentment. The newcomers tended to encounter particular hostility in small, isolated rural communities which were heavily dependent on farming. They also frequently suffered discrimination by the 'political elites' at local level, especially in regard to housing. But what were the causes of the conflicts which developed between the refugees and the native inhabitants? How far were the poor relations between the two groups in the countryside an inevitable consequence of the enormous gulf which existed between the indigenous population who had emerged almost untouched from the war and the refugees who had lost practically everything? These issues will be discussed in the next section.

Causes of poor native–refugee relations in rural areas

The friction which developed between the refugee and native populations in country districts can be fully understood only in the light of the past experiences of both groups, as well as their different cultural and historical roots. However, while these underlying factors undoubtedly had a profound effect on the way in which each group reacted to the other, the actual sources of conflict were primarily of an economic nature. In the harsh economic conditions prevailing between 1945 and 1949, the competing interests of the two groups in the areas of housing and employment formed the basis of many of the disputes which arose.

Economic Factors

Housing

The decision of the Allied Military Governments to billet the refugees with private householders aroused deep hostility among the native inhabitants. In fact, there is general agreement that housing was the most divisive economic issue between the newcomers and the original population. For example, Martina Krug noted that the *Regierungspräsident* of Hanover received more correspondence about housing disputes than any other issue.[72] The opposition of the indigenous inhabitants to sharing their homes with refugees was so great that the intervention of the police was sometimes necessary before the newcomers could move into the rooms they had been allocated. As many as 57 refugees needed police assistance to take up their lodgings in Dossenheim in August 1946,[73] while just one of the 108 rooms set aside for newcomers in the Westphalian parish of Heek was surrendered voluntarily by the householder.[74] While the intervention of the police was usually sufficient to resolve the issue, legal proceedings were initiated against indigenous householders who refused to back down. Although the maximum penalty was a fine of 10,000 reichsmarks and/or a year's imprisonment, the courts in Bavaria often declined to impose these sentences,[75] considering a more appropriate punishment for householders who refused to accept refugees into their homes to be detention in a refugee camp for a period of up to six months.[76]

Of course, some members of the native population treated the refugees assigned to them with kindness and compassion. Frequently, however, disagreements arose and an atmosphere of mutual irritation or dislike developed which sometimes even led to physical violence. The underlying cause of many disputes was the cramped living conditions, which made it difficult for the two groups to live amicably under the same roof.[77] Cooking arrangements were a particular source of discord. Since few refugees had their own stove, they had to share the kitchen with their hosts, an inherently unsatisfactory arrangement which, to quote Franz Bauer, 'made the social gulf between refugees and natives particularly evident'.[78] Other divisive issues included the use of water, electricity, household utensils and washing facilities, as well as the refusal of some householders to give their tenants a house key. In North Rhine-Westphalia, numerous refugees took legal action against the family with whom they were billeted, accusing them of 'slander, actual bodily harm or trespass'.[79]

Less serious cases often revolved around the respective rights of the householder and 'his' or 'her' refugees; for example, the Municipal Court in the Bavarian town of Landshut ruled that a lady who had been compelled to share her home with a doctor's family could not refuse her 'guests' use of the toilet facilities.[80]

Local and regional studies indicate that relations between farmers and refugees were especially fraught.[81] Generally speaking, overcrowding was most severe on medium-size and, above all, small farms.[82] However, the tensions which developed were also due to the reluctance of many refugees to work for the farmer with whom they were billeted. After the collapse of the Reich, German farmers faced a severe shortage of labour. Many former agricultural workers had been killed in the war while thousands were still being held as prisoners-of-war. Moreover, farmers could no longer rely on foreign labour which had accounted for some 40 per cent of Germany's agricultural work force in November 1944.[83] Consequently, they at first viewed the newcomers as an important source of labour. A representative of the Bavarian Farmers' Association summed up these expectations in December 1945: 'Agriculture can absorb many young, healthy refugees who are prepared to work.'[84] Consequently, relations between the farmer and 'his' refugees tended to be least acrimonious when the newcomers acted as farmhands. However, many refugees were unwilling or unable to work on the farms and this provoked deep resentment among the farming community.

The Currency Reform of June 1948 brought about a sharp deterioration in relations between the farmers and refugees. As noted in chapter 2, most newcomers paid only a nominal rent until the middle of 1948 or received free accommodation and food in return for working on the farm. However, after the introduction of the deutschmark, many refugees terminated this arrangement because they enjoyed a higher standard of living by claiming unemployment and welfare benefit than working as agricultural labourers.[85] A refugee widow resident in Neulehe (Emsland) reported in October 1950: 'As is the case with most of the expellees, I am on a war footing with my farmer since I am no longer willing to work for nothing.'[86] Many other refugees, disillusioned at the low wages offered for farm work, found better paid employment in neighbouring towns. But, due to the severe housing shortage in urban areas, the newcomers wanted to continue living with 'their' farmer.[87] In fact, this practice became so widespread that by May 1949 only 9.4 per cent of refugees and evacuees over the age of fourteen accommodated in Bavarian farmhouses worked full-time for the farmer with whom they were billeted.[88] Thus, there was a sense in which the farmers' anger towards the refugees was based on disappointment that they did not prove to be a long-term solution to the migration of the rural population into the towns, a phenomenon which had begun well before 1939 and was to accelerate during the 1950s.

The continuing presence of refugee tenants in farmhouses precipitated deep indignation in the farming community because they prevented the farmer from employing agricultural labourers from outside the village since he was unable to offer them accommodation. As one farmer from Lower Bavaria complained: 'I cannot have female farm-hands sleeping in my room.'[89] In the Rural District of Osnabrück this shortage of accommodation resulted in 650 unfilled vacancies for agricultural labourers in March 1949 and it was a similar story elsewhere.[90] The farmers responded by increasing rent levels sharply or, in some cases, using the absence of a tenancy agreement 'as a pretext to give [the refugees] notice to quit or restrict their use of the garden and cellar'.[91] As a result, the Housing Boards were inundated with requests to settle disputes between house owners and their refugee tenants over rent levels and the Refugee Office in the Rural District of Hanover dealt with no fewer than 6,000 such cases up to 1952.[92]

Rent levels proved to be a particularly acrimonious issue in tourist areas because the presence of the refugees represented a major threat to the livelihood of hoteliers and guest house owners. In fact, 66 per cent of hotel beds in the British and American Occupation Zones were occupied by newcomers in October 1948.[93] Hoteliers responded by demanding higher rents which many refugees were simply unable to afford. This led to considerable friction after the Currency Reform and the Kreis Resident Officer of the Rural District of Eutin (Schleswig-Holstein) reported in August 1948: 'Much ill-feeling has been aroused between refugees ... and hotel and boarding house proprietors ... owing to the fact that rents ... in seaside resorts are still based on prices ... when the same rooms were rented for holiday purposes. Since the Currency Reform refugees find themselves unable to meet these high rentals which usually amount to double the ordinary dwelling house rent.'[94] This was by no means an isolated incident and tension ran high in many resorts.[95]

To sum up, housing represented the most divisive economic issue between the refugee and native populations. This was not just due to the tensions which developed from living together in a confined space but was also a consequence of the adverse economic effects on agriculture and tourism resulting from the billeting of refugees in farming communities and holiday resorts. However, native inhabitants who were engaged in other occupations also viewed the newcomers as a threat to their livelihood and their attempts to stifle competition from the refugees on the employment market constituted another important source of discord between the two groups.

Employment

The native population resented attempts by the State Governments to create employment opportunities for the newcomers and expressed bitterness at the financial concessions granted to firms established by refugees. This view was epitomised in a report by the *Landrat* of Rosenhein (Bavaria) in October 1947: 'In the rural districts there are many complaints that the newcomers are given everything, while local people are repeatedly sent to the very back of the queue.'[96] Consequently, the village elites tended to support refugee firms or businesses only if they posed no threat to the economic interests of the indigenous inhabitants. A meeting of *Landräte* in Middle Franconia in March 1946 confirmed that 'local considerations dictate that refugees will not be employed when there are applicants from the native population'.[97] Similarly, a refugee representative from the Bavarian Rural District of Rothenburg ob der Tauber drew attention to the unwillingness of local people to rent business premises to newcomers or sell them the materials and tools necessary to set up their own business.[98] Other local studies confirm the existence of discrimination against the refugees by employers,[99] though rarely as blatantly as in a job advertisement in a local newspaper in Fallingbostel (Lower Saxony) in February 1946 which expressly stipulated that refugees need not bother to apply.[100]

Discrimination against the newcomers increased sharply in the harsher economic climate prevailing after the Currency Reform. Many employers took the view that, since the refugees had been most recently appointed, they should be the first to be discharged.[101] In the *Regierungsbezirk* of Hanover, the situation was considered to be so serious in July 1948 that the *Regierungspräsident* asked to be personally notified of complaints by newcomers against unfair dismissal,[102] while in North Rhine-Westphalia it was considered necessary to remind the employment offices that a member of the indigenous population could not be appointed to a post if there were better qualified refugee applicants.[103] But these directives were not always followed and in July 1950 refugees comprised 15.5 per cent of the population in the Urban District of Schwandorf (Upper Palatinate, Bavaria) but only 1.2 per cent of those working for the municipal authorities.[104]

The denazification procedure also exacerbated the tense relations between the native and refugee populations. Some newcomers claimed that the denazification tribunals purposely delayed consideration of cases involving refugees in order to protect local businesses from competition.[105] They also considered themselves disadvantaged by their lack of local 'connections'. On the other hand, the indigenous inhabitants believed that they were in greater danger of losing their jobs as a result of their National Socialist connections than the refugees who were sometimes able to retain their anonymity due to the absence of documentary evidence to prove their complicity with the Nazis. One Bavarian civil servant observed in June 1946 that he 'had never seen as many giving the Hitler salute as in the Sudetenland' and went on to suggest that all refugees should be assumed guilty until they could prove their innocence![106] The native population was incensed that, when school teachers were suspended pending their appearance before the denazification panel, they were often replaced by refugees. Due to the acute shortage of teachers in Bavaria, Protestant refugees were often appointed to teaching posts in Catholic schools, giving rise to bitter complaints from parents that their children were being taught by 'Prussians of a different denomination'.[107] While many of the native teachers were reinstated from 1948 onwards, a significant number of newcomers managed to retain their positions and in 1950, 38 per cent of all teachers in Lower Saxony were either refugees or Germans who had been bombed out of their homes, while in Schleswig-Holstein the figure was as high as 43 per cent, well above the proportion they comprised of the total population.[108]

While the conflicts between the native and refugee populations tended to focus on economic issues, religion also represented a major source of friction between the two groups, especially in rural areas, and this issue will be addressed in the next section.

Religion

The arrival of the newcomers had little impact on the overall denominational structure of the Western Occupation Zones of Germany. According to the census of September 1950, 53 per cent of the refugees were Protestant and 45.2 per cent Catholic[109] and, as Table 3.1 indicates, their religious composition closely resembled that of the indigenous population. In theory, it would therefore have been possible to locate Catholic and Protestant refugees in areas where their own denomination was in the majority. However, despite strong representations from leading ecclesiastical figures of both denominations,[110] State Governments were unable to distribute the new population elements according to their religious affiliations. The refugees had been expelled in such large numbers and at such short notice that the sole concern of government officials was to find them suitable accommodation. As a result, many Catholic Sudeten Germans were located in the largely Protestant areas of North Hesse

Table 3.1 The religious composition of the Western Occupation Zones of Germany, 1939–46 (percentage distribution)

	1939			*1946*		
State	*Prot.*	*Cath.*	*Other*	*Prot.*	*Cath.*	*Other*
Bavaria	24.9	73.2	1.9	26.5	71.3	2.2
Hesse	69.6	25.8	4.6	63.4	32.6	4.0
Württemberg-Baden	63.5	31.7	4.8	58.5	37.7	3.8
Bremen	83.8	8.7	7.5	85.3	8.9	5.8
South Württemberg	43.7	54.0	2.3	43.1	54.6	2.3
South Baden	24.7	72.9	2.4	26.0	71.9	2.1
Rhineland-Palatinate	39.3	58.1	2.6	39.6	58.6	1.8
North Rhine-Westphalia	37.0	56.7	6.3	39.0	56.2	4.8
Lower Saxony	78.6	16.4	5.0	76.6	19.2	4.2
Hamburg	79.3	5.9	14.8	80.3	6.5	13.2
Schleswig-Holstein	89.6	3.8	6.6	87.9	6.8	5.3
Totals	49.3	45.7	5.0	50.2	45.7	4.1

Source: BHStA, MArb 27, *Statistischer Informationsdienst*, No. 110. Refugees resident in the western sectors of Berlin have been excluded from this table.

and Franconia, while Catholic newcomers from Silesia and Ermland (East Prussia) were accommodated in the mainly Protestant North German states of Bremen, Hamburg, Lower Saxony and, in particular, Schleswig-Holstein. Similarly, significant numbers of Protestant refugees were settled in the almost exclusively Catholic areas of Lower Bavaria, South Oldenburg, South Emsland and Eichsfeld, as well as parts of the Rhineland. It is clear, then, that the newcomers substantially changed the denominational structure of many parts of the Western Occupation Zones of Germany.

However, the enormous impact of the refugee influx on religious life in Germany after the Second World War can be assessed only at local rather than regional level. As a result of the random distribution of the newcomers, the number of exclusively Catholic or Protestant parishes in Bavaria fell from 1,564 at the outbreak of the Second World War to just nine in 1950.[111] The same trend was apparent in the North German states; in fact, denominationally homogeneous parishes remained a significant feature only in Rhineland-Palatinate, where refugees comprised just 3.6 per cent of the population in July 1950.[112] It is interesting to note that Catholic refugees were affected more severely than Protestants by the failure to distribute them along denominational lines. In September 1950, 1.2 million Catholics were living in overwhelmingly Protestant areas, while only 770,000 Protestant refugees had been settled in almost exclusively Catholic communities. Thus, 33.6 per cent of Catholic refugees were located in diaspora areas as opposed to only 18.7 per cent of Protestant newcomers.[113]

Local studies indicate that religion was generally a less divisive issue between refugees and the native population in the towns and cities than in rural areas. For example, Alexander von Plato concluded that religion exerted little influence on relations between the refugees and the indigenous inhabitants in the Ruhr because of 'the general process of secularisation and the decline in the power of the Catholic Church as a result of the influx of many Protestant refugees'.[114] In Lübeck, the refugees initially found it difficult to come to terms with the different customs and rituals practised in Protestant–Lutheran church services but these problems were largely overcome by the willingness of local church leaders to appoint refugee clergy and permit them to hold their own special services for the newcomers.[115] Town dwellers are, of course, more receptive to 'alien' influences than country people and the inhabitants of the heavily industrialised

Ruhr region had a long history of trading contacts with foreign countries. On the other hand, villages are closed communities where people of different religious beliefs are less likely to encounter tolerance and understanding, and this was certainly the case in many rural parts of Germany after the Second World War.

Religion tended to be a particular source of discord in rural diaspora regions. Eugen Lemberg's empirical study of Northern Hesse, an almost exclusively Protestant area prior to the arrival of Catholic refugees in 1945–46, concluded that 'the antagonism between the indigenous inhabitants and the Upper Silesians was mainly due to denominational differences'.[116] Religious bigotry was also prevalent in rural Bavaria. In the Catholic *Regierungsbezirk* of Lower Bavaria, where the majority of the inhabitants lived in isolated villages largely untouched by economic developments, Protestant newcomers encountered strong prejudice. A number of the National German refugees interviewed by Dr Gerhard Neumann in an empirical survey of a Lower Bavarian community reported being called 'Lutheran bloodhounds' by local Catholic people.[117] A Catholic government official in the Lower Bavarian Rural District of Mainburg was said to have turned down a request by a refugee Protestant minister for a licence to buy the car necessary for him to reach the outlying districts of his parish on the grounds that 'there would then be even more Protestant church services'.[118]

The high degree of denominational homogeneity among both the refugees and the indigenous population was an important reason for their mutual religious intolerance. Neither group was accustomed to living in areas where they came into contact with people holding different religious beliefs. Of the three states which bore the brunt of the refugee influx, Bavaria was more than 70 per cent Catholic in 1939, while Lower Saxony was almost 80 per cent Protestant and Schleswig-Holstein almost 90 per cent Protestant. This trend was equally pronounced in the refugees' homelands. Of the 'Ethnic German' groups, 91.5 per cent of Sudeten Germans were Catholic prior to the Second World War, while more than 80 per cent of Germans living in both Hungary and Yugoslavia belonged to the Catholic Church. Meanwhile, the 'National Germans' were overwhelmingly Protestant, 81.7 per cent of East Prussians, 88.2 per cent of Brandenburgers and 89.5 per cent of Pomeranians being members of the Protestant Church.[119] Only the Silesians had experience of a denominationally 'mixed' environment.

Although religious friction tended to be most pronounced in areas where the refugee and native populations belonged to different denominations, antagonism also arose when they shared the same denomination for, while both groups considered themselves to be 'Catholic' or 'Protestant', they invariably had very different customs and traditions. For example, the Catholic Silesian refugees who settled in Westphalia discovered that the hymns and rites at marriages, christenings and funerals varied greatly from those at home. The Protestant 'National Germans' who set up home in Bavaria experienced similar problems. They adhered to the Lutheran Church, while most Bavarian Protestants belonged to the Reformed Church. In the Lutheran Church, the minister intoned prayers, a custom many Bavarian Protestants associated with Catholicism. For their part, the refugees found it difficult to come to terms with the very sparse rites of the Reformed Church service. The newcomers were also disconcerted by the strict allocation of church pews which meant that they were not guaranteed a seat.[120] The native Bavarians, seeking to retain their own cultural identity in the face of the threat posed by the refugees, expected the newcomers to accept their religious customs and practices. However, the newcomers were often reluctant to do so, especially in parishes where they actually outnumbered the indigenous Protestants. In fact, in the Lower Bavarian District of Viechtach, where refugees comprised no fewer than 74 per cent of the Protestant population in September 1950, relations between the two groups were so strained that the refugees at first declined to join the Bavarian Protestant State Church.[121]

However, it was not just the denominational composition of a parish which influenced the relations between the refugees and the indigenous inhabitants but the reaction of the local priest or minister to the new groups of population. In post-war Germany the clergyman was still a highly respected figure, especially in rural communities. He was therefore capable of exerting a decisive influence on the attitude of his parishioners towards the refugees and expellees. Although some clergy set an excellent example to the faithful, many viewed the refugees with indifference or suspicion. They regarded the newcomers as unwelcome intruders who would have a destabilising effect on religious life in the community.[122] In extreme cases the local priest or clergyman adopted an overtly hostile attitude to the refugees. A notorious example allegedly occurred in

Scheessel (near Hanover) when the Protestant clergyman concluded his sermon on Easter Sunday 1946 as follows:

> The refugees should at last realise that they are only guests in Lower Saxony and do not therefore have the right, let alone a claim to a seat in God's house. It is up to the refugees to conform to the customs practised in Lower Saxony and remain standing until the local people, who are probably held in higher regard in heaven, have taken their usual seats in church. Not until the end of the first verse of the opening hymn should a refugee venture to look for a seat.[123]

Unfortunately, there is no record of how many refugees attended the following week's service! Another example of unusually blatant discrimination against refugees took place in a village in the Rural District of Erding (Bavaria). The Catholic priest organised a strike at the local school because a Rumanian refugee had been appointed to the teaching staff.[124] He took this action not because of her religion – she was, in fact, Catholic – but simply because she was not of Bavarian extraction.

However, it should be stressed that even native clergymen who were personally well disposed towards the newcomers were often reluctant to act against the interests of local people because they were dependent on their support. As one Protestant minister from Hesse put it, the clergyman is likely to identify with the interests of the native population because he 'has to live … among the [indigenous] members of his parish'.[125] Financial factors also came into consideration. A US Military Government official noted that in the Lower Franconian Rural District of Ebern, 'the religious groups are catering more to the local population, [who] … pay the necessary expenses to the parishes rather than supporting the refugees and expellees, many of whom are really destitute'.[126] If, on the other hand, a clergyman was perceived to be too friendly towards the refugees, he was likely to suffer the wrath of the original population. Such was the fate of the vicar in Feuchtwangen (Middle Franconia). In November 1949, he received an anonymous letter purporting to have been written on behalf of the native inhabitants. It accused him of 'holding refugee meetings instead of preaching God's word' and continued: 'It is unacceptable for you to constantly give prominence to the expellees and, in the process, oppress the native inhabitants.' The letter concluded with a warning that, if he continued 'to incite the people from the pulpit', he would be 'the first to be dismissed when the time comes'.[127] While this is an extreme example, it is clear that clergy who concerned themselves with the plight of the refugees risked alienating their indigenous parishioners.

Discrimination against refugees during the burial service was a particularly sensitive issue. In Bavaria, it was the practice at some cemeteries to create separate graveyards for the newcomers, forcing the Government to stipulate in January 1947 that refugees should be granted the same burial rights as the indigenous inhabitants.[128] It is unclear how widespread the practice was of reserving one particular area of the graveyard for refugees but a recent study indicates that it also occurred at the Eichhof cemetery on the outskirts of Kiel. The Cemetery Law in Schleswig-Holstein required that the dead should be buried in consecutive plots in the order that the funerals took place. However, at the Eichhof cemetery, natives of Schleswig-Holstein were laid to rest in the main area of the graveyard, while refugees, as well as foreigners and the former inmates of concentration camps, were buried between 1945 and 1949 in plots on the edge of the graveyard. The authors concluded that, even in death, these refugees were treated as 'second class' citizens.[129]

The attitude of the native clergy to the post-war housing crisis often exacerbated the strained relations between the refugees and the indigenous inhabitants. As noted above, accommodation was in such short supply that many newcomers had to be billeted with the indigenous inhabitants who were naturally reluctant to share their homes with strangers. The local housing officers hoped that the priest or clergyman would set a good example to his parishioners but unfortunately this was not always the case. A commission established by the Parliamentary Council of the *Länderrat* to examine the housing situation in the American Occupation Zone reported in October 1948 that, while non-Bavarian people in Upper Palatinate had to live in very cramped conditions, 'clergymen, in particular, generally had sufficient space'.[130] In fact, the commissioners discovered that one presbytery with fourteen rooms was accommodating just six refugees.[131] In 1946, one of the Bavarian Government's external commissioners noted that a Catholic priest in the Upper Franconian Rural District of Bamberg refused to give up any of his six rooms because 'the peace of God's house would be seriously disturbed if it was occupied by refugees'.[132] In the ensuing exchange of views he expressed his intention of writing to Rome to gain the Pope's support! Such incidents were not confined to Bavaria. In Hesse, for example, the Government considered it necessary to issue a directive stating that, while a clergyman could use two or three rooms for official purposes, his private living quarters were subject to the same regulations as everyone else.[133] It is clear, then, that some native clergy did not set a good example to their parishioners and were unsympathetic to the plight of the refugees, while those who supported the interests of the refugees risked incurring the anger of local people.

Peter Exner's study of Westphalia shows that denominational differences sometimes acted as an important obstacle to social integration in rural communities. Prior to the influx of Protestant Silesian refugees in 1945–46, the village of Ottmarsbocholt (Rural District of Lüdinghausen) was almost exclusively Catholic. Social activities in the village traditionally centred around the rifle club. However, membership was available only to Catholics, thus excluding the refugees from the most important focus for social interaction in the community. However, it is interesting to note that, irrespective of their religious affiliations, Protestant refugees were permitted to play for the village football team, founded in 1946. Thus, while the newcomers were excluded from the rifle club which had a long tradition and was dominated by the 'local elites', young refugees were able to gain access to a newly established football club whose membership traversed the social divide.[134]

There is no doubt, then, that religion constituted a divisive rather than a unifying force between the refugee and native populations in rural areas of the Western Occupation Zones of Germany in the early post-war years. However, religious friction became less of an issue in the major refugee states of Bavaria, Lower Saxony and Schleswig-Holstein during the 1950s. This was partly due to the resettlement of many newcomers from the 'minority denomination'. The number of Catholic refugees in the almost exclusively Protestant state of Schleswig-Holstein dropped from 106,000 in 1946 to 68,000 in 1953[135] and a study by the Catholic International Sociological Institute for Refugee Questions revealed that religious factors were often instrumental in their decision to move to another part of the FRG. In fact, many of the forty-nine Catholic Churches which were built in Schleswig-Holstein between 1945 and 1955 were subsequently abandoned because there were insufficient parishioners to sustain them.[136] The same pattern was discernible in the other major refugee states of Lower Saxony and Bavaria.

Fear of 'foreign' influence

While it has become clear that conflicts over housing, employment and religion were the most frequent outward manifestations of poor relations between the indigenous inhabitants and the refugees, there were deeper underlying causes of the tension between the two groups which, though not always articulated, nonetheless conditioned the response of local people to the newcomers. The generally negative attitude of the native inhabitants towards the refugees was in essence based on the fact that these new population elements were regarded as 'foreign'. The original population perceived the newcomers as a threat to their way of life, their cultural traditions and the very fabric of rural society. This is illustrated by the comments of a clergyman from the Rural District of Celle: 'The influx [of refugees] ... carries the danger that the original character of our national customs and traditions (*Volkstum*) will lose its authenticity through mixing with a character alien to its land and ways.'[137] Local people viewed the employment of refugee teachers with particular misgivings since they were in a position to influence the attitudes and ideas of impressionable young people on whom the prosperity of the village would depend in years to come.

The native inhabitants also displayed a very defensive attitude to the role newcomers were to play in local government. A public opinion poll conducted by the American Military Government in Bad Aibling found that one of the most frequently cited reasons for the native population's hostility towards the refugees was that 'the outsider has a quicker mentality and is rapidly easing the native out of good positions in politics'.[138] The indigenous inhabitants feared that the refugees might gain control over the running of the village[139] and, as a result, local elections were keenly contested in the early post-war years. In fact, the turnout at the Parish Elections (*Gemeindewahlen*) in Bavaria held in April 1948 was 87.3 per cent,[140] an exceptionally high figure. The mobilisation of native voters in the face of the perceived threat from the newcomers appeared to pay off, since only two parishes throughout the whole of Bavaria returned refugee mayors.[141]

The hostility of the native population towards the newcomers was also based on the assumption that the refugees had been enthusiastic supporters of National Socialism. For example, in a public opinion poll carried out by the British Military Government in November 1947, members of the original population explained their dislike for the newcomers on the grounds that 'many were ... Nazis and militarists'.[142] The same point of view was expressed in a petition sent by a group of native Germans from South Schleswig to Field Marshal Montgomery in October 1945 requesting that 'refugees be removed as soon as possible from our state'.[143] A letter accompanying the petition warned that, if the newcomers were allowed to remain in South Schleswig, 'our peaceful Nordic population will be taken over by foreigners on their native soil and ruled by elements who come from the main trouble spots of Europe (Danzig, East Prussia, the Polish corridor, Sudetenland etc.)'.[144] This statement paints a stark contrast between the aggressive, warlike refugees who were considered responsible for the rise of National Socialism and the 'peaceful' inhabitants of South Schleswig who were portrayed as unwitting victims of the Nazis. However, this analysis conveniently forgets that no fewer than 62 per cent of the electorate in South Schleswig voted for the NSDAP in July 1932, some 25 per cent above the national average.

The petition also warned that 'this flood of foreign people from the eastern territories ... represents the most serious danger for centuries of the Prussianisation of our people'.[145] This statement implies that the refugees displayed the negative characteristics traditionally associated with Prussia such as aggression, belligerence and bellicosity. Such a view was not just held in the North German state of Schleswig-Holstein but was perhaps even more prevalent in Southern Germany. For example, the *Landrat* of Rosenheim asserted in October 1945: 'Bavaria wants absolutely nothing more to do with Prussia ... for Prussia signifies to us fascism and militarism.'[146] Since the Bavarians regarded all refugees as 'Prussians', irrespective of whether they actually came from that part of Germany, this remark again confirms that they considered the newcomers responsible for the events of 1933–45. In other words, the refugees from the East were made the scapegoats for the rise of National Socialism and the outcome of the Second World War.[147] There is, in fact, a very real sense in which the native inhabitants sought to project their own guilt about their support for National Socialism on to the refugees and expellees.[148]

The attitude of the indigenous population to the newcomers was also influenced by their experiences with evacuees and forced labourers during the Second World War. Relations between the wartime evacuees and the indigenous inhabitants in rural communities were often so tense that the local people were suspicious of the refugees even before they set foot in the village. For example, a Catholic priest who spent the war years in the Lower Bavarian Rural District of Grafenau reported that 'the attitude of the native population towards the refugees was often very unfriendly; evacuees from Hamburg who came here 2–3 years ago were partly to blame'.[149] The local people complained about the laziness of evacuee women from the towns, as well as their promiscuous sexual behaviour.[150] Religion was another divisive issue and in many isolated uninformed rural communities in Bavaria the indigenous inhabitants blamed the irreligious evacuees for the air-raids on Munich and Nuremberg in the winter of 1943. A typical reaction was: 'We have you lot from Hamburg to thank for that; that is the punishment for not going to church.'[151] Thus, the presence of the evacuees, many of whom came from urban areas, did not practise their religion and had very different customs, traditions and attitudes from the native villagers, fostered an inherent mistrust of 'foreigners' among the indigenous inhabitants which was to impair their relations with the refugees and expellees who began to arrive in the last few months of the war.

The negative reaction of the native population in rural communities can also be partly attributed to their experiences during the Second World War with forced labourers of foreign extraction. In May 1943, as many as 1.5 million foreign workers – mostly from Eastern European countries – were employed as agricultural labourers throughout the Reich.[152] The indigenous inhabitants, influenced by National Socialist ideology, tended to regard these forced labourers from Eastern Europe as racially inferior and, as Martina Krug's study of the rural districts around Hanover shows, this thinking also influenced their attitude towards the German refugees and expellees from the East. To quote Krug: 'The accommodation of the refugees in the camps formerly occupied by the Poles, their employment as agricultural labourers in place of the foreign workers, their language difficulties and their Eastern European origins reinforced the impression that the refugees were the successors to the foreign workers.'[153] The native population's frequent reference to the refugees as 'polacks' – a derogatory term for people of Polish descent – supports the view that the indigenous inhabitants regarded them as nothing more than a cheap work force to replace the forced labourers.[154]

The historical development of Germany promoted the growth of strong local and regional loyalties which encouraged the rejection of 'outsiders' such as the refugees and expellees. After all, in the late eighteenth century Germany still consisted of some 350 small, fiercely independent states. Although Napoleon reduced this number to thirty-nine in 1803 and national feelings began to develop among the middle classes during the first half of the nineteenth century, the unification of Germany did not come about until 1871. Despite the subsequent development of a national identity, local and regional loyalties continued to flourish. The collapse of the Third Reich in May 1945 and the discovery of the concentration camps brought about a loss of national identity and this process was reinforced by the decentralisation policies introduced by the Western Allies. The decision to set up local (*Gemeinde*, *Kreis* and *Bezirk*) and State (*Land*) Governments as early as 1946 but postpone the establishment of the Federal Government until 1949 further promoted the growth of a corporate sense of local and regional identity. However, this, of course, had a detrimental effect on the attitude of the indigenous inhabitants towards 'foreigners'. As the English academic, C. A. Macartney put it: 'The Bavarians cannot be encouraged to call a Berliner a "Prussian pig", yet at the same time be expected to show great sympathy for an expellee from Stettin.'[155]

The native population's desire to retain its own cultural identity in the face of the competing customs and traditions of the refugees provoked much bad blood in rural areas in the early post-war years. As noted above, native churchgoers initially rejected the newcomers' religious customs[156] and the indigenous inhabitants also defended their own cultural traditions against those of the refugees. For example, in 1947, the native Bavarians attempted to prevent newcomers wearing leather shorts on the grounds that it was 'a purely Bavarian costume'.[157] Conflicts arose over the Sudeten German tradition of erecting a maypole during May Day celebrations and their practice of lighting bonfires to mark the summer solstice. In fact, in some villages the indigenous inhabitants revived old Bavarian cultural customs in a conscious attempt to ward off this perceived threat to their own identity. Some parishes reintroduced annual carnivals, while others held country fairs.[158] The refugees themselves often kept their own company at first – especially when newcomers from the same village had managed to settle en masse in their new homeland and therefore preserve their social network. However, in the 1950s refugee and native traditions began to intermingle and in many respects the arrival of the newcomers represented a cultural enrichment for isolated villages; the refugees founded singing clubs and organised dances, much to the regret of the local clergy who warned that these developments would lead to the moral degeneration of the village.[159]

Conclusion

There is considerable evidence from rural areas of the Western Occupation Zones of Germany in the early post-war years to support the view expressed in the *Süddeutsche Zeitung* in May 1947 that an 'atmosphere of latent civil war' had developed between the native and refugee populations.[160] In fact, the situation became so serious in some farming communities that local officials predicted outbreaks of political radicalisation among the newcomers.[161] Although, in rural communities, the hostility of the indigenous inhabitants towards the refugees often found expression in conflicts over housing or employment, their rejection of the new population groups was, in essence, based on the threat the refugees were perceived to represent to the original nature and fabric of rural society. The local people believed that the refugees' cultural and religious traditions and customs would undermine traditional rural life as they knew it. They blamed the newcomers for the fundamental changes taking place in the countryside – such as the exodus from the land and the process of industrialisation – even though these developments had begun prior to the influx of the refugees. Similarly, technological changes in German agriculture would have taken place after 1945 irrespective of the arrival of the newcomers. Moreover, it was the evacuees and forced labourers rather than the refugees who first introduced 'urban' culture and mentalities into rural areas previously immune from outside influences. But the native inhabitants made the newcomers the scapegoats for all these developments which they regarded as a threat to their own identity.[162]

The widely expressed fears that the friction between the refugees and indigenous inhabitants might lead to outbreaks of political radicalisation among the new population elements placed a heavy responsibility on the fledgling political parties in the Western Occupation Zones of Germany. What attitude would they adopt to the refugees and expellees? To what extent would they be willing to represent the interests of the newcomers, especially when their demands conflicted with those of the more numerous indigenous voters? How far were the native and refugee politicians prepared to set a good example to their constituents by co-operating closely to improve the newcomers' disastrous economic position? There is no doubt that the response of the political parties to the refugee problem was of critical importance, and this issue will be explored in chapter 4.

Notes

1 Bayerisches Staatsministerium für Arbeit und Sozialordnung (ed.), *30 Jahre Flüchtlingsverwaltung in Bayern* (Munich 1975), p. 24.
2 Glensk, *Die Aufnahme und Eingliederung.*
3 Weiher, *Flüchtlingssituation und Flüchtlingspolitik.*
4 Grosser, '*Wir brauchten sie nicht zu nehmen*'.
5 See: Schier, *Die Aufnahme und Eingliederung*; Parisius, 'Flüchtlinge und Vertriebene in Osnabrück', pp. 13–91; K. Mundhenke, 'Hameln. Eine Fallstudie zur Eingliederung von Flüchtlingen 1945–1952', in M. Krug/ K. Mundhenke, *Flüchtlinge im Raum Hannover und in der Stadt Hameln 1945–1952* (Hildesheim 1988), pp. 83–206; A. von Seggern, *'Großstadt wider Willen': Zur Geschichte der Aufnahme und Integration von Flüchtlingen und Vertriebenen in der Stadt Oldenburg nach 1944* (Münster 1997).
6 A. von Plato, 'Fremde Heimat: Zur Integration von Flüchtlingen und Einheimischen in die Neue Zeit', in Niethammer and von Plato (eds), '*Wir kriegen jetzt andere Zeiten*', pp. 172–219.
7 Brosius, 'Zur Lage der Flüchtlinge im Regierungsbezirk Lüneburg', pp. 3–86.
8 Hohenstein, 'Aufnahme und Eingliederung', in Brosius and Hohenstein, *Flüchtlinge im nordöstlichen Niedersachsen*, pp. 87–181.
9 M. Krug, 'Das Flüchtlingsproblem im Raum Hannover (Die Altkreise Burgdorf, Hannover, Neuburg a. Rbge. und Springe) 1945–1950', in Krug and Mundhenke, *Flüchtlinge im Raum Hannover*, pp. 1–81.
10 R. Schulze (ed.), *Unruhige Zeiten: Erlebnisberichte aus dem Landkreis Celle 1945–1949* (Munich 1990). See also Schulze, 'Growing Discontent', pp. 332–49.
11 Von der Brelie-Lewien, '*Dann kamen die Flüchtlinge*'.
12 Erker, *Vom Heimatvertriebenen zum Neubürger.*
13 P. Exner, 'Integration oder Assimilation? Vertriebeneneingliederung und ländliche Gesellschaft – eine sozialgeschichtliche Mikrostudie am Beispiel westfälischer Landgemeinden', in D. Hoffmann and M. Schwartz (eds), *Geglückte Integration? Spezifika und Vergleichbarkeiten der Vertrie-*

benen-Eingliederung in der SBZ/DDR (Munich 1999), pp. 57–88.

14 Lüttig, *Fremde im Dorf.*

15 IfZ, DK 110.001, OMGUS, Information Control Division (ICD), Report No. 14A, 'German Attitudes towards the Expulsion of German Nationals from Neighbouring Countries', 8 July 1946.

16 Pfeil, *Der Flüchtling*, p. 123.

17 A.J. and R.L. Merritt (eds), *Public Opinion in Occupied Germany: The OMGUS Surveys 1945–1949* (Urbana, Chicago and London 1970), p. 20.

18 Quoted in Schulze, 'Growing Discontent', p. 345.

19 *Ibid.*, pp. 345–6. See also M. Frantzioch-Immenkeppel, 'Die Vertriebenen in der Bundesrepublik Deutschland. Flucht, Vertreibung, Aufnahme und Integration', *APZ*, B 28 (1996), p. 4.

20 D. von der Brelie-Lewien and H. Grebing, 'Flüchtlinge in Niedersachsen', in B.U. Hucker, E. Schubert and B. Weisbrod (eds), *Niedersächsische Geschichte* (Göttingen 1997), p. 630. See also D. von der Brelie-Lewien, 'Flüchtlinge in einer ländlichen Region – Aspekte des Strukturwandels zwischen "Drittem Reich" und Nachkriegszeit', in D. von der Brelie-Lewien, H. Grebing, A. Hohenstein, D. von Reeken, H. Rinklake and G. J. Trittel, *Niedersachsen nach 1945: Gesellschaftliche Umbrüche, Reorganisationsprozesse, sozialer und ökonomischer Strukturwandel* (Hanover 1995), p. 123. This view is confirmed by Rainer Schulze's study of the Rural District of Celle. See R. Schulze, 'Zuwanderung und Modernisierung – Flüchtlinge und Vertriebene im ländlichen Raum', in K.J. Bade (ed.), *Neue Heimat im Westen: Vertriebene, Flüchtlinge, Aussiedler* (Münster 1990), p. 85.

21 BSL (ed.), *Die Vertriebenen in Bayern: Ihre berufliche und soziale Eingliederung bis Anfang 1950*, Beiträge zur Statistik Bayerns, No. 151 (Munich 1950), p. 31.

22 Exner, 'Integration oder Assimilation?', pp. 84–5.

23 T. Grosser, 'Das Assimilationskonzept der amerikanischen Flüchtlingspolitik in der US-Zone nach 1945', in C. Grosser, T. Grosser, Müller and Schraut (eds), *Flüchtlingsfrage – das Zeitproblem*, pp. 17–18. In distributing the refugees, German officials were instructed by the US Military Government to 'preserve the unity of families but not communities'.

24 R. Müller, 'Von den Schwierigkeiten einer Bergstraßengemeinde im Umgang mit den Heimatvertriebenen. Dossenheim 1945–1950', in C. Grosser, T. Grosser, Müller and Schraut, *Flüchtlingsfrage – das Zeitproblem*, pp. 197–223.

25 E. Glensk, 'Großstädtischer Arbeitsmarkt und Vertriebenenintegration', p. 254.

26 Glensk, *Die Aufnahme und Eingliederung*, p. 364.

27 Grosser, '*Wir brauchten sie nicht zu nehmen*', p. 74.

28 Quoted in *ibid.*, p. 106.

29 Parisius, 'Flüchtlinge und Vertriebene in Osnabrück', p. 86.
30 Von Plato, 'Fremde Heimat'.
31 Quoted in Grosser, '*Wir brauchten sie nicht zu nehmen*', pp. 107–8.
32 Von Plato, 'Fremde Heimat', p. 204.
33 *Ibid.*, p. 203.
34 Grosser, '*Wir brauchten sie nicht zu nehmen*', pp. 70–1.
35 Weiher, *Flüchtlingssituation und Flüchtlingspolitik*, pp. 40–1.
36 Grosser, '*Wir brauchten sie nicht zu nehmen*', p. 115. See also Glensk, 'Großstädtischer Arbeitsmarkt und Vertriebenenintegration', pp. 269–70.
37 Parisius, 'Flüchtlinge und Vertriebene in Osnabrück', p. 55.
38 The argument in this paragraph is based on T. Grosser, 'Von der freiwilligen Solidar- zur verordneten Konfliktsgemeinschaft: Die Integration der Flüchtlinge und Vertriebenen in der deutschen Nachkriegsgesellschaft im Spiegel neuerer zeitgeschichtlicher Untersuchungen', in Hoffmann, Krauss and Schwartz (eds), *Vertriebene in Deutschland*, pp. 77–8.
39 Schier, *Die Aufnahme und Eingliederung* , p. 27.
40 *Ibid.*, p. 308.
41 *Ibid.*, p. 77.
42 *Ibid.*, p. 50.
43 Von Seggern, '*Großstadt wider Willen*', p. 77.
44 *Fränkische Landeszeitung*, 21 September 1948. Quoted in Erker, *Vom Heimatvertriebenen zum Neubürger*, p. 37.
45 See for example, E. Pfeil, *Fünf Jahre später: Die Eingliederung der Heimatvertriebenen in Bayern bis 1950* (Frankfurt a. M. 1951), p. 101.
46 Von der Brelie-Lewien, 'Flüchtlinge in einer ländlichen Region', p. 123.
47 Quoted in Bauer, 'Der Bayerische Bauernverband', p. 443.
48 *Ibid.*, p. 444.
49 Schulze, 'Growing Discontent', p. 339.
50 See for example, *ibid.*, p. 338 and Erker, 'Revolution des Dorfes?', pp. 392–3. Hans Joachim Malecki's study of Lower Saxony concluded that, although a higher proportion of refugees than the native population were engaged in petty theft, the overall crime rate among the newcomers was below that of the indigenous inhabitants. See Malecki, *Die Heimatvertriebenen in Niedersachsen*, p. 18.
51 PRO, FO 1006/337, Special Report of the Public Opinion Research Office for Schleswig-Holstein, 13–24 May 1948, p. 5.
52 Erker, 'Revolution des Dorfes?', p. 393.
53 See for example, Schulze, 'Growing Discontent', pp. 337–8 and Exner, 'Integration oder Assimilation?', p. 67.
54 Schulze, 'Growing Discontent', pp. 338–9 and von der Brelie-Lewien, 'Flüchtlinge in einer ländlichen Region', p. 122.
55 Quoted in Schulze, 'Growing Discontent', p. 341.

56 Von der Brelie-Lewien, 'Flüchtlinge in einer ländlichen Region', p. 123.
57 Landeskirchliches Archiv, Nuremberg (LKA), LKR 2745, Report from a Protestant Refugee Aid Worker, 1946.
58 M.H. Böhm, 'Gruppenbildung und Organisationswesen', in Lemberg and Edding (eds), *Die Vertriebenen in Westdeutschland*, Vol.1, p. 522.
59 Quoted in Schulze, 'Growing Discontent', p. 341.
60 Quoted in Erker, *Vom Heimatvertriebenen zum Neubürger*, p. 35.
61 *Bayerischer Staatsanzeiger*, 26 November 1948. Quoted in R. Koller, *Das Flüchtlingsproblem in der Staatsverwaltung: Entwickelt am Beispiel der bayerischen Flüchtlingsbetreuung* (Tübingen 1949), pp. 42–4.
62 Wennemann, 'Flüchtlinge und Vertriebene in Niedersachsen', p. 95.
63 H. Grebing, *Flüchtlinge und Parteien in Niedersachsen: Eine Untersuchung der politischen Meinungs- und Willensbildungsprozesse während der ersten Nachkriegszeit 1945–1952/53* (Hanover 1990), p. 38.
64 Quoted in Erker, *Vom Heimatvertriebenen zum Neubürger*, p. 147.
65 BHStA, MArb II/3a 1857/1, Pirner (Bavarian Red Cross) to Jaenicke, 15 March 1946.
66 M. Krauss, 'Die Integration Vertriebener am Beispiel Bayerns – Konflikte und Erfolge', in Hoffmann and Schwartz (eds), *Geglückte Integration?*, p. 54.
67 Parisius, 'Flüchtlinge und Vertriebene in Osnabrück', p. 44.
68 Müller, 'Von den Schwierigkeiten einer Bergstraßengemeinde', p. 214. Emphasis in text.
69 J. Isaac, *Die Assimilierung der Flüchtlinge in Deutschland* (London 1948), p. 5. in GStA, MA 130674.
70 Führer, *Mieter, Hausbesitzer*, p. 358.
71 Erker, *Vom Heimatvertriebenen zum Neubürger*, p. 25.
72 Krug, 'Das Flüchtlingsproblem im Raum Hannover', p. 46.
73 Müller, 'Von den Schwierigkeiten einer Bergstraßengemeinde', p. 216.
74 Exner, 'Integration oder Assimilation?', p. 66–7.
75 Bauer, *Flüchtlinge und Flüchtlingspolitik*, pp. 188–9.
76 Erker, *Vom Heimatvertriebenen zum Neubürger*, p. 25.
77 See for example, Hohenstein, 'Aufnahme und Eingliederung', p. 151.
78 Bauer, *Flüchtlinge und Flüchtlingspolitik*, p. 366.
79 Quoted in Exner, 'Integration oder Assimilation?', p. 67.
80 Koller, *Das Flüchtlingsproblem in der Staatsverwaltung*, p. 27.
81 See for example, Bauer, *Flüchtlinge und Flüchtlingspolitik*, pp. 341–80 and von der Brelie-Lewien, 'Flüchtlinge in Niedersachsen', pp. 91–109.
82 Bauer, *Flüchtlinge und Flüchtlingspolitik*, p. 366–7.
83 *Ibid.*, p. 350.
84 Quoted in Krauss, 'Die Integration Vertriebener am Beispiel Bayerns', p. 53.
85 This applied particularly to refugees with families. See Bauer, *Flüchtlinge und Flüchtlingspolitik*, p. 362.

86 Quoted in Parisius, 'Flüchtlinge und Vertriebene in Osnabrück', p. 61.
87 See for example, *ibid.*, pp. 61–2 and Exner, 'Integration oder Assimilation?', p. 71.
88 Bauer, 'Der Bayerische Bauernverband', p. 446.
89 Bauer, *Flüchtlinge und Flüchtlingspolitik*, p. 359.
90 Parisius, 'Flüchtlinge und Vertriebene in Osnabrück', p. 61.
91 Erker, *Vom Heimatvertriebenen zum Neubürger*, p. 30.
92 Krug, 'Das Flüchtlingsproblem im Raum Hannover', p. 47.
93 Führer, *Mieter, Hausbesitzer*, p. 257.
94 PRO, FO 1006/54, Monthly Report of the Kreis Resident Officer of the Rural District of Eutin to the Regional Commissioner of Schleswig-Holstein, 21 August 1948, p. 5.
95 For example, the *Landrat* of Bad Aibling petitioned the Bavarian Parliament in November 1949 to transfer the refugees living in hotels to nearby barracks, while local officials in Bad Harzburg demanded in June 1949 that the refugees occupying hotel rooms be resettled in the French Occupation Zone. See Bayerisches Landtagsarchiv (BLA), Petition submitted to a Meeting of the Committee for Refugee Questions on 21 November 1949, and NHStA Hanover, Nds 380, 62/65, 555, Minister of Economics and Transport to the Economic Administration of Bizonia, 7 June 1949.
96 StA, LRA 57248, Situation Report of the *Landrat* of Rosenheim to the Rural Police of Upper Bavaria, 1 October 1947.
97 Quoted in Erker, *Vom Heimatvertriebenen zum Neubürger*, p. 170.
98 *Ibid.*, p. 171.
99 See for example, Brosius, 'Zur Lage der Flüchtlinge im Regierungsbezirk Lüneburg', pp. 41–2.
100 *Ibid.*, p. 52.
101 Independent observers such as the academic Julius Isaac drew attention to this problem in 1949: 'The employer, who is, in most cases, an old citizen, is inclined to protect his fellow citizens with whom he has often worked for many years and the ... slogan ... "The last fired, the first hired" has some validity for the refugees in Western Germany.' See IfZ, RG 260, 3/165–1/15, 'German Refugees in the U.S. Zone 1948/1949', pp. 3–4, July 1949.
102 NHStA Hanover, Nds 120 Hanover, Acc 58/65, 151, *Regierungspräsident* of Hanover to the District Employment Officer, 31 July 1948.
103 HStA Düsseldorf, Landesarbeitsamt, 32, President of the State Labour Office to District Labour Offices, 25 August 1948.
104 BLA, Committee for Refugee Questions, Minutes of the Meeting of 10 July 1950, p. 14.
105 See for example, Erker, *Vom Heimatvertriebenen zum Neubürger*, p. 55.

106 Information Control Division Report, Regensburg, 3 June 1946. Quoted in L. Niethammer, *Entnazifizierung in Bayern: Säuberung und Rehabilitierung unter amerikanischer Besatzung* (Frankfurt a. M. 1972), p. 387.
107 Erker, 'Revolution des Dorfes?', p. 421.
108 Wennemann, 'Flüchtlinge und Vertriebene in Niedersachsen', p. 121.
109 H. Braun, 'Demographische Umschichtungen im deutschen Katholizismus nach 1945', in A. Rauscher (ed.), *Kirche und Katholizismus 1945–1949* (Paderborn 1977), p. 13.
110 See for example, ADW, ZB, 858, Dr Wolf von Gersdorff (Departmental Head in the *Evangelisches Hilfswerk* in Stuttgart) to Dr Gerstenmaier, 12 July 1946. Von Gersdorff wanted to exert pressure on the Bavarian Government to exchange Protestant newcomers living in the Catholic parts of Bavaria with Catholic refugees resident in Protestant areas of Württemberg. Similarly, the Catholic Bishop of Hildesheim warned the *Oberpräsident* of the Province of Hanover in September 1946 about the negative consequences of locating Catholic refugees in exclusively Protestant districts. See Parisius, 'Flüchtlinge und Vertriebene in Osnabrück', pp. 78–9.
111 W. Menges, 'Wandel und Auflösung der Konfessionszonen', in Lemberg and Edding (eds), *Die Vertriebenen in Westdeutschland*, Vol. 3, p. 13.
112 Statistisches Amt des Vereinigten Wirtschaftsgebietes (ed.), *Statistische Unterlagen zum Flüchtlingsproblem*, No. 7, np.
113 Menges, 'Wandel und Auflösung', p. 11.
114 Von Plato, 'Fremde Heimat', p. 212.
115 For further details, see Schier, *Die Aufnahme und Eingliederung*, pp. 259–61.
116 E. Lemberg and L. Krecker (eds), *Die Entstehung eines neuen Volkes aus Binnendeutschen und Ostvertriebenen: Untersuchungen zum Strukturwandel von Land und Leuten unter dem Einfluß des Vertriebenenzustroms* (Marburg 1950), p. 69.
117 F. Spiegel-Schmidt, 'Religiöse Wandlungen und Probleme im evangelischen Bereich', in Lemberg and Edding (eds), *Die Vertriebenen in Westdeutschland*, Vol. 3, p. 75.
118 LKA, LKR 2765, Protestant–Lutheran District Deanery (Munich) to Hellmuth Bunzel (Council of the Bavarian State Church), 12 April 1948.
119 Menges, 'Wandel und Auflösung', p.3.
120 Spiegel-Schmidt, 'Religiöse Wandlungen', p. 49.
121 *Ibid.*, p. 56.
122 For example, a native Bavarian priest from Dachau, Balthazar Ranner, characterised his colleagues' reaction as follows: 'What will be the effect on my parish?'. According to Ranner, 'many priests saw their work in ruins like a cornfield after a hailstorm'. See BA, Z18, 122,

Ranner to *Kirchliche Hilfsstelle* representatives, nd.

123 Evangelisches Zentralarchiv, Berlin (EZA), 2/643, Herbert Mochalski (Chancellery of the Protestant Church of Germany) to Protestant–Lutheran Bavarian State Church Office, 11 September 1946.

124 Quoted in U. Enders, 'Die Kirchliche Hilfsstelle München', in Prinz (ed.), *Integration und Neubeginn*, Vol. 1, p. 184.

125 H. Rudolph, *Evangelische Kirche und Vertriebene 1945 bis 1972*, Vol. 1 (Göttingen 1984), p. 219.

126 IfZ, Fig. 02/01, Military Government for Land Bavaria, Historical Report (July–September 1947), pp. 426–7.

127 LKA, LKR 2798, Anonymous letter to clergyman Löhr, 15 November 1949.

128 LKA, LKR 2745, Pfügel (Protestant–Lutheran Bavarian State Church Council) to District Deaneries, 13 January 1947. See also Erker, *Vom Heimatvertriebenen zum Neubürger*, p. 36.

129 For further details, see A. Krippner and S. Wiechmann, 'Diskriminierung und Ausgrenzung bis ins Grab: Flüchtlinge auf dem Friedhof Eichhof', in T. Herrmann and K.H. Pohl (eds), *Flüchtlinge in Schleswig-Holstein nach 1945: Zwischen Ausgrenzung und Integration* (Bielefeld 1999), pp. 127–48.

130 GStA, MA 130674, *Bericht über die Prüfung der Wohnverhältnisse und der Unterbringung der Flüchtlinge in Bayern, Hessen und Württemberg*, p. 6.

131 Bauer, *Flüchtlinge und Flüchtlingspolitik*, pp. 199–200.

132 BHStA, MArb 275, General Morale Report, 12 February 1946.

133 ADW, ZB 859, Directive from Dr F. Schramm (Minister of Cultural and Educational Affairs) and Oskar Müller (Minister of Labour and Public Safety) to the Presidents of the Administrative Districts of Darmstadt, Kassel and Wiesbaden, nd.

134 This paragraph is based on Exner, 'Integration oder Assimilation?', pp. 57–88.

135 Menges, 'Wandel und Auflösung', p. 19.

136 *Ibid.*, pp. 16–17.

137 Quoted in Schulze, 'Growing Discontent', p. 339.

138 Erker, 'Revolution des Dorfes?', p. 416.

139 See for example, *ibid.*, pp. 409–17 and Schulze, 'Growing Discontent', p. 340.

140 BSL (ed.), *Die Wahlen in den Gemeinden und Kreisen Bayerns 1946 und 1948*, Beiträge zur Statistik Bayerns, No. 147 (1949), p. 4.

141 Erker, 'Revolution des Dorfes?', p. 413.

142 Quoted in von der Brelie-Lewien and Grebing, 'Flüchtlinge in Niedersachsen', p. 627.

143 Quoted in M. Jessen-Klingenberg, '"In allem widerstrebt uns dieses Volk": Rassistische und fremdenfeindliche Urteile über die Heimat-

vertriebenen und Flüchtlinge in Schleswig-Holstein 1945–1946', in K.H. Pohl (ed.), *Regionalgeschichte heute: Das Flüchtlingsproblem in Schleswig-Holstein nach 1945* (Bielefeld 1997), p. 85.

144 *Ibid.*, p. 86.

145 *Ibid.*, pp. 85–6

146 StA, LRA 56632, Report on the mood of the population from the *Landrat* of Rosenheim to the Municipal Court, 10 October 1945.

147 For a more detailed discussion of this issue, see M. Krauss, 'Das "Wir" und das "Ihr": Ausgrenzung, Abgrenzung, Identitätsstiftung bei Einheimischen und Flüchtlingen nach 1945', in Hoffmann, Krauss and Schwartz, *Vertriebene in Deutschland*, pp. 28–39.

148 *Ibid.*, p. 35.

149 BA, Z18, 174, Report from O. Nowak, nd.

150 For further details, see Erker, 'Revolution des Dorfes?', pp. 377–9.

151 Report of 18 November 1943. Quoted in H. Böberach (ed.), *Meldungen aus dem Reich: Auswahl aus den geheimen Lageberichten des Sicherheitsdienstes der SS 1939–44*, 2nd edn (Munich 1968), p. 365.

152 Bauer, *Flüchtlinge und Flüchtlingspolitik*. p. 350.

153 Krug, 'Das Flüchtlingsproblem im Raum Hannover', p. 42.

154 Wennemann, 'Flüchtlinge und Vertriebene in Niedersachsen', p. 121; see also, Krauss, 'Die Integration Vertriebener am Beispiel Bayerns', p.53 and Lüttig, *Fremde im Dorf*, p. 83.

155 C.A. Macartney, *Das Flüchtlingsproblem in der amerikanischen Zone Deutschlands* (unpublished ms, 1948), p. 2, in GStA, MA, 130674.

156 See pp. 74–7.

157 Krauss, 'Das "Wir" und das "Ihr"', p. 33.

158 Erker, 'Revolution des Dorfes?', p. 404.

159 *Ibid.*, p. 405.

160 *Süddeutsche Zeitung*, 3 May 1947, in GStA, Bev. Stuttgart, 17.

161 Erker, 'Revolution des Dorfes?', p. 384.

162 For a more detailed discussion of these issues, see *ibid.*, pp. 367–425, Erker, *Vom Heimatvertriebenen zum Neubürger*, pp. 35–6 and Krauss, 'Das "Wir" und das "Ihr"', pp. 27–39.

Plate 1 The flight of German refugees from Pillau (East Prussia), December 1944.

Plate 2 German refugees fleeing from Braunsberg (East Prussia), January 1945.

Plate 3 The flight of German refugees from Danzig as Soviet troops advance westwards, February 1945.

Plate 4 Refugee children on Lankwitz station.

Plate 5 Living accommodation of a refugee family with nine children in the British Occupation Zone, 1947.

Plate 6 Waldfriedhof Refugee Camp (near Munich).

Plate 7 Sleeping accommodation for refugee camp occupants.

Plate 8 A refugee camp in Bavaria. Overcrowding and lack of privacy was an enormous problem.

Plate 9 Egon Herrmann delivers a speech in Dachau Refugee Camp whose occupants vote to begin a hunger strike in protest at the deplorable conditions, September 1948.

Plate 10 A refugee making shoes out of straw. Up to the Currency Reform of June 1948, it was essential to have material goods to exchange on the flourishing black market.

4

Refugees and political parties, 1945–50

Introduction

Historians and political scientists have so far devoted little attention to the refugees' impact on political life in the Western Occupation Zones of Germany. This is surprising since the newcomers undoubtedly represented an important factor in post-war West German politics simply by dint of their numerical strength. They made up some 16 per cent of the West German electorate at the first *Bundestag* Election held in August 1949, while in Schleswig-Holstein, the state most severely affected by the refugee influx, one in three voters was a newcomer. The political dimension of the refugee problem is also very important because leading West German and Allied politicians frequently expressed fears that the economically impoverished newcomers might be attracted to the overtures of radical right- and left-wing parties. In fact, in the early post-war years, it was widely believed that the refugees represented a potentially serious threat to the political stability of the Western Occupation Zones of Germany.

This chapter will analyse the attitude and policies of the political parties to the German refugees and expellees. It will also explore the tensions which often developed within the parties between refugees and their indigenous counterparts. Particular attention will be paid to the Social Democratic Party of Germany (*Sozialdemokratische Partei Deutschlands*, SPD) and the Christian Democratic Union (*Christlich-Demokratische Union*, CDU)/Christian Social Union (*Christlich-Soziale Union*, CSU). Brief reference will also be made to the Free Democratic Party (*Freie Demokratische Partei*, FDP) which, though justifiably regarded as a party representing the interests of the indigenous inhabitants, did make a belated attempt to woo refugee voters at the first *Bundestag* Election. The chapter will evaluate the strenuous efforts of the Communist Party of Germany (*Kommunistische Partei Deutschlands*, KPD) to win support among the newcomers, as well as examining the attitude of radical right-wing parties to the refugees and expellees.

This chapter will also seek to analyse the newcomers' voting behaviour between 1946 and 1950 in the three main refugee states of Bavaria, Lower Saxony and Schleswig-Holstein. Although electoral research in the early post-war period was not highly developed, the statistical data do make it possible to draw conclusions about the voting behaviour of a particular group of the electorate such as the refugees. However, it should be borne in mind that all political parties were closely supervised by the Occupying Authorities at this time and in 1946 both the British and American Military Governments forbade the establishment of a refugee party.[1] General Lucius Clay, Deputy Military Governor in the American Occupation Zone, justified his decision by arguing that the existence of a refugee party would prove detrimental to the US policy of 'assimilating' the refugees in their new homelands. He was also concerned that the Sudeten Germans, in particular, were attempting to create a 'state within a state' and reminded the Minister-Presidents of the American Occupation Zone states in February 1947 of 'the difficulties that minority groups have caused in the past'.[2] In private, Clay expressed more fundamental objections to the formation of refugee political organisations, arguing that since the newcomers were 'strongly Nazi',[3] a refugee party might become a centre of nationalism and irredentism.

The decision to outlaw refugee organisations pursuing political objectives was greeted with relief by the leaders of the CDU/CSU and SPD. At the same time, they found themselves in a serious dilemma because by banning a refugee party the Occupying Authorities placed the onus on the established parties to integrate the newcomers into their ranks. However, the political elites recognised that, at a time of general economic hardship, any party which was perceived to be placing too much emphasis on improving the refugees' material welfare was likely to lose the support of large sections of the indigenous voters who, after all, made up the vast majority of the electorate. In fact, an independent study of the refugee problem in the American Occupation Zone concluded that at the District Elections of 1948 'a considerable number of *Landräte* and mayors who had the reputation of being sympathetic to the refugees were not re-elected and were replaced by candidates who were less co-operative'.[4]

It should be borne in mind that the relationship between the refugees and individual political parties was very fluid in the early post-war years. There were huge variations between and within the eleven *Länder*. The refugees' voting behaviour was characterised by volatility and there is evidence to suggest that the personality of the candidate – and, in particular, whether he or she was a refugee – represented a more important influence on how the newcomers voted than ideological considerations or previous party affiliations. In essence, then, the refugees supported the party they considered most likely to improve their precarious economic plight.

Social Democratic Party of Germany (SPD)

The electoral prospects of the SPD appeared to be very favourable at the outset of the Occupation. After delivering a speech at an election rally in Bad Segeberg (Schleswig-Holstein) in July 1946, a Social Democrat from Hamburg concluded that 'the majority of the refugees will vote for the SPD'[5] and reports compiled by British Military Government officials in northern Germany confirmed this assumption.[6] At that time the SPD seemed to have several advantages over its political rivals. Having been founded in 1875, it was better known than either the CDU or the FDP, neither of which had come into existence until after the Second World War. In fact, the influx of refugees included several who had been prominent SPD politicians in their homelands such as Richard Reitzner, the former leader of the Social Democratic Workers' Party in the Czechoslovakian Republic (*Deutsche Sozialdemokratische Arbeiterpartei in der Tschechoslowakei*, DSAP), and Hinrich Wilhelm Kopf who led a 'trek' of refugees from Upper Silesia to Lower Saxony between January and April 1945.[7] More important still, the SPD's reputation as a party which fought for social justice appeared to make it the 'natural home' of refugees and expellees who were experiencing poverty and economic deprivation.

On the other hand, the SPD faced two major challenges in its attempt to attract the newcomers' votes. One problem was that the economic and social background of some refugees made them unlikely SPD voters. While the party could expect significant support among the Sudeten Germans, Lower Silesians and, to a lesser extent,

Upper Silesians, its long-term electoral prospects among refugees from the mainly agricultural areas of East Prussia and Pomerania, where attitudes and mentalities were conservative, appeared to be bleak. Another major challenge facing the SPD was to banish its reputation as a party with ideological links to the KPD since the refugees and expellees were deeply hostile to communism as a result of their suffering at the hands of Soviet troops at the end of the Second World War.

The SPD was the first party to recognise the importance of the refugee problem. At the party's first national post-war conference in Hanover in May 1946, its leader, Kurt Schumacher, announced that 'we will make the refugee issue our own'.[8] Conscious of the importance of distancing the SPD from the KPD at every opportunity, Schumacher denounced the expulsion of the refugees from their homelands and upheld their right to return, arguing at the SPD's party conference in Nuremberg in June 1947: 'We Social Democrats are not willing to accept the loss of the entire area east of the Oder–Neisse [rivers]. This does not only concern our national right of self-determination but is a matter of simple economic necessity.'[9] Recognising, however, that there was no immediate prospect of a change in the territorial status quo, the SPD's leaders urged the newcomers to channel all their energies into integrating in their new homelands. They also underlined at every opportunity that the newcomers should enjoy economic and political equality with the indigenous inhabitants. A key element of SPD policy towards the refugees and expellees was its demand for a 'social' Equalisation of Burdens (*Lastenausgleich*) measure based on the newcomers' present material position as opposed to their property losses.[10] It is interesting to note that, at a time when a far-reaching Land Reform measure was being introduced in the SBZ, the SPD leadership in the Western Occupation Zones also advocated the introduction of Land Reform which aimed to provide land for former refugee farmers by dispossessing large landowners.[11]

During the first half of 1946 the SPD attempted to create an organisational structure which involved the newcomers in the decision-making machinery of the party in an advisory capacity but precluded the establishment of a refugee 'lobby group' within it. In Bavaria, the SPD set up a State Refugee Committee on 14 March 1946, which had the task of advising the party on issues affecting the refugees.[12] It was also responsible for building up the party organisation at district (*Kreis*) level and by the end of 1946 refugee committees had been established in as many as 151 districts.[13] Similar bodies were set up in the other *Länder*. In Schleswig-Holstein, for example, the SPD leadership stipulated in June 1946 that, at both district and local level, the party executive should include at least one refugee.[14] After the SPD's poor performance at the Federal Election of August 1949, the party elites in Kiel made more intensive efforts to woo refugee voters, including the appointment of a party representative to each of Schleswig-Holstein's 478 refugee camps.[15]

Despite public expressions of support for the refugees, the SPD leadership in private adopted a more ambivalent attitude to the newcomers. They voiced particular concern about the presence of former Nazis among the refugees and expellees; the provisional executive of the SPD in Kiel responded to the first applications for party membership by urging local party officials in August 1945 to scrutinise carefully the applicants' political record during the Third Reich, adding that 'this applied particularly to the refugees whose past is in most cases shrouded in mystery'.[16] SPD leaders were also wary about the infiltration of communist spies into the party and at a meeting of the party executive in March 1947, Schumacher warned that '2,000 SED functionaries from the eastern zone' were residing in the Western Occupation Zones.[17] To combat this threat, district associations were instructed to send applications from refugees who claimed to have fled from the SBZ to the party headquarters in Hanover where they were individually checked by a member of the party executive.[18]

Relations between the indigenous and refugee elites within the SPD varied from state to state. In the American Occupation Zone, SPD leaders in Hesse generally cooperated well with their Sudeten German counterparts, while in Bavaria relations between the two groups were frequently strained and in Württemberg the situation was even worse.[19] Josef Seifried, Bavarian Interior Minister between 1945 and 1947, gained a reputation for being particularly hostile towards the refugees. For example, during negotiations in 1946 on the terms of the Refugee Law, he systematically sought to introduce amendments detrimental to the newcomers. He attempted to exclude from the Refugee Law newcomers from those areas east of the Oder-Neisse line which had formed part of Germany on 31 December 1937, even though their former homelands had been ceded to Poland and the Soviet Union in the post-war territorial settlement.[20] However,

Minister-President Wilhelm Hoegner, under pressure from refugees in his own party, rejected Seifried's recommendation.

While the SPD leadership attempted to keep these disagreements out of the public eye, the frustration of those who supported the refugees' interests was expressed publicly at the party conference in Düsseldorf in September 1948 by Hermann Lüdemann, Minister-President of Schleswig-Holstein, and his Refugee Minister, Walter Damm. Against the background of hunger strikes by refugees in several camps in Bavaria, Damm criticised what he saw as the failure of the party elites to provide positive leadership, regretting, in particular, the SPD's reluctance to co-operate with the newly established refugee organisations. Lüdemann was even more outspoken, claiming that the party had failed to translate its promises to the refugees into deeds.[21] Divisions between the party elites were also aired publicly at the SPD's national conference in May 1950, when Lüdemann criticised the national party executive for failing to support the resettlement of refugees from overburdened states such as Schleswig-Holstein to less overcrowded areas in southern Germany. While vigorously rejecting this claim, Schumacher argued that the SPD leadership in Kiel was too preoccupied with refugee resettlement programmes and should have placed more emphasis on creating employment opportunities and building residential housing for the newcomers in Schleswig-Holstein.[22]

However, it was at local level that the arrival of the refugees and expellees had the greatest impact on political life. In fact, they enabled the SPD to gain a foothold in many rural areas where it had previously enjoyed negligible support. In Lower Saxony, for example, Lower Silesian refugees set up local SPD associations in rural constituencies where local people still viewed the party as a radical organisation to be shunned at all costs.[23] Similarly, Sudeten German newcomers played a dominant role in many local party organisations in Catholic areas of Southern Bavaria where the SPD had traditionally been weak. This was reflected in party membership figures. In December 1947, refugees comprised 33 per cent of SPD members in Upper Bavaria, 37 per cent in Lower Bavaria/Upper Palatinate and 52 per cent in Swabia.[24] However, it was at district and parish level that the impact of the newcomers was most keenly felt. For example, in the Rural District of Ansbach (Middle Franconia) membership of the SPD increased from 150 in 1946 to 1,000 in 1948 as a result of the influx of Sudeten Germans,[25] while in the parish of

Marke (near Osterode, Lower Saxony) there was not a single representative of the native population in the local SPD organisation.[26]

Relations between native and refugee members at local level varied enormously. In some constituencies such as Oldenburg (Schleswig-Holstein), where the party unanimously selected Paul Stech, a refugee from Königsberg, as its candidate for the *Bundestag* Election of 1949, the two groups cooperated amicably.[27] However, this was by no means always the case. In Bavaria, for example, Benno Schmeidl, Head of the SPD's Department for Expellees and Refugees, reported to the party's Vice Chairman in January 1948 that 'generally speaking, there is little co-operation with the indigenous party members, who have little or no interest in our situation'.[28] Helga Grebing's study of Lower Saxony reached a similar conclusion, observing that tensions between the two groups increased as the refugees established themselves in the party.[29] Many of the SPD's district associations in Bavaria, Lower Saxony and Schleswig-Holstein ignored the party executive's directive in 1946 to establish refugee committees in each district.[30] An unusually flagrant example of prejudice against refugees occurred in the small town of Wyk, on the remote island of Föhr (Schleswig-Holstein), where the indigenous SPD leaders refused to allow the *Landtag* delegate Kurt Pohle, a refugee from Breslau, to deliver a speech in February 1946 because 'a stranger should not, in our opinion, make public declarations on behalf of our party'.[31] The hostility of the SPD's party executive in Wyk towards refugees was confirmed by its decision to select only natives of Schleswig-Holstein to contest the District Elections of October 1948.[32]

However, there is also evidence that, when refugees succeeded in gaining control of a local party, they were apt to discriminate against native functionaries in the same way. In Rendsburg (Schleswig-Holstein) the newcomers succeeded in strengthening their position by introducing a regulation in December 1946 excluding from the district party executive anyone who had not belonged to the SPD before 1933.[33] In the Rural District of Segeberg (Schleswig-Holstein), where the newcomers held the upper hand, only refugees were nominated as SPD candidates in the District Elections of October 1948.[34] Bruno Verdieck, who spoke at meetings throughout Schleswig-Holstein during the campaign for the *Bundestag* Election of August 1949, observed that in constituencies where refugees had established control of the party, native SPD functionaries often withdrew from politics altogether.[35] A number of studies confirm that the refugees' domination of some constituency organisations was not always due to their numerical superiority over the indigenous members but was because of their greater commitment and energy.[36]

But what was the attitude of refugee and expellee voters to the SPD? Helga Grebing has argued convincingly that in Lower Saxony the SPD was the party of the refugees in the initial stages of the Occupation and this conclusion is equally valid for the neighbouring state of Schleswig-Holstein. At the first *Landtag* Election in Schleswig-Holstein held on 20 April 1947, the SPD polled 43.8 per cent, an excellent result in a region which did not have a strong tradition of Social Democracy. Significantly, the SPD performed well in constituencies heavily populated with newcomers and the party executive concluded that 'the election victory was to a large extent due to the refugees'.[37] The Social Democrats captured 53.3 per cent of the vote in the refugee camps in Kiel, more than 16 per cent ahead of its nearest rival, the CDU,[38] and in the Bülow-Kaserne camp in Ratzeburg (Lauenburg-Ost), the SPD's lead over the CDU was some 30 per cent.[39] The SPD also attracted significant support from refugees in Bavaria. Although the party suffered a heavy defeat at the first *Landtag* Election in December 1946, its respectable performance in Lower Bavaria, a predominantly rural and overwhelmingly Catholic area where the SPD had attracted negligible support in the past, was undoubtedly due to the influx of refugee voters.[40]

The widespread support for the SPD among refugee voters at the *Landtag* Elections of 1946–47 was based predominantly on its reputation as a party representing the interests of the 'poor, oppressed and underprivileged'.[41] In other words, the economically distressed and needy refugees saw the SPD as the party most likely to introduce measures to alleviate their poverty, especially Land Reform and Equalisation of Burdens legislation.[42] Initial reservations among some newcomers about voting for a 'left-wing' party were allayed by Kurt Schumacher's fierce attacks on the KPD.[43] In addition, some SPD refugee politicians such as Heinrich Albertz and Hinrich Wilhelm Kopf, who served as Lower Saxony's Minister-President between 1946 and 1955, attracted a personal following among the newcomers. In fact, Kopf won 47.6 per cent of the vote in Fallingbostel (Lower Saxony) at the *Landtag* Election of April 1947. It is also clear that the SPD's organisational structure at local level was far superior to that of its rivals in the early post-war years

Table 4.1 Electoral support for the SPD in the main refugee states, 1946–51

Election	*% of total vote*		
	Bavaria	*Lower Saxony*	*Schleswig-Holstein*
Landtag (1946–47)	28.6	43.4	43.8
District (1948)	23.7	39.6	39.7
Bundestag (1949)	22.7	33.4	29.6
Landtag (1950–51)	28.0	33.7	27.5

Source: Adapted from: Forschungsinstitut der Konrad-Adenauer-Stiftung (ed.), *Wahlergebnisse in der Bundesrepublik Deutschland und in den Bundesländern 1946–1988*, pp. 3, 5, 11 (Sankt Augustin 1988); BSL (ed.), *Die erste Bundestagswahl in Bayern am 14. August 1949*, Beiträge zur Statistik Bayerns, No.150, p. 42 and Archiv der sozialen Demokratie der Friedrich Ebert-Stiftung, Bonn (AdsD), LV S-H, 79, Statistisches Landesamt Schleswig-Holstein (ed.), *Vorläufiges Ergebnis der Bundestagswahlen vom 14. August 1949 im Vergleich zu den Wahlen 1947 und 1948.*

and in the Rural District of Göttingen the party held no fewer than 40 meetings for refugees during the autumn of 1946.[44]

The *Landtag* Elections of 1946–47 proved to be the high point of the SPD's electoral fortunes in the early post-war years. As Table 4.1 shows, its share of the vote fell by some 4–5 per cent at the District Elections of 1948 in Bavaria, Lower Saxony and Schleswig-Holstein and this was due mainly to the defection of the newcomers. Many refugee voters who had previously supported the SPD now turned to their own independent candidates. In Schleswig-Holstein, for example, the party suffered heavy losses in each of the districts where it was competing against independent refugee candidates – Plön, Stormarn, Pinneberg, Oldenburg and Norderdithmarschen.[45] The same pattern was evident in Bavaria.[46] On the other hand, its best performances tended to be in districts where it cooperated closely with refugee organisations such as the administrative district of Oldenburg (Lower Saxony) where the party registered an increase of 3.4 per cent at the District Elections of 1948.[47]

At the *Bundestag* Election held on 14 August 1949 the SPD suffered a heavy defeat, especially in Lower Saxony and Schleswig-Holstein, and the loss of refugee votes contributed significantly to its demise. Electoral returns from refugee camps in Kiel and Bad

Segeberg indicated a sharp fall in the SPD's vote,[48] while in Bavaria the party incurred losses in as many as 23 of the 27 constituencies where it had enjoyed some success in 1948 in the absence of independent refugee candidates. This development foreshadowed the spectacular successes achieved by the newly established refugee party – the Bloc of Expellees and Dispossessed Persons (*Block der Heimatvertriebenen und Entrechteten*, BHE) at *Landtag* elections in Bavaria and Schleswig-Holstein in 1950.

Divisions and conflicts within the SPD concerning the refugee problem played an important part in the erosion of its support among the newcomers in the period 1948–50. The public disagreement between Schumacher and Lüdemann over the resettlement issue at the party conference took place in May 1950, shortly before the *Landtag* Election in Schleswig-Holstein, and undoubtedly cost the party refugee votes. Conflicts at local level were often more intense and the SPD's inquest into its disappointing performance at the Bavarian District Elections in 1948 concluded that 'in many places the necessary degree of co-operation within the party between refugee and indigenous comrades was lacking'.[49] Local reports indicate that many newcomers living in outlying areas of rural Schleswig-Holstein felt neglected by the SPD leadership and during the campaign for the *Bundestag* Election of August 1949, refugees in Böel (Rural District of Segeberg) and other small localities complained that they had had no contact with the party executive in Kiel since the *Landtag* Election of April 1947.[50]

The view that the SPD had lost touch with its grass roots support is confirmed by the failure of its refugee politicians in Schleswig-Holstein to gain influence in the Homeland Societies (*Landsmannschaften*) even though these organisations exerted increasing political influence on the newcomers in 1949–50. The SPD's Refugee Advisory Committee discussed in November 1949 whether it should emulate the tactics of the FDP at the first *Bundestag* Election when it achieved some success by nominating a number of refugee candidates who were active in the *Landsmannschaften*.[51] But the Committee failed to reach a consensus and the party's loss of contact with the refugees at local level was once again underlined at the *Landtag* Election of 1950 by the fact that several of the BHE's leaders such as Dr Alfred Gille and Hans Adolf Asbach played a prominent role in the *Landsmannschaften*.

However, the most important reason for the refugees' defection from the SPD was their disillusionment at what they saw as the inability or unwillingness of the party to improve their economic position.[52] This was particularly the case in Schleswig-Holstein, the only state where, as the sole governing party in the period 1947–50, it had ultimate responsibility for the refugee problem. A report by the British Military Government, based on interviews conducted in Schleswig-Holstein, concluded in July 1949 that 'refugees frequently express disgust with the treatment they receive at the hands of the government'.[53] The SPD was blamed for the delay in passing the Emergency Refugee Law,[54] as well as the deterioration in the refugees' material wellbeing in the aftermath of the Currency Reform.[55] Another important grievance was the delay in introducing the much-vaunted Land Reform and by 1949 the patience of the some 32,000 refugees who had applied for a share of the land to be confiscated from the large landowners was wearing thin.[56] They were particularly incensed at the long delays in implementing the programme to resettle them from Schleswig-Holstein to areas where overcrowding was less serious or where the prospects for economic integration were more favourable (in particular, North Rhine-Westphalia).

To sum up, the SPD gained significant support from refugee voters in Bavaria, Lower Saxony and Schleswig-Holstein at the beginning of the Occupation because they believed that it was the party most likely to alleviate their severe economic deprivation. But this support dwindled steadily from 1947 onwards as the newcomers' economic position showed little sign of improvement and in some cases actually deteriorated. In fact, after the SPD's disastrous performance in the *Landtag* Election in Schleswig-Holstein in July 1950, Hermann Lüdemann concluded: 'The SPD has lost Schleswig-Holstein for a long time (one might almost say for ever) and the reason is our mistakes in the way we handled the refugee problem.'[57] Although Lüdemann's claim that the SPD's demise was due solely to the expellee issue was overstated, there is no doubt that the party's standing among the newcomers had been tarnished.

Christian Democratic Union (CDU)/Christian Social Union (CSU)

Although the refugees and expellees are traditionally regarded as supporters of the CDU and its Bavarian counterpart, the CSU, this view requires much qualification as regards the early post-war years. At the beginning of the Occupation, the electoral prospects of the

CDU appeared to be good in Northern Germany since most of the refugees and expellees who had settled there came from the predominantly rural eastern territories and had a conservative outlook. This applied particularly to the East Prussians and Pomeranians who comprised 71 per cent of the newcomers in Schleswig-Holstein in September 1950[58] and a substantial proportion of those in Lower Saxony. On the other hand, the CSU was, from an ideological perspective, not in such a good position to attract refugee voters in Bavaria since some 80 per cent of them were Sudeten Germans or Silesians, groups who were more likely to support the SPD than the CSU.[59]

Another advantage for the CDU was that it attracted a number of energetic refugee politicians in the early post-war years, in particular Dr Linus Kather, a Protestant lawyer from East Prussia. He jointly founded the CDU in Hamburg and was the driving force behind the establishment of an organisational structure to represent refugee interests within the party. Kather was an ambitious, uncompromising and outspoken politician who saw the CDU as a focal point for all native and refugee voters who did not subscribe to Marxist ideas.[60] Another leading refugee in the CDU was Dr Hans Lukaschek, a former *Oberpräsident* of Upper Silesia who was appointed Minister for Expellees in Adenauer's first government. The most prominent refugee in the CSU was Dr Hans Schütz, a former leader of the Sudeten German Textile Workers' Union who had also represented the German Christian Social People's Party (*Deutsche Christlich-Soziale Volkspartei*, DCSVP) in the Czechoslovakian Parliament from 1935 to 1938.

The policies of the CDU/CSU towards the refugees were in some respects similar to those of the SPD, but there were also important differences. In common with the SPD, the CDU/CSU advocated the legal, political and economic equality of the refugees with the indigenous population.[61] It also advocated the introduction of Equalisation of Burdens legislation to compensate war-damaged groups such as the refugees. Some CDU politicians favoured an 'individual' Equalisation of Burdens Law, based on the refugees' property losses in their former homelands, but the majority supported a 'social' measure which would allocate funds according to the material needs of the recipients.[62] Despite pressure from prominent CDU refugee spokesmen such as Kather,[63] the party leadership, in contrast to the SPD, opposed the introduction of Land Reform legislation to provide land for former refugee farmers (*Landwirte*). In Bavaria, where, under pressure from the Americans, a Land Reform measure was introduced in September 1946, the CSU Minister of Agriculture Josef Baumgartner undermined its effectiveness by introducing a lengthy appeals' procedure.[64] CDU politicians, like their counterparts in the SPD, publicly underlined the refugees' right to return to their homelands and Adenauer stressed on 31 December 1946 that his party would never 'sign a peace treaty which recognise[d] the Oder–Neisse line'.[65] However, some of his colleagues went much further by encouraging the refugees to believe that they would be able to reclaim their homelands in the near future. Carl Schröter, CDU Chairman in Schleswig-Holstein, maintained in October 1948 that the day when the refugees would be permitted to go back was 'nearer than most people dare to imagine',[66] while Günther Gereke predicted a speedy return since 'the Western Powers had already been forced to revise many of their decisions in the last three years'.[67] Such statements were criticised by politicians from both the major parties because they were apt to discourage the refugees from channelling their full energies into integrating in their new homelands.

The CDU leadership took steps to involve the refugees and expellees in the party organisation, albeit in a purely advisory capacity. In June 1946 it authorised the establishment of a Zonal Refugee Committee in the British Occupation Zone under the chairmanship of Kather, based in Hamburg where he had taken up residence. The party also set up refugee committees in Schleswig-Holstein, Hamburg, Bremen, the Rhineland, Westphalia, Hanover, Oldenburg, Braunschweig and Lippe. It was envisaged that a refugee committee would be formed in each district (*Kreis*), comprising not just newcomers but also members of the native population.[68] Similar developments took place elsewhere. In Bavaria, for example, the CSU set up its own state refugee committee in May 1946 which had the task of establishing representation for the newcomers at *Regierungsbezirk* and district level. In June 1947, the Chairman of the CSU, Dr Josef Müller, attempted to integrate the newcomers more closely into the party by replacing the state refugee committee with a 'Union of Expellees' under the chairmanship of Hans Schütz.[69] However, its importance should not be overestimated because it had little influence within the CSU and at the end of 1949 boasted a membership of just several hundred in the whole of Bavaria.[70]

Despite official declarations of support for the refugees, the

CDU was justifiably regarded as a party of the native population in the early post-war years. This was particularly true of mainly Catholic states such as North Rhine-Westphalia where the party was dominated by middle-class indigenous Catholics. In these areas, some CDU leaders had particular reservations about Protestant refugees and Wilhelm Boden, who later became Minister-President of Rhineland-Palatinate, justified his request to the French Military Government to ban refugees from the state on the grounds that 'the influx of mainly Protestant Germans from the East would strongly dilute the Catholic character of the Rhineland'.[71] In the mainly Catholic state of Bavaria, the CSU elites adopted an equally negative attitude to the newcomers. Many considered it their duty to defend the interests of the native population against the refugees and other 'outsiders'. Rather than viewing the newcomers' integration into their new homelands as a bilateral process involving compromises from both groups, many CSU politicians interpreted 'integration' as the adoption by the refugees of the mentality, customs and traditions of the Bavarian people. In fact, this view was even held by the CSU Chairman of the Bavarian Parliament's Committee for Refugee Questions, Josef Scharf, who argued in February 1948 that 'the main aim' of refugee welfare legislation was to promote 'the integration of the refugees in the indigenous population', adding that 'it was essential ... that ... [they] consider themselves to be part of the Bavarian people'.[72]

In the mainly Protestant states of Lower Saxony and Schleswig-Holstein prominent CDU politicians also often adopted a negative attitude to the newcomers. Carl Schröter gained a reputation for hostility towards the refugees, arguing on one occasion that the interests of the indigenous population should take precedence over those of the newcomers.[73] However, in some of these mainly Protestant constituencies the refugees themselves were able to gain control of the CDU because the native population identified with one of the other parties. In Schleswig-Holstein, for example, this was the case in the Urban District of Flensburg, where large numbers of indigenous voters supported the Party of the Danish Minority, the South Schleswig Voters' League (*Südschleswigscher Wählerverband*, SSW),[74] and also in Steinburg, where the majority of the native population voted for either the SPD or the FDP.[75] A similar pattern was discernible in parts of Lower Saxony and in Soltau refugees comprised 90 per cent of the CDU's membership in mid-1949,[76] a development which horrified the local Catholic priest who claimed that it had become 'a radical refugee party'.[77]

The grudging and in some cases even hostile attitude of the CDU/CSU elites to the refugees and expellees was reflected in their reluctance to represent the newcomers' interests adequately within the party. Despite intense pressure from Kather, there was just one refugee among the CDU's 16 members in the Economic Council and none at all among its 27 representatives in the Parliamentary Council.[78] Similarly, newcomers were consistently underrepresented among the CDU's candidates at regional and national elections. In fact, they made up just 7 per cent of the CDU's 115 successful candidates at the *Bundestag* Election of 1949, even though they comprised some 16 per cent of the electorate.[79] The prejudice of CDU leaders towards the refugees was exemplified by events in Lower Saxony where the party decided to nominate only indigenous candidates to contest individual constituencies.[80] In Bavaria, CSU leaders at both regional and local level also consistently failed to represent the newcomers' interests. At the State Election of December 1946, just one of the 104 delegates the CSU returned to the *Landtag* was a refugee, while at the *Landtag* Election of November 1950 none of the CSU's constituency parties nominated a newcomer as its candidate.[81] The refugees fared no better at local level. At the District Elections held in Bavaria in April 1948 they comprised 22.8 per cent of the population in the rural districts but just 3.6 per cent of the CSU's delegates elected to the District Councils.[82]

The failure of the CDU/CSU elites to represent the newcomers' interests adequately provoked great bitterness among its refugee politicians. Kather was a particularly outspoken critic of his native counterparts in the CDU and his pugnacious disposition contributed to the bad blood between the two groups. He was the driving force behind the so-called 'Schneverding' letter sent to Konrad Adenauer in March 1948 by prominent refugee politicians in the CDU. The letter contained examples illustrating what its authors considered to be the party's failure to represent the refugees' interests and concluded that the way in which indigenous CDU politicians had treated the newcomers was 'neither christian nor democratic'.[83] Later that year one of the signatories of this letter, Franz Schmucker, Chairman of the CDU Refugee Committee in Schleswig-Holstein, resigned from the party because 'he could no longer reconcile his conscience with the negative policy of the CDU to the refugees'.[84]

Meanwhile, Dr Franz Ryba, a refugee from Upper Silesia whose hopes of becoming Minister-President of Schleswig-Holstein after the *Landtag* Election of July 1950 failed to materialise, informed Adenauer that, 'as a Catholic – and especially with the taint of having a birth certificate issued outside Schleswig-Holstein', he 'was fighting a losing battle'.[85] In Bavaria, where the CSU Government under Hans Ehard systematically reduced the powers of the State Secretary for Refugees, Wolfgang Jaenicke, the party's refugee politicians also considered themselves to be discriminated against by their indigenous colleagues. This prompted Ernst Glaser, a leading Sudeten German who later became Chairman of the CSU's 'Union of Expellees', to claim that the newcomers were 'only regarded as a necessary evil by leading figures in the government'.[86] There is no doubt, then, that relations between refugee and native politicians in the CDU/CSU were invariably characterised by friction and even hostility.

What was the attitude of refugee voters to the CDU in the early post-war years? The outcome of the *Landtag* Elections in Schleswig-Holstein and Lower Saxony in April 1947 indicated that the party had failed to gain significant support from the newcomers. In Schleswig-Holstein, for example, the CDU achieved its best results in constituencies such as Schleswig and Südtondern which had a small refugee population.[87] The voting returns from refugee camps in Kiel, Lübeck and Lauenburg-Ost confirm that refugee support for the CDU lagged well behind that for the SPD.[88] It is clear that the newcomers regarded the CDU as a middle-class party representing the interests of the indigenous population. The widespread support it received from the local farming community discouraged refugees from voting for the party because of the unsympathetic treatment many had received from the farmers with whom they were billeted.[89] In fact, no fewer than 15 of the 42 CDU candidates at the first post-war *Landtag* election in Schleswig-Holstein were farmers.[90] In Lower Saxony, the CDU suffered a heavy defeat at the *Landtag* Election, polling just 19.9 per cent of the vote, and it attracted little support from the newcomers. In 21 of the 95 constituencies it formed an electoral pact with the anti-refugee Regional Party of Lower Saxony (*Niedersächsische Landespartei*, NLP), a decision which prompted most newcomers in these constituencies to abstain from voting, cast their vote for the SPD or, in the cases of Lüneburg and Stade, re-establish the Centre Party.[91]

Table 4.2 Electoral support for the CDU/CSU in the main refugee states, 1946–51

Election	*% of total vote*		
	Bavaria	*Lower Saxony*	*Schleswig-Holstein*
Landtag (1946–47)	52.3	19.9	34.1
District (1948)	37.8	24.3	38.0
Bundestag (1949)	29.2	17.6	30.7
Landtag (1950–51)	27.4	23.7[a]	19.8

Note [a] At this election the CDU merged with the German Party to form the 'Low German Union'.

Source: Adapted from: Forschungsinstitut der Konrad-Adenauer-Stiftung (ed.), *Wahlergebnisse in der Bundesrepublik Deutschland und in den Bundesländern 1946–1988*, pp. 3, 5, 11; BSL (ed.), *Die erste Bundestagswahl*, pp. 42–3 and AdsD, LV S-H, 79, Statistisches Landesamt Schleswig-Holstein (ed.), *Vorläufiges Ergebnis der Bundestagswahlen vom 14. August 1949 im Vergleich zu den Wahlen 1947 und 1948.*

As Table 4.2 shows, the CDU improved its overall performance at the District Elections of 1948 in both Lower Saxony and Schleswig-Holstein. This was partly due to the influence of the refugees, especially in Lower Saxony, but the most striking feature of the election was the volatility of the newcomers' voting behaviour. The CDU undoubtedly benefited from the fact that the refugees tended to vote against the party which had controlled their District Council in the period 1946–48, in protest at its failure to improve their economic plight. For example, this contributed significantly to the CDU's success in the *Regierungsbezirk* of Lüneburg (Lower Saxony), an area heavily populated with refugees where the SPD had been in power since 1946.[92] The outcome of the District Elections also indicated that the newcomers' voting behaviour was not primarily determined by the policies of the major parties but the number of refugees they nominated as candidates. This is again illustrated by events in Lüneburg. Although the SPD remained the largest party in the *Regierungsbezirk* as a whole, the CDU obtained good results in districts where it was dominated by refugees. In Soltau, for example, it polled 28 per cent, well above its average in the state, due to the newcomers who comprised 80 per cent of the party's successful candidates.[93] The same pattern was evident in Dannenberg, where 75 per cent of the CDU's delegates in the district council were refugees.[94] An important contributory factor to the success of the CDU in Dannenberg and elsewhere was their close co-operation with the refugees' newly established cultural and welfare organisations and in this respect the CDU generally outmanoeuvred the SPD.[95] However, as a rule, neither the CDU nor the SPD won widespread support from the newcomers when they were competing against independent refugee candidates, a development which did not bode well for their future electoral prospects.

The CDU/CSU advocated the introduction of special constituencies at the *Bundestag* Election of August 1949 where parties would be permitted to nominate only refugee candidates but this proposal was rejected in the Parliamentary Council by the other parties. CDU/CSU politicians hoped that on polling day refugee voters would give them credit for this initiative but these expectations did not materialise. As Table 4.2 shows, the CDU's share of the vote fell sharply in all three of the main refugee states and this was partly due to the fact that many newcomers supported their own independent candidates. In Schleswig-Holstein 'independents' polled 7.6 per cent of the vote and in Lower Saxony, 8.1 per cent, while in Hesse, where the CDU also suffered heavy losses, they garnered 11.5 per cent of the votes cast.[96] The CDU's poor showing among refugee voters can also be attributed to the electoral pacts it formed in some states with parties known to be unsympathetic to the newcomers. For example, in Hamburg, where the CDU formed an electoral pact with the FDP, the share of the vote gained by the CDU or FDP candidate was almost 12 per cent lower in refugee camps than in the rest of the constituency.[97] In Lower Saxony, the standing of the CDU among the newcomers was damaged by the open hostility between two of the party's best-known refugee politicians, Linus Kather and Günther Gereke.[98] However, the most important underlying factor for the refugees' growing alienation from the CDU/CSU and SPD in 1949 was that they blamed these parties for the material deprivation they continued to suffer more than four years after the end of the war.

In Bavaria, the political fortunes of the CSU slumped sharply during the Occupation period. As Table 4.2 shows, the party won an absolute majority at the *Landtag* Election held on 1 December 1946 but, after a series of setbacks, its share of the vote slumped to just 27.4 per cent in November 1950. This can be partly attributed to the defection of former CSU voters to the Bavarian Party,[99] a particularist organisation founded by Jakob Fischbacher and Ludwig Lallinger which adopted a violently anti-refugee platform and espoused the grievances of native Bavarians who had been compelled to share their homes with the newcomers. However, the erosion of the CSU vote was also due to the loss of support from refugee voters. As was the case with the CDU and SPD, the party invariably sustained heavy losses at the District Elections of 1948 in areas such as Swabia where it was competing against independent refugee candidates.[100] The growing alienation of refugees in Bavaria from the CSU was confirmed by the outcome of the first *Bundestag* Election in 1949 and the *Landtag* Election of November 1950. According to a survey undertaken by the Bavarian Statistical Office, the CSU's best results in rural areas in both elections were achieved in constituencies with a small refugee population, while some of its worst performances were recorded in constituencies densely inhabited with newcomers. This trend was especially pronounced at the *Landtag* Election of 1950 when the CSU polled 44 per cent in constituencies where refugees comprised up to 14 per cent of the population but only 28.6 per cent in constituencies in which newcomers made up more than 26 per cent of the inhabitants.[101] Significantly, the CSU fared disastrously in Bavaria's *Flüchtlingsgemeinden* – municipalities where newcomers comprised at least 90 per cent of the inhabitants. It polled only 8.8 per cent in Geretsried (Rural District of Wolfratshausen), 7.7 per cent in Traunreut (Rural District of Traunstein), 7.6 per cent in Neugablonz (Urban District of Kaufbeuren) and 5.4 per cent in Waldkraiburg (Rural District of Mühldorf).[102]

It is clear, then, that by 1950 the CSU held little attraction for the refugees. One reason was that, as with the SPD in Schleswig-Holstein, the CSU, as the sole governing party in Bavaria after September 1947, was held responsible by the newcomers for their continuing material deprivation. Another key factor was the lack of solidarity that CSU politicians displayed towards the refugees at both regional and local level. As Alf Mintzel put it: 'Almost everywhere the indigenous Bavarians in the CSU isolated themselves in their "native party" against the "strangers", the "intruders" and "Prussians".'[103] Under these circumstances, it is not surprising that many newcomers who had voted for the party in 1946 had become alienated from it by 1950.

Free Democratic Party (FDP)

Following the collapse of the Third Reich, a number of different 'liberal' parties were established in the various states of the Western Occupation Zones of Germany. In Württemberg-Baden, for example, a Democratic People's Party (*Demokratische Volkspartei*, DVP) came into existence, while its counterpart in Hesse was initially called the Liberal Democratic Party (*Liberal-Demokratische Partei*, LDP). However, in the three states most heavily populated with refugees – Bavaria, Lower Saxony and Schleswig-Holstein – the liberals adopted the name 'FDP' from the outset.

In the early post-war years, the FDP was justifiably regarded as a party of the indigenous inhabitants which adopted an apathetic or even hostile attitude towards the German refugees and expellees from the East. This is shown by an incident at a Special Party Conference convened in Neumünster (Schleswig-Holstein) in July 1948 when no one contradicted a speaker who argued that the FDP should exclusively represent the interests of the native population.[104] Only when the delegates became aware of a refugee in their midst did they see fit to amend the original motion. Similarly, the FDP in Lower Saxony gained a reputation among refugees for 'representing the selfish interests of the propertied classes',[105] while Hans Woller's study of the Bavarian town of Ansbach concluded that it was the party of local businessmen and professional groups and 'kept the newcomers at arm's length'.[106]

Against this background, refugee politicians in the FDP seeking to promote the interests of the newcomers faced an uphill struggle. The party's leading refugee politician in the British Occupation Zone was Dr Fritz Oellers, a lawyer who had fled to the West from Halle in 1946. He enjoyed an excellent reputation and was elected Chairman of the FDP's Refugee Committee in the British Occupation Zone in June 1947. However, his efforts to support the newcomers were frustrated by the lack of commitment among the party leadership. Noting that the FDP's nominations to the Economic Council did not include a single refugee, Oellers warned Franz Blücher, Chairman of the FDP in the British Occupation Zone, in January 1948 that 'a dangerous antipathy to the political parties is spreading among the refugees who feel that they have been let down'.[107] However, this warning appeared to fall on deaf ears and two months later Oellers reiterated a plea to Blücher to authorise the printing of the FDP's refugee programme which had been approved in August of the previous year.[108] This was not an isolated example of the dilatoriness of the FDP leadership in the British Occupation Zone and the party's District Association in Osterode (Lower Saxony) wrote as many as twelve different letters to the Zonal Headquarters between May 1947 and February 1948 in an attempt to discover party policy towards the refugees and expellees.[109] Problems arose again in the autumn of 1948 and, five weeks before the District Elections in Schleswig-Holstein, the FDP leadership in Kiel had received no election literature on the refugee issue.[110]

The FDP's policies towards the refugees and expellees had much in common with those of the SPD and CDU/CSU. It demanded the return of the eastern territories, expressed support for the implementation of the Refugee Law and stressed that the newcomers should enjoy exactly the same rights as the indigenous inhabitants. However, in several other respects the FDP's policies differed from those of the mainstream political parties. It favoured the introduction of an 'individual' as opposed to a 'social' Equalisation of Burdens measure and proposed that private building contractors be offered tax incentives to construct new homes for refugees. While the FDP opposed the compulsory expropriation of indigenous landowners to help refugee farmers, it advocated that land belonging to public corporations should be redistributed among the newcomers.[111]

While some local FDP parties had reached an informal agreement with refugee groups at the District Elections of 1948,[112] it was not until the first *Bundestag* Election of August 1949 that the party leadership recognised the electoral potential of the newcomers. In Schleswig-Holstein, for example, where Oellers had been elected party chairman in February 1949, no fewer than 10 of the FDP's 14 candidates at the first *Bundestag* Election were refugees.[113] A number of these candidates were active in the Homeland Societies and therefore enjoyed a certain following among refugee voters. Similarly, 11 of the FDP's 31 names on its *Land* list in Bavaria were newcomers,[114] while in North Rhine-Westphalia refugees occupied three of the first five places.[115] In several regional elections held in 1950, the FDP again paid particular attention to attracting refugee votes and in Hesse it actually formed an electoral pact with the newly established BHE.[116]

It is clear that the FDP gained negligible electoral support from the refugees and expellees in the early post-war years. At the first *Landtag* elections, held in 1946–47, the party's share of the vote was small, winning just 5.7 per cent in Bavaria (1 December 1946), 5.0 per cent in Schleswig-Holstein (20 April 1947) and 8.7 per cent in Lower Saxony (20 April 1947). The district elections held in 1948 produced equally disappointing results for the FDP.[117] The party's failure to attract significant support in the early years of the Occupation was due partly to its organisational shortcomings. Significantly, it failed to nominate a candidate in many parishes in Bavaria at the local elections in April 1948, while in Schleswig-Holstein the party's constituencies north of the River Eider boasted just 25 members between them in July 1948.[118] However, the FDP's electoral defeats can also be attributed to its apathetic attitude towards the newcomers. In his postmortem on the FDP's poor performance in the *Landtag* Election in Schleswig-Holstein in April 1947, Oellers highlighted the fact that the party 'had shown too little initiative on the refugee question'.[119] The 21 constituency parties in Schleswig-Holstein were dominated by members of the indigenous population and when they were asked in June 1948 to nominate a representative to the party's state refugee committee, just three of them responded.[120]

An analysis of the outcome of the *Bundestag* Election of August 1949 indicates that the FDP's campaign to win the support of the refugees met with a mixed response. An empirical study revealed that in Bavaria the FDP achieved its best results in constituencies with a small refugee population and performed least well in constituencies most heavily populated with newcomers.[121] However, the results from individual constituencies in Schleswig-Holstein indicate that refugees were prepared to vote for the FDP when it put forward a refugee candidate who had close links to the *Landsmannschaften*. For example, in Husum/Südtondern/Eiderstedt, where Dr Palaschinski, the Chairman of the Union of Expellees (*Bund der Heimatvertriebenen*) in Eiderstedt, fought a very active campaign, the FDP's share of the vote rose from 1 per cent in the District Elections of October 1948 to 12.7 per cent in August 1949.[122] The same pattern was evident in Lübeck where the FDP's candidate was Dr Alfred Gille, a former mayor of Lötzen (East Prussia) and Secretary of the town's 'Emergency Association of East German Homeland Societies' (*Notgemeinschaft Ostdeutscher Landsmannschaften*).[123] On the strength of refugee votes, the FDP polled 15.8 per cent in Lübeck at the *Bundestag* Election, as opposed to 9 per cent in October 1948.

However, while Palaschinski, Gille and others were able to win refugee votes for the FDP in 1949 through their own personal following, this success proved to be short-lived. When Gille resigned from the party in January 1950 to become one of the founding members of the BHE, FDP membership figures in Lübeck fell by 50 per cent.[124] At the *Landtag* Election in Schleswig-Holstein in July 1950 most of the refugees who had voted FDP in 1949 switched their allegiance to the BHE, which won no less than 23.4 per cent of the vote. Similarly, the FDP obtained negligible support from the refugees in the *Landtagswahl* in Bavaria in November 1950 and that in Lower Saxony in May 1951.

To sum up, the FDP in the early post-war years was essentially a middle-class party representing the interests of the indigenous population. Neither the party elites nor its local functionaries displayed much commitment to the refugee problem up to mid-1949. Although its belated attempt to attract refugee votes at the *Bundestag* Election of August 1949 achieved some success in individual constituencies, these successes were not sustained in subsequent elections.

Communist Party of Germany (KPD)

In the early post-war years, leading Allied and German politicians expressed deep concern that the refugees' acute poverty would make them susceptible to the propaganda of the German Communist Party. In June 1949, the British Foreign Secretary, Ernest Bevin, warned that 'heavy unemployment in Western Germany ... would provide a breeding-ground for communism'[125] and noted, with particular disquiet, the large number of refugees who were out of work on a long-term basis. In fact, some prominent German politicians argued that the Soviet Union's decision to expel millions of refugees to the West was a deliberate attempt to create the severe economic distress on which communism was thought to prosper.[126] They also expressed concern that the large influx of refugees from the SBZ and Czechoslovakia included communist spies whose aim was to provoke unrest among the newcomers in order to destabilise the political situation in the Western Occupation Zones of Germany.[127]

The fears of the Allied and German authorities about the newcomers' vulnerability to left-wing radicalism were reinforced by the high quality of several of the KPD's spokesmen on the refugee problem. In particular, Kurt Müller, appointed Chair of the KPD in Lower Saxony in 1945, enjoyed an excellent reputation even among his political opponents and was elected Chair of the Refugee

Committee in the British Occupation Zone in 1947.[128] Another Communist, Karl Hefter, was regarded as an energetic administrator during his short tenure as acting Bavarian State Commissioner for Refugees at the end of 1945.[129]

There is no doubt that the KPD made strenuous efforts to win the newcomers' electoral support. It advocated generous Equalisation of Burdens legislation at the expense of former Nazis, proposed the introduction of work creation schemes and campaigned for a radical measure of Land Reform which would provide land for the refugees and expellees. Communist Party spokesmen argued that the newcomers should harbour no illusions about being able to return to their former homes and should devote all their energies to integrating into the West. Recognising that the refugees held the Soviet Union (and therefore the Communists) responsible for the loss of their homelands and the atrocities many of them had suffered during their expulsion to the West, the KPD leadership sought to shift the blame for these events on 'Hitler's wicked, fanatical policies'.[130]

A feature of the KPD's campaign to win the support of the newcomers was to disguise its events as 'all-party' (*überparteilich*) rather than KPD initiatives. Communist functionaries attracted some 500 delegates to a conference on the refugee question in Munich on 16 February 1947 by giving the false impression that it was an all-party venture.[131] The conference established a committee which submitted a number of demands to the Bavarian Government on 28 February. Without waiting for a response, the KPD claimed that, since its proposals had been rejected, it had no alternative but to organise a petition to compel the Government to hold a referendum on the refugee problem. The instigator of this plan, Alfred Hadek, was initially able to conceal its party political nature and the KPD claimed to have as many as 200,000 signatures by the end of March 1947.[132] However, support fell away sharply after the Bavarian Government launched a campaign to inform public opinion about the origins of the petition. Many refugees were duped into signing the document and only later discovered that it contained a clause renouncing their claim to their homelands. Similar incidents were reported from other parts of the Western Occupation Zones[133] and it is clear that the KPD used unscrupulous methods to try to win the support of the refugees and expellees.

Communist Party functionaries were particularly active in refugee camps. In Bavaria, the KPD's most prominent refugee leader was

Egon Herrmann, a Sudeten German who had secured illegal entry to the West from the SBZ. He exploited the dissatisfaction of refugee camp occupants with their food rations and living conditions and in September 1948 organised a hunger strike in Dachau camp where he was based which soon spread to other camps in southern Bavaria.[134] Although Herrmann denied that he had any links with the KPD, he stood as a KPD candidate in Dachau at the *Bundestag* Election of August 1949. In his election speeches, Herrmann poured scorn on government and church leaders, as well as the occupying authorities. He sought to exacerbate the tension between the native and refugee populations and at an election rally in Kaufbeuren on 29 July 1949 lost all control, arguing that 'hundreds of farms must be burnt down and thousands of farmers and local Bavarians must be hanged' if the refugee problem was to be solved.[135] There is no doubt that Herrmann represented one of the most dangerous demagogues in post-war Bavaria.

The KPD, unlike the other political parties, had ample funds at its disposal in the early post-war years and was receiving financial aid from outside the Western Occupation Zones of Germany. At a time of severe economic hardship after the Currency Reform, Herrmann had sufficient money to make 100,000 copies of an invitation to a meeting at Dachau Refugee Camp in October 1948.[136] He was also able to establish a newspaper for refugees in Aachen in May 1949,[137] a venture which would not have been possible without considerable external financial support. Local branches of the KPD in Schleswig-Holstein also had no financial worries and the Kreis Resident Officer in Steinburg observed in July 1948 that, although none of the main political parties had been able to hold meetings in the first month after the Currency Reform, the KPD had staged no fewer than four during this period.[138]

Despite the energetic propaganda campaign mounted by KPD leaders to win the support of the refugees in the early post-war years, a brief examination of the newcomers' voting behaviour in the 1946–50 period indicates that the overwhelming majority of them were immune to the overtures of the Communists. At the *Bundestag* Election of August 1949, the KPD polled well below the national average in the three states most severely affected by the refugee influx, winning just 4.1 per cent of the vote in Bavaria and 3.1 per cent in both Lower Saxony and Schleswig-Holstein. However, the number of refugees who voted for the Communists was even smaller than these figures suggest since the KPD generally gained its best results in constituencies where newcomers made up a small proportion of the electorate and suffered its most comprehensive defeats in constituencies heavily populated with refugees. This is shown by the performance of the KPD in Bavaria at the *Bundestag* Election of 1949, when the party obtained 8.1 per cent of the vote in constituencies where refugees made up less than 14 per cent of the inhabitants but only 1.9 per cent in constituencies in which they comprised over 26 per cent of the population.[139] The same pattern was evident at the Bavarian State Election of November 1950.

The antipathy of the refugees and expellees towards communism is illustrated by local examples. The KPD attracted negligible support at the State Election of November 1950 in Bavaria's *Flüchtlingsgemeinden*. In fact, it polled just 1.1 per cent in Traunreut (Rural District of Traunstein), 0.8 per cent in Geretsried (Rural District of Wolfratshausen) and 0.7 per cent in Bubenreuth (Rural District of Erlangen).[140] Although KPD officials pursued a vigorous campaign in refugee camps, the voting returns in parishes dominated by such camps reaffirmed the newcomers' antipathy towards left-wing radicalism. For example, at the *Bundestag* Election of August 1949, the parishes of Kaltenkirchen and Seedorf in the constituency of Segeberg-Neumünster (Schleswig-Holstein) recorded votes for the KPD of just 1.5 per cent and 1.4 per cent respectively,[141] while Egon Herrmann collected just three of the 198 votes cast in Dachau refugee camp at the same election.[142]

It is clear, then, that the German refugees and expellees emphatically rejected the Communists at successive elections in spite of the severe economic distress they were experiencing. While it is clear that communism held little ideological attraction for the refugees even before the Second World War, their hostility to the KPD can be primarily attributed to the events of 1944–45 when many of them fled or were expelled from their homes as the Red Army advanced westwards. The outbreak of the Cold War, and in particular the Berlin Blockade of 1948–49, reinforced the refugees' antipathy towards the KPD.

Radical right-wing parties

The Western Allies also expressed apprehension that the refugees and expellees might be attracted to the slogans of nationalist parties and this fear of a resurgence in right-wing radicalism increased from mid-1948 onwards due to the adverse effects of the Currency Reform on the refugees' economic and social position. For example, Brian Robertson, Military Governor of the British Occupation Zone, warned Foreign Secretary Bevin in February 1949 that 'the loss of self-respect which ... [the refugees] have undergone and the discontent which their mode of life engenders lay them open to the temptations of nationalist agitation and provides ready made material for the first unscrupulous leader that comes to power'.[143]

Election results in 1949–50 gave credence to these fears about a revival of right-wing radicalism, especially in Lower Saxony, a former stronghold of the National Socialist Workers' Party of Germany (*Nationalsozialistische Deutsche Arbeiterpartei Deutschlands*, NSDAP) and a state heavily populated with refugees. One prominent nationalist party was the German Right-Wing Party (*Deutsche Rechtspartei*, DRP) whose members included Otto Ernst Remer, who had become infamous for his part in foiling the plot to assassinate Hitler on 20 July 1944, and Fritz Dorls, who had joined the NSDAP as early as 1929 and, according to the US High Commission, ranked as 'the most capable leader in the rightist–nationalist fringe'.[144] At the *Bundestag* Election in August 1949, the DRP won 8.1 per cent of the vote in Lower Saxony, an outstanding achievement for a party which had not been granted a zonal licence until two weeks before the names of parliamentary candidates had to be submitted.[145] Although no firm conclusions can be drawn about the basis of the DRP's electoral support, it would seem that the refugees contributed significantly to the party's success in protestant, rural constituencies such as Helmstedt, Gandersheim, Wolfenbüttel and Celle-Land.[146]

On 2 October 1949, just a few days after the end of the Allied Occupation of Germany, Dorls and Remer founded the Socialist Reich Party (*Sozialistische Reichspartei*, SRP), an organisation which openly displayed its contempt for the democratic principles of the Bonn Republic. In fact, Remer observed on one occasion that the only distinction 'between the SRP and the NSDAP lies ... in the time period'[147] and the party was eventually banned by the Federal Constitutional Court in October 1952. The SRP directed its appeals at groups who harboured grievances against the new political system such as former army officers, those convicted by the denazification tribunals, the unemployed and the refugees and expellees from the East. The party underlined the expellees' right to return to their homelands and appealed in particular to the refugees from the GDR whose economic plight was sometimes even worse than that of the refugees and expellees from the East who had fled or been expelled in 1945–46.[148] At the *Landtag* Election in Lower Saxony in May 1951 the SRP won no less than 11 per cent of the vote, much to the consternation of political observers in West Germany and abroad. Many contemporaries attributed this success primarily to the votes of the expellees but subsequent research has refuted this assumption, arguing that the majority of them voted for the BHE.[149] However, Heiko Buschke's case study of Lüneburg indicates that the SRP did gain significant support from the refugees from the GDR, who considered themselves neglected by the BHE.[150]

There is also evidence of refugee support for radical right-wing groups in southern Germany. In Württemberg-Baden an Emergency Association (*Notgemeinschaft*, NG) was established under the leadership of Franz Ott, a Catholic priest from Dachau who had studied in Prague during the war. Ott, a former member of the NSDAP, gained control of the NG's district branch in Esslingen in 1948 and appointed almost entirely former Nazis to run it.[151] His brilliant oratory and 'rabid anticommunist, but extreme nationalist' attitudes were a constant source of concern to US Military Government officials.[152] By exploiting the refugees' economic discontent and campaigning for their swift return to their homelands, Ott attracted a strong following among the newcomers. In fact, although the NG failed to gain a licence to contest the first *Bundestag* Election, he stood as an independent in Esslingen and was directly elected to the Federal Parliament.

However, it was in Bavaria that the refugees proved most susceptible to the overtures of nationalist groups. One of the first radical right-wing parties to woo the expellee vote was the Economic Reconstruction Union (*Wirtschaftliche Aufbau-Vereinigung*, WAV), founded in December 1945 by Alfred Loritz, an immensely controversial figure whose superb oratory inspired one political commentator to call him 'the blond Hitler'.[153] In common with other nationalist groups, the WAV portrayed itself as the only party which had taken up the cause of disaffected elements such as demobilised soldiers, small-time Nazis resentful of the denazification procedure and, of course, the refugees and expellees. After achieving some success at the *Landtag* Election of December 1946, the WAV suffered an

Table 4.3 Refugee composition and support for the WAV in Bavaria: the *Bundestag* Election of 1949 and the *Landtag* Election of 1950

% of refugees in population	*% voting WAV (all areas)*		*% voting WAV in rural districts*	
	1949	*1950*	*1949*	*1950*
Under 14	14.1	4.6	12.1	0.1
14–18	12.2	3.7	11.0	1.1
18–22	13.3	1.2	13.1	1.0
22–26	15.4	2.3	15.3	2.0
Over 26	17.4	2.7	17.5	2.6
Bavaria	14.4	2.8	14.3	1.9

Source: BSL (ed.), *Die erste Bundestagswahl*, p. 13 and BSL (ed.), *Wahl zum Bayerischen Landtag*, p. 31.

ignominious defeat at the District Elections of 1948, winning just 1.7 per cent of the total votes cast. Torn apart by internal disputes, the party appeared to be in total disarray. Yet it staged a remarkable recovery, obtaining no less than 14.4 per cent of the vote in Bavaria in the *Bundestag* Election of August 1949, and it is clear that this success can be attributed primarily to the refugees. As Table 4.3 indicates, the WAV's share of the vote generally increased in relation to the proportion of refugees in a particular constituency. The widespread support for the WAV among refugee voters is confirmed by the electoral returns from refugee camps and in the St. Nikolakloster camp in Passau it gained no fewer than 476 of the 782 votes cast, 61 per cent of the total.[154]

The key to the WAV's success was its electoral pact with the New Citizens' Alliance (*Neubürgerbund*, NB), a refugee organisation established in Passau in 1948 by Günther Goetzendorff. Although independent refugee groups had achieved impressive results at the District Elections in 1948, the US Military Government forbade their participation in the first *Bundestag* Election. As a result, Goetzendorff and Loritz forged an agreement whereby the NB would urge its supporters to vote for the WAV in return for nominating half of the candidates on the party's electoral list.[155] Goetzendorff was a radical nationalist from Silesia whose outspoken oratory at election rallies rivalled that of Loritz himself, arguing on one occasion that he 'would force the government to introduce Equalisation of Burdens legislation, even if it necessitated burning down houses in the process'.[156] It is evident, then, that the sizeable number of refugees who supported the WAV at the *Bundestag* Election were voting for a radical nationalist party.

There is no doubt that the outcome of the *Bundestag* Election in August 1949 demonstrated the refugees' growing vulnerability to the overtures of radical right-wing parties. Deprived by the Occupying Authorities of the right to establish their own political party, many newcomers rejected the CDU/CSU, SPD and FDP for demagogues such as Ott, Goetzendorff and Loritz. The fears of the Western Allies that the refugees would become a source of political instability in post-war Germany appeared to have become a reality.

The emergence of a refugee party

Even before the Allied High Commission formally lifted the ban on refugee organisations pursuing political objectives in January 1950, steps were being taken in Schleswig-Holstein to set up a refugee party. This culminated in the establishment of the BHE in Kiel on 8 January 1950 under the chairmanship of Waldemar Kraft. The party leadership was dominated by former Nazis. Kraft, a former captain in the SS, was interned by the Allies from 1945 until 1947 in connection with his war record in Poland.[157] Theodor Oberländer, who was elected Chairman of the BHE in Bavaria in 1950, was another prominent nationalist who had to resign his post as Federal Minister for Expellees in 1960 when it was alleged that he had taken part in the murder of Jews in the Ukraine in 1941.[158]

The BHE's primary concern was to represent the interests of the refugees and expellees but it also sought to attract other groups who had suffered as a result of the war and its aftermath such as returning German soldiers, the victims of war-time bombing, the Currency Reform and denazification tribunals. In fact, the BHE leaders launched fierce attacks on the denazification policy of the Western Allies, dismissing it as a Communist inspired plot to remove those elements most likely to oppose a Soviet takeover of the FRG.[159] Yet although the BHE curried favour with all groups harbouring grievances against the new West German state, it directed its appeals primarily at the refugees and expellees. It demanded economic and social justice for the newcomers and advocated generous Equalisation of Burdens legislation which granted compensation on an individual basis for all those who had lost property during the war.[160]

The formation of the BHE transformed refugee politics during the early years of the FRG. To the astonishment of political commentators inside and outside Germany, it captured 23.4 per cent of the vote at the *Landtag* Election in Schleswig-Holstein held on 9 July 1950, a sensational result for a fledgling party. The BHE enjoyed further success in the Bavarian *Landtag* Election in November 1950. It concluded an electoral pact with the German Association (*Deutsche Gemeinschaft*, DG), led by August Haußleiter, a strident nationalist who had taken part in the Munich Putsch in November 1923,[161] and the combined vote of the BHE–DG totalled a creditable 12.3 per cent. The BHE achieved an even better result in the *Landtag* Election in Lower Saxony in May 1951 when it won 14.9 per cent of the votes cast.

Although the BHE's election propaganda was aimed at all 'war-damaged' groups, practically all its support came from the refugees and expellees. In fact, in the *Landtag* Elections of 1950–51, the BHE gained 72 per cent of the votes cast by refugees in Schleswig-Holstein, 58 per cent in Bavaria and 55 per cent in Lower Saxony.[162] Support for the BHE was particularly strong among refugees who were still suffering acute economic hardship. This is illustrated by the outcome of the election in Schleswig-Holstein. Three of the BHE's best results were achieved in Oldenburg-Ost (33.1 per cent), Eutin-West (34.7) and Eutin-Ost (39.9), unemployment black spots which were heavily populated with refugees.[163] On the other hand, the BHE returned below-average results in the three Pinneberg constituencies, situated on the outskirts of Hamburg, even though they also had a very high refugee population. Here a significant proportion of refugee voters remained loyal to the established parties. This was due to the more favourable economic conditions prevailing in Pinneberg, where unemployment figures were considerably lower than in other parts of Schleswig-Holstein and thousands of newcomers commuted daily to work in Hamburg.[164] To sum up, the BHE emerged in 1950 as an important factor in West German political life and by the end of 1951 it was represented in no fewer than five of the country's state assemblies, often holding the balance of power between the established parties. The fears of Allied and West German politicians that the refugees would become an organised political force had materialised.

Conclusion

The Western Allies' decision in 1946 to ban the formation of refugee parties pursuing political objectives placed a heavy responsibility on the mainstream political parties to integrate the newcomers into their ranks. The SPD was the first party to recognise the importance of the refugee problem and, as the party of 'social justice', attracted considerable support from the newcomers in the *Landtag* Elections in Bavaria, Lower Saxony and Schleswig-Holstein in 1946–47. However, this support fell away in subsequent elections due to internal divisions and the party's failure to improve the refugees' economic position when in government. In the early post-war years, the CDU/CSU and FDP were justifiably regarded as parties of the native population and refugee politicians in these parties often encountered prejudice and even hostility. It is clear, then, that most refugees had lost faith in the mainstream political parties by the end of the Occupation period. However, the widespread fears of contemporary politicians that the newcomers' material deprivation would make them vulnerable to communism proved to be unfounded as the refugees repeatedly spurned the overtures of the KPD. Memories of their flight or expulsion from their homelands in 1944–45 as the Red Army advanced westwards rendered them immune to communism irrespective of their economic plight. On the other hand, the refugees' voting behaviour at the *Bundestag* Election in August 1949 indicated their susceptibility to the slogans of radical right-wing parties. However, the most significant political development was the striking successes achieved by the newly founded BHE in a series of *Landtag* Elections in 1950–51. As a result, the BHE became a junior coalition partner in several State Governments and for the first time since 1945 the newcomers believed that they had a political voice.

The fact that the refugees and expellees set up their own political party as soon as the Allied restrictions were relaxed underlined that many had not been integrated into the mainstream political parties by 1950. The newcomers' support for the BHE in 1950–51 reflected the material hardship they were still experiencing more than five years after the end of the war – unemployment in the FRG did not peak until February 1950. In addition, the wide gap which emerged between the 'haves' and 'have-nots' following the Currency Reform in June 1948 exacerbated the tensions between the expellee and indigenous populations, while the emergence of a 'refugee party' threatened to intensify the conflicts between the two groups. Against this background, chapter 5 will assess the economic, social and political integration of the refugees and expellees from 1950 onwards.

Notes

1 This ban was not lifted in the British Occupation Zone until March 1950. See T. Schäfer, *Die Schleswig-Holsteinische Gemeinschaft 1950–1958: Mit einem Beitrag zur Entstehung des 'Blocks der Heimatvertriebenen und Entrechteten'* (Neumünster 1987), p. 29.

2 Quoted in Grosser, 'Das Assimilationskonzept der amerikanischen Flüchtlingspolitik', p. 29.

3 Quoted in D.E. Rogers, *Politics after Hitler: The Western Allies and the German Party System* (London 1995), p. 109.

4 Isaac, *Die Assimilierung der Flüchtlinge*, p. 5, in GStA, MA 130674.

5 Quoted in H. Martens, *Die Geschichte der Sozialdemokratischen Partei Deutschlands in Schleswig-Holstein 1945 bis 1959*, Vol. 1 (Malente 1998), pp. 157–8.

6 See for example, PRO, FO 1006/331, Report on interviews with political leaders in the Rural District of Husum, 25 May 1946. Even the CDU representatives acknowledged privately that, in the forthcoming District Elections, 'the majority of the refugees will vote SPD as a safe bet'.

7 H. Grebing, 'Politischer Radikalismus und Parteiensystem: Die Flüchtlinge in der niedersächsischen Nachkriegspolitik', in B. Weisbrod (ed.), *Rechtsradikalismus in der politischen Kultur der Nachkriegszeit: Die verzögerte Modernisierung in Niedersachsen* (Hanover 1995), p. 262.

8 Quoted in Grebing, *Flüchtlinge und Parteien in Niedersachsen*, p. 11.

9 *Ibid.*

10 M. L. Hughes, *Shouldering the Burdens of Defeat: West Germany and the Reconstruction of Social Justice* (Chapel Hill and London 1999), p. 192.

11 For a more detailed discussion of the measure in the SBZ, see A. Bauerkämper, 'Social Conflict and Social Transformation in the Integration of Expellees in Rural Brandenburg, 1945–1952', in Ther and Siljak (eds), *Redrawing Nations*, pp. 285–305.

12 Archiv für Christlich-Soziale Politik der Hanns-Seidel Stiftung, Munich (ACSP), NL Schütz, Vol. 1.2.1., *Die Entwicklung der politischen Parteien der Flüchtlinge*, p. 3.

13 A. Mintzel, *Die CSU: Anatomie einer konservativen Partei, 1945–72* (Opladen 1975), p. 208.

14 Martens, *Die Geschichte der Sozialdemokratischen Partei Deutschlands*, Vol. 1, p. 257.

15 AdsD, Landesverband (LV) Schleswig-Holstein (S-H), 107, Plan for the

Reorganisation of the Work for Refugees, 7 November 1949.

16 AdsD, LV S-H, 1, Theodor Werner and Wilhelm Kuklinski to SPD members, 27 August 1945. This was a real problem for the SPD hierarchy since some refugees were able to conceal their complicity with the Nazis due to the absence of documentary evidence to prove their guilt. On the other hand, refugees who were unfairly accused of having National Socialist connections were unable to prove their innocence.

17 Quoted in W. Albrecht (ed.), *Kurt Schumacher: Reden – Schriften – Korrespondenzen 1945–1952* (Bonn 1985), p. 175.

18 Archiv der Hansestadt Lübeck (AHL), SPD-Kreisverband Lübeck, 299, Instructions on how to deal with refugees from the SBZ, May 1951.

19 H.-W. Martin, *'nicht spurlos aus der Geschichte verschwinden': Wenzel Jaksch und die Integration der sudetendeutschen Sozialdemokraten in die SPD nach dem II. Weltkrieg (1945–1949)* (Frankfurt a. M. 1996), pp. 162–3.

20 BA, NL Jaenicke, 30, Jaenicke to Hoegner, 13 October 1946; BHStA, StK 114841, Seifried to Hans Menzel, 11 June 1946, and Menzel to Seifried, 21 June 1946.

21 Grebing, *Flüchtlinge und Parteien in Niedersachsen*, pp. 97–9.

22 AdsD, LV S-H, 237, Lüdemann to Schumacher, 7 July 1950.

23 H. Grebing, 'Politischer Radikalismus und Parteiensystem', p. 262.

24 IfZ, Ed. 120, Vol. 227, SPD Landesverband Bayern, *Jahresbericht 1947/48*, p. 8.

25 H. Woller, *Gesellschaft und Politik in der amerikanischen Besatzungszone: Die Region Ansbach und Fürth* (Munich 1986), p. 228.

26 Grebing, *Flüchtlinge und Parteien in Niedersachsen*, p. 15.

27 AdsD, LV S-H, 80, Secretary of the SPD in the Rural District of Oldenburg to the Party Executive, 19 August 1949.

28 AdsD, SPD LV Bayern, 191, Schmeidl to von Knoeringen, 26 January 1948.

29 Grebing, *Flüchtlinge und Parteien in Niedersachsen*, p. 118.

30 See for example, *ibid.*, p.54; IfZ, Ed. 120, Vol. 226, Martin Albert to SPD District Executive Committees, July 1946; AdsD, LV S-H, 107, Gerhard Strack to Refugee Advisory Committee, 14 November 1949.

31 Quoted in Martens, *Die Geschichte der Sozialdemokratischen Partei Deutschlands*, Vol. 1, p. 255.

32 *Flensburger Tageblatt*, 23 October 1948, in AdsD, LV S-H, 128.

33 Martens, *Die Geschichte der Sozialdemokratischen Partei Deutschlands*, Vol. 1, pp. 255–6.

34 AdsD, LV S-H, 1139, Report on a Meeting of the SPD Party Executive, 27 October 1948.

35 Martens, *Die Geschichte der Sozialdemokratischen Partei Deutschlands*, Vol. 1, p. 255.

36 Martin, *'nicht spurlos aus der Geschichte verschwinden'*, pp. 151–2.

37 AdsD, LV S-H, 1139, Report on a Meeting of the SPD Party Executive, 10 September 1947, p. 4.
38 AdsD, LV S-H, 415, *Wahlergebnisse in den Flüchtlingslagern*, nd.
39 AdsD, LV S-H, 106, *Bericht über die Auswertung der Nachwahl im Wahlkreis Lauenburg-Ost am 9. November 1947.*
40 For further details, see I. Connor, 'Flüchtlinge und die politischen Parteien in Bayern 1945–50', *Jahrbuch für deutsche und osteuropäische Volkskunde*, Vol. 38 (1995), pp. 146–7.
41 AdsD, NL Franz Osterroth, 245, *Der Weckruf: Informationen an die Mitglieder der Sozialdemokratischen Partei Deutschlands*, June 1948.
42 'Das Haus auf der Wanderdüne', *Die Gegenwart*, 15 July 1950, in AdsD, LV S-H, 110.
43 Martens, *Die Geschichte der Sozialdemokratischen Partei Deutschlands*, Vol. 2, p. 355.
44 Grebing, *Flüchtlinge und Parteien in Niedersachsen*, p. 16.
45 AdsD, LV S-H, 129, *Schleswig-Holsteinische Zeitung*, 26 October 1948.
46 For further details, see Connor, 'Flüchtlinge und die politischen Parteien', p. 147.
47 Grebing, *Flüchtlinge und Parteien in Niedersachsen*, p. 107.
48 AdsD, LV S-H, 415, *Wahlergebnisse in den Flüchtlingslagern*, nd and LV S-H, 79, *Statistische Untersuchungen über die Bundeswahl in Schleswig-Holstein (Flüchtlinge)*, p. 3.
49 IfZ, Ed. 120, Vol. 228, *Landeskonferenz der SPD in Rosenheim*, 4–6 June 1949.
50 Martens, *Die Geschichte der Sozialdemokratischen Partei Deutschlands*, Vol. 1, p. 255.
51 AdsD, LV S-H, 107, Short minutes of a meeting of the SPD's Refugee Advisory Committee, 12 November 1949, p. 2.
52 See for example, *Hamburger Echo*, 19 October 1948, in AdsD, LV S-H, 128. In response to criticism at the newcomers' decision to put forward their own candidates at the election, the Chairman of the Refugee Committee in Elmshorn (Rural District of Pinneberg) retorted that 'the refugees … no longer had any faith in the political parties and wanted to take control of their own predicament by representing their own interests'.
53 PRO, FO 1005/1859, Morale Report for Schleswig-Holstein for period 25 June–12 July 1949, p. 3.
54 See for example, AdsD, LV S-H, 1139, Minutes of the Meeting of the SPD Party Executive, 1 April 1948, p. 5. Paul Dölz reported that 'there was a lot of dissatisfaction with the Emergency Refugee Law and the fact that its supplementary provisions have still not appeared'.
55 For further details, see Connor, 'The Refugees and the Currency Reform', pp. 301–24.

56 See for example, AdsD, LV S-H, 1140, Minutes of a meeting of government and party representatives, 18 November 1949. According to party secretary Walter Eilsberger, 'the crisis in confidence among those refugees interested in farming expropriated land will become a crisis among the refugees as a whole' unless the Land Reform came into force soon.

57 AdsD, LV S-H 237, Lüdemann to Schumacher, 23 August 1950.

58 Statistisches Landesamt Schleswig-Holstein (ed.), *Das Flüchtlingsgeschehen in Schleswig-Holstein*, p. 28.

59 BSL (ed.), *Volks- und Berufszählung am 13. September 1950*, p. 19.

60 Grebing, *Flüchtlinge und Parteien in Niedersachsen*, p. 26.

61 ACDP, NL Kather, 1–377–01/2, Minutes of the Meeting of the CDU Refugee Committee of Schleswig-Holstein, 8 October 1947, p. 3.

62 Hughes, *Shouldering the Burdens of Defeat*, pp. 192–8.

63 For details, see ACDP, NL Kather, 1–377–01/2, Minutes of a Meeting of the CDU Refugee Committee in the British Occupation Zone, 18 July 1946.

64 K. Schreyer, *Bayern – ein Industriestaat: Die importierte Industralisierung. Das wirtschaftliche Wachstum nach 1945 als Ordnungs- und Strukturproblem* (Munich and Vienna 1969), pp. 85–6.

65 Quoted in Ahonen, *After the Expulsion*, p. 55.

66 PRO, FO 1006/205, 'Monthly Political Notes for October 1948', compiled by the Schleswig-Holstein Intelligence Office.

67 Quoted in *Hannoversche Neue Nachrichten*, 29 April 1948, in ACDP, NL Kather, 1–377–01/3.

68 ACDP, NL Kather, 1–377–01/2, Report by Kather on the Work of the Zonal Refugee Committee, 20 October 1946.

69 ACSP, NL Schütz, Vol. 1.4.1., *Die Union und die Ausgewiesenen*, nd (but probably originates from 1947), p. 11.

70 Mintzel, *Die CSU*, p. 209.

71 Quoted in F. Bösch, 'Die politische Integration der Flüchtlinge und Vertriebenen und ihre Einbindung in die CDU', in R. Schulze, R. Rohde and R. Voss (eds), *Zwischen Heimat und Zuhause: Deutsche Flüchtlinge und Vertriebene in (West-)Deutschland 1945–2000* (Osnabrück 2001), p. 108.

72 Minutes of a meeting of the Bavarian Committee for Refugee Questions, 5 February 1948. Quoted in Bauer, *Flüchtlinge und Flüchtlingspolitik*, p. 121.

73 ACDP, NL Kather, 1–377–01/2, Kather to Adenauer, 13 May 1947.

74 H. J. Varain, *Parteien und Verbände: Eine Studie über ihren Ausbau, ihre Verflechtung und ihr Wirken in Schleswig-Holstein 1945–1958* (Cologne 1964), p. 38.

75 *Ibid.*, pp. 41–2.

76 Bösch, 'Die politische Integration der Flüchtlinge', p. 109.

77 Quoted in Grebing, *Flüchtlinge und Parteien in Niedersachsen*, p. 75.
78 ACSP, NL Schütz, Vol. 2.2.3, Kather to Adenauer, 14 June 1954 and ACDP, NL Kather, 1–377–03/2, Kather to Dr Friedrich Holzapfel (Chair of CDU Parliamentary Party in the Economic Council), 26 November 1948.
79 Schraut, *Flüchtlingsaufnahme in Württemberg-Baden*, p. 464.
80 Bösch, 'Die politische Integration der Flüchtlinge', p. 112. In the event, just two of the CDU's twelve MPs from Lower Saxony were refugees, both elected through the *Land* list.
81 BA, NL Jaenicke, 38, Jaenicke to Holzapfel, 8 February 1951.
82 BHStA, MArb, 27, *Statistischer Informationsdienst*, No. 74.
83 ACDP, NL Kather, 1–377–01/2, Letter from representatives of the CDU State and Zonal Refugee Committees to Adenauer, 14 March 1948.
84 PRO, FO 1006/205, 'Monthly Political Notes for October 1948', compiled by the Schleswig-Holstein Intelligence Office.
85 Quoted in Bösch, 'Die politische Integration der Flüchtlinge', p. 114.
86 ACSP, NL Glaser, Glaser to Willi Ankermüller, 9 February 1950.
87 Martens, *Die Geschichte der Sozialdemokratischen Partei Deutschlands*, Vol. 2, p. 356.
88 For example, in the Flender II refugee camp in Lübeck the CDU polled just 14.6 per cent, while the SPD gained 72 per cent of the vote. See AHL, SPD-KV Lübeck, 579, Analysis of the outcome of the *Landtag* Election of April 1947 by the SPD District Association in Lübeck.
89 For example, the SPD claimed that in Lauenburg-Ost, farmers refused to give milk to refugees who attended SPD election rallies. See AdsD, LV S-H, 106, *Bericht über die Auswertung der Nachwahl im Wahlkreis 41 Lauenburg-Ost am 9.11.1947*, p. 2.
90 Varain, *Parteien und Verbände*, p. 149.
91 Grebing, *Flüchtlinge und Parteien in Niedersachsen*, p. 47.
92 For example, Osker Wackerzapp observed that the CDU's good performance at the District Elections could be attributed 'to a large extent to dissatisfaction with the SPD's running of the local authorities'. See AdsD, LV Baden-Württemberg, 445, O. Wackerzapp, *Praktische Vorschläge für eine wirksame Propaganda der CDU unter den Ostvertriebenen*, 20 February 1949.
93 Quoted in Bösch, 'Die politische Integration der Flüchtlinge', p. 110.
94 *Ibid.*
95 Grebing, *Flüchtlinge und Parteien in Niedersachsen*, pp. 99–100.
96 A. Mintzel and H. Oberreuter (eds), *Parteien in der Bundesrepublik Deutschland* (Opladen 1992), pp. 519–20, 524.
97 Glensk, *Die Aufnahme und Eingliederung*, p. 346.
98 Grebing, *Flüchtlinge und Parteien in Niedersachsen*, p. 135.
99 I. Unger, Die *Bayernpartei: Geschichte und Struktur 1945–1959* (Stuttgart 1979), p. 94.

100 BSL (ed.), *Die erste Bundestagswahl*, pp. 42–3.
101 BSL (ed.), *Wahl zum Bayerischen Landtag am 26. November 1950*, Beiträge zur Statistik Bayerns, No. 163, p. 31.
102 BSL (ed.), *Landtagswahlergebnisse 1950 bis 1974 in den Flüchtlingsgemeinden*, nd.
103 Mintzel, *Die CSU*, p. 209.
104 Archiv des Deutschen Liberalismus der Friedrich-Naumann-Stiftung (ADL), FDP Britische Zone, 8, Hans Kraaz to Dr Fritz Oellers, 13 July 1948.
105 Grebing, *Flüchtlinge und Parteien in Niedersachsen*, p. 44.
106 Woller, *Gesellschaft und Politik*, pp. 218–19.
107 ADL, FDP Britische Zone, 8, Oellers to Blücher, 22 January 1948.
108 ADL, FDP Britische Zone, 8, Oellers to Blücher, 4 March 1948.
109 ADL, FDP Britische Zone, 8, Chairman of the FDP District Association in Osterode to FDP Headquarters in the British Occupation Zone, 17 February 1948.
110 ADL, FDP Britische Zone, 8, Oellers to Blücher, 17 September 1948.
111 This paragraph is heavily based on ADL, A 1–3, *Beschluß Nr. 14 des Parteitages der Freien Demokratischen Partei vom 11. und 12. Juni 1949 in Bremen zu den Fragen der Heimatvertriebenen*, pp. 1–8.
112 Grebing, *Flüchtlinge und Parteien in Niedersachsen*, p. 108.
113 AdsD, LV S-H, 77, Dr Herbert Mücke (*Bund der Heimatvertriebenen* [BdH] Plön) to local BdH associations, 22 July 1949.
114 B. Mauch, 'Die bayerische FDP: Porträt einer Landespartei 1945–49', PhD thesis, University of Erlangen-Nuremberg, 1965, pp. 88–9.
115 J.-D. Steinert, *Vertriebenenverbände in Nordrhein-Westfalen 1945–1954* (Düsseldorf 1986), p. 189.
116 Messerschmidt, *Aufnahme und Integration*, p. 203. As a result of this pact, the FDP polled 31.8 per cent at the *Landtagswahl* in Hesse, by far its best result in a state election in the period 1946–92.
117 It polled 5.1 per cent in Bavaria, 5.7 per cent in Schleswig-Holstein and 9.4 per cent in Lower Saxony.
118 ADL, FDP Britische Zone, 8, Kraaz to Oellers, 13 July 1948.
119 ADL, FDP Britische Zone, 8, Oellers to Blücher, 28 April 1947.
120 ADL, FDP Britische Zone, 8, Kraaz to Oellers, 13 July 1948.
121 BSL (ed.), *Die erste Bundestagswahl*, p. 13. The FDP polled 10 per cent in constituencies where newcomers comprised fewer than 14 per cent of the inhabitants but only 6.9 per cent in areas with a refugee population of more than 26 per cent.
122 AdsD, LV S-H, 79, *Schleswig-Holsteinische Volks-Zeitung*, 16 August 1949, and AdsD, LV S-H, 80, Paul Dötz (SPD District Association in Eiderstedt) to District Executive in Kiel, 15 August 1949.
123 Schier, *Die Aufnahme und Eingliederung*, pp. 217 and 223.
124 Varain, *Parteien und Verbände*, p. 48.

125 PRO, FO 944/318, Ernest Bevin to Dean Acheson, 4 June 1949.

126 For example, the Bavarian Minister-President Hans Ehard claimed at a CSU rally in October 1948 that 'the expulsion had been planned in Moscow in the expectation that the Germans would tear themselves apart in their ... overcrowded rump-state'. See *Fränkischer Tag*, 19 October 1948, in Kriegsarchiv, Munich (KA), Bayerische Innenpolitik, 1948/22.

127 The Bavarian State Secretary for Refugees, Wolfgang Jaenicke, argued in a speech in Iphofen (Lower Franconia) on 20 October 1948 that 'the continuous illegal influx of refugees is preparing the ground for the Russian seeds'. See *Fränkische Landeszeitung*, 21 October 1948, in KA, Bayerische Innenpolitik, 1948/22.

128 Grebing, 'Politischer Radikalismus und Parteiensystem', p. 261.

129 Bauer, *Flüchtlinge und Flüchtlingspolitik*, pp. 49–52.

130 Quoted in Grebing, *Flüchtlinge und Parteien in Niedersachsen*, p. 35.

131 BHStA, StK 114843, Main Committee of Refugees and Expellees in Bavaria to Hans Ehard, 7 May 1947.

132 BLA, Committee for Refugee Questions, Minutes of Meeting of 25 March 1947, p. 33.

133 For example, early in 1948 the British Military Government in Schleswig-Holstein rejected an application by the 'all-party' Refugee Committee in Lübeck to hold a conference on the refugee problem since 'it is forbidden to use the word "all-party" to describe any refugee organisation which is known to enjoy the support of one party only'. See PRO, FO1006/482, Headquarters of the *Land* Schleswig-Holstein to HQ District groups of Kiel, Flensburg and Itzehoe, 3 March 1948.

134 *Süddeutsche Zeitung*, 7 September 1948.

135 IfZ, RG 260, OMGUS, 7/34–1/6, Intelligence Report to the Director of the Office of Military Government for Bavaria (OMGB), nd.

136 IfZ, RG 260, OMGUS, 1948/146/1, Clarence Bolds (Acting Director of OMGB) to Lucius Clay, 15 October 1948.

137 BA, Z18, 142, *Kirchliche Hilfsstelle* to Johann Baumgartler, 27 May 1949.

138 PRO, FO1006/78, Monthly Report of the KRO of Steinburg to the Regional Commissioner of Schleswig-Holstein, 22 July 1948.

139 BSL (ed.) *Die erste Bundestagswahl*, p. 13 and BSL (ed.), *Wahl zum Bayerischen Landtag*, p. 31.

140 BSL (ed.), *Wahl zum Bayerischen Landtag*, pp. 24, 27, 100.

141 AdsD, LV S-H, 79, *Statistische Untersuchungen über die Bundeswahl in Schleswig-Holstein (Flüchtlinge)*, p. 3 and *S.-H. Volks-Zeitung*, 16 August 1949.

142 IfZ, RG 260, OMGUS, 7/34–1/6, Donald T. O'Shea (Acting Director of Intelligence Division OMGB) to Director of Intelligence for OMGUS (Bad Nauheim), 16 August 1949.

143 Quoted in Schulze, 'Growing Discontent', p. 347.

144 Quoted in F. Buscher, 'The Great Fear: The Catholic Church and the Anticipated Radicalization of Expellees and Refugees in Post-War Germany', *GH*, Vol. 21(2) (2003), p. 214.

145 K. Tauber, *Beyond Eagle and Swastika: German Nationalism since 1945* (Middletown, Conn. 1967), p. 89.

146 Bösch, 'Die politische Integration der Flüchtlinge und Vertriebenen', p. 112.

147 L. McGowan, *The Radical Right in Germany 1870 to the Present* (London 2002), p. 152.

148 H. Buschke, 'Die Sozialistische Reichspartei im Raum Lüneburg 1949–1952', in Weisbrod (ed.), *Rechtsradikalismus in der politischen Kultur der Nachkriegszeit,* p. 93.

149 G. J. Trittel, 'Die *Sozialistische Reichspartei* als Niedersächsische Regionalpartei', in Weisbrod (ed.), *Rechtsradikalismus in der politischen Kultur der Nachkriegszeit*, p. 81.

150 Buschke, 'Die Sozialistische Reichspartei', p. 99.

151 Schraut, *Flüchtlingsaufnahme in Württemberg-Baden*, p. 439

152 *Ibid.*, p. 440.

153 *Die Zeit*, 4 August 1949. For a comprehensive study of the WAV, see H. Woller, *Die Loritz-Partei: Geschichte, Struktur und Politik der Wirtschaftlichen Aufbau-Vereinigung (WAV) 1945–1955* (Stuttgart 1982).

154 BHStA, MArb 958, Fuchs (Head of the Refugee Office in Passau) to the Lower Bavarian Government, 17 August 1949.

155 D. Thränhardt, *Wahlen und politische Strukturen in Bayern 1848–1953* (Düsseldorf 1973), p. 277.

156 BA, Z18,119, *Radikalisierung der Vertriebenen: Kirchliche Hilfsstelle stellt beunruhigende Syptome fest*, 8 February 1950.

157 Hughes, *Shouldering the Burdens of Defeat*, p. 136.

158 P. Ó Dochartaigh, *Germany since 1945* (Basingstoke 2004), p. 53. For a biography of Oberländer, see P.-C. Wachs, *Der Fall Theodor Oberländer (1905–1998): Ein Lehrstück deutscher Geschichte* (Frankfurt a. M. 2000).

159 *Sonderrundschreiben Nr. 1 des Landesverbandes Bayern des BHE*, 14 November 1950. Quoted in Neumann, *Der Block der Heimatvertriebenen und Entrechteten*, p. 56.

160 Hughes, *Shouldering the Burdens of Defeat*, p. 135.

161 Tauber, *Beyond Eagle and Swastika*, p. 126.

162 Neumann, *Der Block der Heimatvertriebenen und Entrechteten*, p. 306.

163 Schäfer, *Die Schleswig-Holsteinische Gemeinschaft*, p. 53.

164 Edding, *Die wirtschaftliche Eingliederung*, p. 61 and Glensk, *Die Aufnahme und Eingliederung*, p. 265.

5

The integration of the refugees into (West) Germany after 1950

Introduction

Chapters 1–4 have demonstrated the immensity of the refugee problem in the Western Occupation Zones of Germany during the early post-war years showing, in particular, the acute material hardship that many newcomers suffered after their flight or expulsion to the West. While the general food situation had improved by 1950, many refugees continued to live in squalid housing conditions and unemployment remained a major issue in the early years of the *Bundesrepublik*, especially in Bavaria, Lower Saxony and Schleswig-Holstein. This chapter will discuss the progress made in the newcomers' economic integration during the 1950s and 1960s. It will also examine the political dimension of the refugee problem, analysing the fall of the BHE and the changing relationship between the expellees and the major political parties from 1950 to 1972. The chapter will also briefly assess the role of the expellee associations during the post-war period. Finally, it will discuss the relations between the refugee and native populations from the early 1950s until the present day, exploring the newcomers' search for a new identity in post-war Germany.

Economic Integration

Housing

Housing is widely regarded as one of the most important indicators of the refugees' economic integration into their new homelands. As chapter 2 showed, many newcomers in the Western Occupation Zones of Germany had to live in cramped, overcrowded conditions in the early post-war years. In fact, the census of September 1950 revealed that the newly established West German state had a shortage of 4.4 million homes.[1] However, as Table 5.1 indicates, the housing situation of the refugees and expellees improved greatly between 1950 and 1956 and in the next four years consolidated further. The most noticeable development was the huge rise in the number of expellee tenants. The vast majority of this group rented a flat or house but it also included a minority of expellees (17 per cent in 1960) who actually owned their own home.[2] This reflected the newcomers' disinclination to be subtenants as a result of the problems many had experienced when billeted with native householders in the early post-war years. They preferred their own space and privacy even if their flat or house was of indifferent quality.[3]

Another feature of expellee housing aspirations in the 1950s was the desire to move from rural to urban areas. In 1950, 47 per cent of expellees in the FRG resided in parishes with a population of fewer than 3,000 but this figure fell dramatically during the following decade.[4] On the other hand, the proportion of expellees living in towns and cities with more than 100,000 inhabitants increased from 17.2 per cent in 1950 to 27.6 per cent in 1961.[5] Generally speaking, however, the newcomers preferred to migrate to small or middle-sized towns where employment prospects tended to be more favourable.[6] Of those who continued to live in the rural areas, some found employment locally but many commuted each day to work in a nearby town or city. In Hamburg, for example, where the housing shortage remained acute in 1950, refugees and expellees comprised almost a third of the city's daily commuters.[7]

Table 5.1 Expellee and native housing, 1950–60 (% distribution)

	Tenants		*Subtenants*		*Temporary housing*[a]	
	Expellees	*Natives*	*Expellees*	*Natives*	*Expellees*	*Natives*
1950	22.4	69.0	66.6	27.3	11.0	3.7
1956	62.9	79.3	30.5	17.7	6.6	3.0
1960	70.1	78.8	22.1	14.9	7.8	6.3

Note [a] The term 'temporary housing' includes refugee camps.

Source: M. Frantzioch, *Die Vertriebenen: Hemmnisse, Antriebskräfte und Wege ihrer Integration in der Bundesrepublik Deutschland* (Dietrich Reimer Verlag, Berlin 1987), p. 204.

The striking improvement in expellee housing during the 1950s can be primarily attributed to the major housing building programmes introduced by the Federal Government in Bonn. The First Housing Construction Law of April 1950 envisaged the construction of 1.8 million houses over a six-year period.[8] In the early 1950s official house building programmes concentrated on providing cheap rented accommodation for the newcomers and particular attention was paid to closing down the refugee camps. The Federal Government gave subsidies to building contractors on the condition that the houses they constructed were rented to refugees and expellees. However, from 1953 onwards greater emphasis was placed on building properties for private ownership and this trend was reinforced by the Second Housing Construction Law of 1956.[9] The key issue, of course, was finance. In the period 1952–56, as much as 40 per cent of public housing expenditure in the FRG was devoted to the expellees.[10] These monies were partly provided from the budgets of the Federal and State Governments but the Immediate Aid Law (August 1949) and Equalisation of Burdens Law (August 1952) also provided key sources of funding. Initially, foreign aid was important and in 1950, 100 million DM were allocated from Marshall Aid funds to finance a major housing construction programme in Bavaria, Lower Saxony and Schleswig-Holstein.[11] The importance of this pilot project was that the availability of employment opportunities dictated where the housing was built and this became the cornerstone of Federal housing policy towards the expellees. Consequently, the largest beneficiary of public housing assistance was the industrial state of North Rhine-Westphalia, where employment prospects were favourable but much of the housing stock had been damaged or destroyed during the war.[12] In fact, as a result of official government resettlement schemes and the initiative of individual newcomers, North Rhine-Westphalia accommodated more expellees than any other Federal State by mid-1954.[13] The Federal Government's house building programme gained momentum in the second half of the 1950s and an average of 500,000 houses were constructed each year between 1955 and 1960.[14]

Both the major churches were also involved in refugee housing projects. In the Protestant Church the driving force behind these initiatives was Dr Eugen Gerstenmaier, Head of the Protestant Church Welfare Organisation in Germany (*Das Hilfswerk der Evangelischen Kirche in Deutschland*, EHW) from 1945 until 1951. He argued that the most important antidote to the growth of radicalism among the refugees and expellees was to provide them with their own property. By the end of 1956, some 23,000 homes for refugees had been constructed under the auspices of the EHW and, significantly, 81 per cent of them were owned as opposed to rented.[15] Among the EHW's most successful projects was the establishment in 1949 of the refugee settlement of Espelkamp (North Rhine-Westphalia). By 1959 it had a population of 10,000.[16] Leading Catholic churchmen shared Gerstenmaier's philosophy about the social and political importance of promoting home ownership among the newcomers. In February 1947 Bishop Maximilian Kaller re-established the Catholic Housing Development Service and by the end of 1968 it had built no fewer than 225,000 homes.[17] Although these homes were not exclusively for the use of newcomers, they received preferential treatment and comprised 70 per cent of successful applicants in Hesse in 1949.[18] The Catholic Housing Development Service, like its Protestant counterpart, was based on the principle of self-help and successful applicants were expected to devote at least 1,000 hours of their time to the construction of their home.

However, even though the expellees' housing conditions improved considerably during the 1950s, serious problems persisted at both regional and local level. For example, according to the 1956 census, as many as 30 per cent of all households in Hamburg and 29 per cent in Lower Saxony were not connected to the mains water or electricity supply.[19] Meanwhile, more than 24,000 people were still living in temporary dwellings in Lübeck in September 1956, three times the number in towns of comparable size such as Kassel or Karlsruhe.[20] Letters to the Federal Expellee Ministry also illustrate that some refugees still had to endure appalling housing conditions in the second half of the 1950s. For example, a widow living in the granary of a farmhouse complained in March 1957, twelve years after the end of the war, that her 'room is 5 metres square and the walls are made of chipboard. As there is no chimney, I cannot heat the room, let alone cook.'[21]

One of the main priorities of successive Federal Expellee Ministers during the 1950s was to close down the refugee camps and the Bonn Government launched a house construction programme in 1953 to provide cheap rented accommodation for former camp occupants. But this policy enjoyed only partial success. Although the number of refugees residing in camps fell from some 400,000 at the beginning of 1952 to 185,750 in June 1955,[22] huge regional variations persisted. Bavaria (29,906), Schleswig-Holstein (53,776) and Lower Saxony (62,564) continued to accommodate the vast majority of West Germany's refugee camp occupants, while Rhineland-Palatinate's 10 camps held just 345 refugees.[23] Although further government measures were taken in the second half of the 1950s to phase out refugee camps, they continued to exist in towns and cities in the main *Flüchtlingsländer* in the 1960s. In Kiel, for example, the last camps were not closed until 1966,[24] while in Lübeck the Johann-Baltzer-Platz camp was finally shut down in November 1967.[25] In fact, it was not until 1971 that the last refugee camp in the FRG was finally closed down.[26]

The main reason for the failure of the efforts of the Adenauer Government to eliminate refugee camps was the influx of some 2.6 million refugees from East Germany between 1949 and 1961 who competed with the expellees from the East for scarce housing resources.[27] At the same time, it should be borne in mind that some expellees refused to leave the camps. In fact, just 400 of the 13,000 refugee camp occupants in Lübeck in 1952 took advantage of the opportunity to apply to be resettled in southern Germany.[28] A significant number, particularly large families and those relying on welfare benefits, were unable to afford the rent for a new house or flat,[29] while other camp occupants were unwilling to give up the standard of living they enjoyed because they paid no or only a nominal rent.[30] For example, a newspaper reporter in Osnabrück referred in 1962 to an expellee who was willing to live in deplorable conditions in a camp because the low rent gave him the disposable income to purchase 'a brand-new car of the most modern design'.[31] In addition, some elderly expellees had become so accustomed to life in the camps that they lacked the willpower or initiative to look after themselves in private accommodation. A further problem was that even those refugees and expellees who were prepared to move out of the camps had much higher expectations in the 1950s than in 1945–46. They often turned down good-quality housing if it was located in a rural area, insisting instead on being accommodated in an urban environment.[32]

To sum up, the expellees' housing conditions improved considerably during the 1950s but, according to the census of 1960, still remained below those enjoyed by the native population. However, the census of October 1968, the last one to classify expellees separately, indicated that the gap had been closed. The number of expellee subtenants had fallen to just 1.6 per cent, fewer than the native population, while the number of expellee tenants had risen to 94.1 per cent, as opposed to 95.6 per cent for the native inhabitants.[33] In terms of housing, integration had been achieved.

Employment

There is a general consensus that the refugees' employment situation represents the most important criterion for measuring their economic integration into West German society.[34] As shown in chapter 2, the refugees' disadvantaged position on the labour market, initially concealed by the availability of 'economically meaningless'[35] jobs as a result of the huge drop in the value of the reichsmark, became starkly apparent after the introduction of the deutschmark in mid-1948. The unemployment rate in the Western Occupation Zones of Germany rose from just 3.2 per cent in June 1948 to a peak of 10.8 per cent in February 1950[36] and the refugees bore the brunt of this increase. In fact, in March 1950 they made up 34.3 per cent of those out of work in the FRG, more than twice their proportion of the population at that time (16.1 per cent).[37] During the first half of the 1950s, unemployment figures fell steadily and the discrepancy in the unemployment rates of the refugee and native populations narrowed significantly. In fact, between March 1950 and September 1955 the percentage refugees comprised of those out of work fell from 34.3 to 24.3.[38]Yet there were still wide regional variations and in Bavaria, Lower Saxony and Schleswig-Holstein refugee unemployment remained a major issue in the mid-1950s.[39] In addition, newcomers in work were more likely to be made redundant than their native counterparts. However, as the West German economy expanded rapidly in the second half of the 1950s, employers increasingly expressed concern about a labour shortage, despite the constant influx of refugees from the GDR. Against this background, the unemployment rate among the refugees and expellees from the East was by 1959 no higher than that of the indigenous work force[40] and in 1961 just 14,000 refugees were out of work in the whole of the FRG.[41]

However, while the refugees had effectively achieved full employment by the end of the 1950s, Table 5.2 indicates that in terms of occupational structure they were still disadvantaged in relation to the indigenous inhabitants. The sharp rise in the period 1939–50 in the number of refugees classified as 'workers' indicated that many who had formerly been self-employed (often as independent farmers) had been compelled to accept unskilled or manual jobs after their arrival in the West. Although the number of refugee 'workers' fell from some 75 per cent in 1950 to 60 per cent in 1961, this figure remained far higher than among the indigenous population (46.5 per cent). At the same time, the refugees were in 1961 still heavily underrepresented among the self-employed and this reflected the loss of social status many had suffered.

These conclusions were reinforced by several empirical studies. Paul Lüttinger concluded that the economic and social integration of the refugees and expellees at the beginning of the 1970s was by no means as advanced as had been previously assumed. He found that, in times of economic recession, older newcomers, in particular, continued to be more susceptible to unemployment than the native population. He also confirmed that the refugees' employment structure in 1971 remained less favourable than that of the native population and established that the refugees generally had lower pensions than the indigenous inhabitants. According to Lüttinger's findings, 51.9 per cent of expellee pensioners as opposed to 41.2

Table 5.2 Refugee and native employment structure, 1939–61 (percentage distribution)

	1939		*1950*		*1961*	
	Refugees	*Natives*[a]	*Refugees*	*Natives*	*Refugees*	*Natives*[b]
Self-employed	15.4	17.4	5.2	16.5	6.0	13.3
Assisting family members	19.6	11.0	1.8	16.7	3.1	11.2
Civil servants	4.5	6.9	3.7	4.0	5.7	4.5
Employees	10.3	13.0	14.3	16.3	24.6	24.4
Workers	50.2	51.7	75.0	46.5	60.6	46.5

Notes: [a] This figure refers to the area which became West Germany in 1949.
[b] Does not total 100 per cent due to rounding.

Source: M. Frantzioch, *Die Vertriebenen: Hemmnisse, Antriebskräfte und Wege ihrer Integration in der Bundesrepublik Deutschland* (Dietrich Reimer Verlag, Berlin 1987), p. 209.

per cent of their native counterparts had a pension of less than 600 DM net per month in 1971.[42] Lüttinger concluded that in 1971 'the older cohorts [of expellees] were certainly not completely integrated. Successful integration is only fully achieved by the refugees' children and grandchildren'.[43] An empirical study of the refugees' economic and social integration in Bavaria in 1971, undertaken by Johann Handl and Christa Herrmann,[44] and a series of interviews with 215 refugees in Bavaria, conducted by Michael von Engelhardt in 1992–93, reached the same conclusion.[45]

Despite these findings, there is no doubt that the employment situation of the refugees registered a marked improvement during the 1950s. This owed much to legislation introduced by the Federal Government. One of the most controversial measures was the voluntary resettlement of newcomers from Bavaria, Lower Saxony and Schleswig-Holstein to states which provided more favourable prospects for their economic integration. The Federal Refugee Ministry in Bonn announced a series of resettlement programmes between November 1949 and June 1956 but progress was at first painfully slow through the resistance of the states earmarked to accept the refugees (*Aufnahmeländer*). By 1951, there was a general consensus that refugees would be resettled only if they could be provided with a suitable job and satisfactory housing in their new place of residence. However, as a result of the vague wording of the Resettlement Law of May 1951, the *Aufnahmeländer* often refused to accept the refugees unless the Federal Government met the cost of constructing the new houses required,[46] an undertaking Federal Refugee Minister Hans Lukaschek was unwilling to give. A further obstacle to the success of the resettlement programme was the continuing influx of new refugees from East Germany. Despite these difficulties, as many as 915,000 refugees were eventually relocated as a result of official resettlement schemes, mainly to Rhineland-Palatinate, Baden-Württemberg and, in particular, North Rhine-Westphalia.[47]

However, many refugees and expellees chose to remain in the rural areas where they had settled directly after the war and some of them, particularly the Sudeten Germans, set up their own commercial or industrial concerns. These refugee enterprises, described by Klaus Schreyer as 'imported industrialisation',[48] had an important long-term impact on the structure of West Germany's rural economy. While the refugee industries were concentrated in Bavaria, others were established in states such as Schleswig-Holstein, Lower Saxony and Hesse. One of the most successful refugee firms in the 1950s and 1960s was the glass and jewellery makers from the Czechoslovakian town of Gablonz, who established the refugee municipality of Neugablonz (near Kaufbeuren, Bavaria) after the Second World War. In 1952–53 the 993 firms from Gablonz employed 14,400 people at seven different locations in the FRG and this figure had dropped only slightly to 14,100 by 1965.[49]

Both the Federal and State Governments gave financial aid, loans and tax incentives to promote refugee industries. The Immediate Aid Law entitled refugees to apply for grants to set up business concerns, while loans of up to 15,000 DM were available for the same purpose under the Equalisation of Burdens Law.[50] Many refugee industries and businesses experienced severe difficulties in the early 1950s and were heavily dependent on government assistance. For example, the State Government in Schleswig-Holstein invested 107 million DM in refugee enterprises in the period 1949–53.[51] An example of the industrialisation of a rural community as a result of the influx of refugees was Allendorf, an isolated backwater in Hesse where 23 per cent of the working population was unemployed in 1953.[52] In Allendorf, as in Bubenreuth (Bavaria), Geretsried (Bavaria) and Trappenkamp (Schleswig-Holstein),[53] refugee industries were established on the site of a former military installation and, supported by the State Government, some 7,500 jobs were created between 1954 and 1966.[54] The State Government also financed the construction of 2,103 homes in Allendorf in the period 1953–63, approximately two-thirds of which were occupied by refugees.[55] However, many small businesses set up by refugees in rural areas in the early post-war years failed in the first half of the 1950s as large numbers of newcomers moved from the countryside to urban areas.

Of all the occupational groups who fled or were expelled from their homelands, independent refugee farmers (*Landwirte*) proved the most difficult to integrate in West German society. In 1939 National Germans (*Reichsdeutsche*) owned some 172,000 farms larger than 2 hectares (ha) but by the end of 1949 just 13,500 of them had been able to resume their former occupation in the newly established FRG.[56] The most important legislative measure to ameliorate this problem was the Refugee Land Resettlement Law of 10 August 1949 which aimed to encourage the West German farming community through tax incentives to sell property to the newcomers or lease it for a period of not fewer than 12 years.[57] At the same time, refugees would receive interest-free loans of up to 5,000 DM to help them purchase or rent land.[58] Between 1949 and 1958, 2.8 billion DM of public money was spent on providing land for the refugees through this measure, but the results were modest.[59] Although over 105,000 homesteads for refugees were founded in West Germany from 1949 to 1958, only 16.2 per cent were larger than 10 ha and many were so small that they could maintain farming only on a part-time basis.[60] Attempts were also made to reclaim moorland, woodland and waste ground for cultivation by refugees but the process turned out to be both slow and prohibitively expensive. The failure to meet the aspirations of independent refugee farmers was due partly to the reluctance of the Western Allies to support the expropriation of large landowners after 1945.[61] As a result, there was insufficient farmland to give to the refugees. In addition, the CDU/CSU-led Government in Bonn was disinclined to risk losing the native farming vote by supporting the redistribution of land to the newcomers.

The refugees themselves also made a huge contribution to their integration in the labour market since they proved to be a flexible, geographically mobile and well-educated work force. They had to display greater flexibility than their indigenous counterparts and large numbers were forced to retrain or accept jobs for which they were overqualified because they could not initially find employment in their former occupation. This process continued in the first half of the 1950s and many refugees who resettled in North Rhine-Westphalia accepted manual work in the coal mining or construction industry, while the indigenous work force tended to move to better-paid, more secure jobs in service industries or in commerce.[62] Another positive feature of the refugees was their willingness to move to those areas where employment opportunities were available and, in addition to those who took part in official government resettlement programmes, more than 900,000 relocated on their own initiative in the period up to 1956.[63] As a work force, the refugees were generally well qualified, especially the industrially orientated Sudeten Germans, the majority of whom settled in Bavaria. In fact, Handl and Herrmann's empirical study concluded that, for both male and female expellees, the 'average level of education was higher than that of the native Bavarian population'.[64]

However, it should also be borne in mind that the improvement in the refugees' employment prospects during the 1950s could not have been achieved but for the remarkable post-war revival of the West German economy. Between 1950 and 1961 the economy grew by an average of 8.3 per cent per annum[65] and in the period 1950–64 the gross national product (GNP) increased by 300 per cent.[66] By 1961 West Germany had become the world's third largest producer of industrial goods. Initially, the economy relied heavily on Marshall Aid monies which paid for no fewer than 37 per cent of the imports into the FRG in late 1949.[67] The turning point, however, was the outbreak of the Korean War in June 1950, because it provided a market for the modern machinery that West Germany was producing.

To sum up, it is clear that, due to their own efforts, government legislation and West Germany's swift post-war economic recovery, the refugees made impressive progress on the labour market during the 1950s and 1960s. Nonetheless, their overall employment structure remained less favourable than that of the native population in 1971. This view is also substantiated by the refugees' own retrospective perception of their professional life. Rainer Schulze concluded from a series of interviews conducted in the 1990s with former refugees living in the Rural District of Celle (Lower Saxony) that, even though they enjoyed much the same standard of living as the indigenous population, they did not necessarily regard themselves as professionally successful.[68] Many felt that they had experienced a loss of social status since they had been unable to resume their former profession in Celle, while others spoke of inferior promotion prospects in relation to their native counterparts. Indeed, even those who did perceive themselves to be professionally successful believed that they had had to work much harder than the local people to achieve that success.[69]

At the same time, it should be stressed that the refugees themselves made a decisive contribution to the revival of the West German economy in the 1950s as a source of cheap, mobile labour but also as consumers. Moreover, the commercial and industrial concerns they established in the countryside played a crucial role in the modernisation and diversification of West Germany's rural economy. In fact, Werner Abelshauser has even argued that an important reason for the slower economic growth in South West Germany during the 1950s was the relatively small number of refugees who lived in these *Länder* of the former French Occupation Zone.[70]

Political integration

The decline of the BHE

As noted in chapter 4, the remarkable electoral success achieved by the newly established refugee party, the BHE, at the State Election in Schleswig-Holstein in July 1950 had a profound effect on West Germany's fledgling political system and by the end of 1951 the BHE was represented in the state assemblies of Schleswig-Holstein, Hesse, Bavaria, Lower Saxony and Bremen. However, the 23.4 per cent of the vote the BHE won in Schleswig-Holstein in 1950 proved to be its best result by some distance at State level and as early as November 1952 the party changed its name to the All German Bloc (*Gesamtdeutscher Block*, GB)/BHE in an attempt to broaden its appeal. Although the BHE still retained representation in five state assemblies at the beginning of 1962 and did not lose its seats in Hesse and Bavaria until November 1966, its success at national level was much more limited. At the Federal Election of September 1953, the party won 5.9 per cent of the vote and gained 27 seats in the *Bundestag*. However, at the Federal Election in September 1957, its share of the vote slumped to 4.6 per cent, thus failing to overcome the 5 per cent hurdle necessary to obtain any seats. In 1961 the GB/BHE merged with the German Party to establish the All German Party (*Gesamtdeutsche Partei*, GDP), but it secured just 2.8 per cent of the vote at the *Bundestag* Election of 1961.

The BHE's approach to politics was determined by pragmatic rather than ideological considerations. Waldemar Kraft, the party's leader between 1951 and 1954, was willing to form a coalition with any of the major parties, arguing that the BHE could only improve the refugees' economic and social position if it was in government. As a result, the BHE entered into a coalition with the CDU, FDP and the German Party (*Deutsche Partei*, DP) in Schleswig-Holstein in September 1950, the SPD and the German Centre Party (*Deutsche Zentrumspartei*, DZP) in Lower Saxony in June 1951, the SPD and FDP in Baden-Württemberg in 1952, while in Bavaria it formed a coalition with both the CSU and SPD after the inconclusive *Landtag* Election of November 1950.[71] The party also responded positively to Konrad Adenauer's overtures to join the coalition he formed after the *Bundestag* Election of September 1953. In fact, two GB/BHE politicians gained ministerial positions, Theodor Oberländer as Minister for Expellees and Waldemar Kraft as Minister without Portfolio. However, the GB/BHE's influence on Federal refugee legislation should not be overestimated since the most important measures were already on the statute book when it entered Adenauer's Government. Even though the party advocated amendments to the Equalisation of Burdens Law during the Federal Election campaign of 1953, these demands were quietly dropped after the election.[72] Similarly, the party enjoyed only limited success in securing the appointment of its supporters as administrators responsible for implementing Federal refugee legislation.[73] At State level, however, it was a different story, especially when the BHE held the balance of power. In Lower Saxony, for example, the Welfare Law for Expellees, Refugees, War Victims and Evacuees of May 1952 stipulated that the officials responsible for its implementation were to be appointed in consultation with the refugee organisations.[74] To sum up, the GB/BHE played an important role because it campaigned in government for measures to improve the expellees' economic and social position, exerted pressure by its very existence on the SPD, CDU/CSU and FDP to be more responsive to the needs of the refugees and gave hope in the early 1950s to many economically deprived newcomers who had lost confidence in the mainstream political parties.

Although the BHE appealed to all 'war-damaged' groups, the overwhelming majority of its support came from the refugees and expellees. In fact, according to an exit poll at the 1953 *Bundestag* Election, 95 per cent of the 1,616,000 who voted for the party were newcomers.[75] It polled particularly heavily in small rural communities and at the *Bundestag* Election in 1953 garnered 9.7 per cent of the vote in parishes with a population of fewer than 3,000 but just 2.9 per cent in towns of over 50,000 inhabitants.[76] However, the most striking characteristic of the BHE's electoral support was its heavy reliance on economically impoverished refugees, especially agricultural workers and those such as refugee farmers and other formerly self-employed groups who had suffered a sharp fall in their economic and social status after their arrival in the West. In fact, a survey carried out in 1956 revealed that 32 per cent of GB/BHE voters had an income of fewer than 250 DM a month, a higher proportion than any other political party.[77]

It is clear, then, that the BHE's spectacular electoral successes in 1950–51 can be largely attributed to the severe material distress many refugees were experiencing. However, the fragile nature of this support was exposed as soon as the newcomers' economic position began to improve. This is illustrated by the crushing defeat the GB/BHE experienced in North Rhine-Westphalia at the *Bundestag* Election in 1953 when a mere 21 per cent of refugee voters supported the party, the lowest in any *Bundesland* except Rhineland-Palatinate.[78] Significantly, refugee unemployment in North Rhine-Westphalia was very low, especially in the industrial Ruhr where the GB/BHE suffered some of its heaviest defeats. As Franz Neumann put it: 'The expellees who saw the newly established BHE as a saviour from their economic predicament forgot the party when, following their resettlement, they had found new homes and good jobs'.[79] This pattern was also reflected in the changing age profile of the party's electoral support during the 1950s. While many young voters turned their back on the BHE as their economic integration advanced, refugees over the age of 60, who as a rule integrated less well into West German society and still harboured hopes of returning to their homelands, generally remained loyal to the party.[80]

In an attempt to arrest the decline in the BHE's electoral fortunes, its leaders placed greater emphasis on demands for the return of the refugees' homelands after the party changed its name from BHE to GB/BHE in November 1952. But this strategy proved to be misguided and public opinion polls revealed that the refugees' voting behaviour was determined by domestic issues rather than foreign policy considerations. At the *Bundestag* Election of 1953, just 9 per cent of GB/BHE voters attributed their support for the party to its policy on German reunification and the eastern territories, a figure which fell to just 3 per cent in 1957.[81]

Internal divisions between moderate and right-wing elements in the BHE also played an important part in its decline. For example, in Lower Saxony friction between a moderate group under the leadership of Friedrich von Kessel, a former Junker from Silesia, and a right-wing, nationalist faction led by Dr Schulz led to tumultuous scenes at the party's state conference in Helmstedt in October 1951. The outcome was the re-election of von Kessel as *Land* party chairman but the emergence of Schulz and Dr Wilhelm Stuckart, a prominent former Nazi, as his deputies.[82] However, it was the controversy over the Paris Treaties of October 1954 which ultimately led to the demise of the GB/BHE. After the party joined Adenauer's coalition government in 1953, its nationalist elements became increasingly critical of Kraft's leadership, arguing that his support for Adenauer's foreign policy of western integration undermined the prospects for German unification. This disagreement came to a head on one aspect of the Paris Treaties, the Saar agreement between France and Germany which envisaged the Saar as an autonomous area administered by a European commissioner under the auspices of the Western European Union (WEU).[83] While Kraft, Oberländer and nine other GB/BHE *Bundestag* delegates supported the agreement, 16 voted against because it involved the 'voluntary abandonment of German soil'.[84] This led to a split in the GB/BHE in July 1955. Kraft and Oberländer, together with five other *Bundestag* delegates, joined the CDU, while two others transferred their allegiance to the FDP. For the GB/BHE, this represented the beginning of the end. Its remaining delegates left the Federal coalition in October 1955 and adopted more strident right-wing policies. Its failure to overcome the 5 per cent hurdle at the 1957 *Bundestag* Election came as no great surprise although, as we have seen, it continued to be represented in a number of State assemblies until well into the 1960s.

To sum up, the refugees and expellees initially voted in large numbers for the BHE after it was established in January 1950. However, support for the party began to erode when the refugees' economic situation improved. As Hans-Adolf Asbach, BHE Minister for Expellees in Schleswig-Holstein from 1951 to 1957, put it: 'The tragedy of our party is simply that, although we gave thousands [of refugees] hope, employment and a livelihood, they switched their allegiance to the self-satisfied parties after their integration.'[85] But to which parties did the refugees transfer their support? This issue will be addressed in the next section.

Adenauer, the CDU and refugees in the 1950s

As seen in chapter 4, the disappointing results achieved by the CDU/CSU and SPD at the first *Bundestag* Election in August 1949 were at least partly due to the defection of refugee voters disillusioned at what they perceived to be the failure of the established parties to improve their precarious economic position. However, despite further setbacks at a number of *Landtag* Elections in 1950–51 the CDU/CSU under Federal Chancellor Konrad Adenauer won an impressive victory at the *Bundestag* Election in 1953, winning 45.2 per cent of the vote, more than 16 per cent higher than the SPD. The refugees and expellees from the East undoubtedly made an important contribution to this success. A public opinion poll conducted in 1953 revealed that 26 per cent of the refugees would vote for the CDU as opposed to 21 per cent for the SPD and 19 per cent for the BHE.[86] Analyses of the outcome of the election confirm that the Union parties increased their support among refugee voters, mainly at the expense of the SPD,[87] while the CDU/CSU's own electoral strategists concluded that the party had secured more than half of all the votes cast by the newcomers.[88] By all accounts, the CDU was particularly successful at attracting the support of refugees who had fled from East Germany.[89] At the 1957 *Bundestag* Election, the CDU/CSU won a landslide victory, polling 50.2 per cent of the total vote, the only occasion since the establishment of the FRG that a party has won an outright majority at Federal level. Once again, the Union parties increased their share of the refugee vote, mainly at the expense of the FDP and BHE. The SPD, while remaining well behind the CDU/CSU, achieved approximately the same level of support among the newcomers as in 1953.[90]

How can we explain the growing identification of the refugees and expellees with the CDU/CSU during the 1950s? There is no doubt that the formation of the BHE prompted the established parties to pay more attention to the refugee problem and at the CDU's first national party conference, held in Goslar in October 1950, steps were taken to integrate the newcomers more closely into the party by founding an association for refugees and expellees (*Landesverband Oder–Neisse*) and a separate organisation (*Exil-CDU*) for party members in the GDR. The combined votes of these two groups exceeded any of the CDU's other sixteen regional branches.[91]

Another significant factor was Adenauer's strategy of co-operating closely with the BHE's leaders with the ultimate aim of integrating them and their supporters into the ranks of the CDU. In fact, the Federal Chancellor was so apprehensive at the prospect of a possible SPD–BHE coalition in Schleswig-Holstein after the 1950 *Landtag* Election that the matter was discussed in the cabinet.[92] A key consideration was that Adenauer's coalition government of 1949–53 had such a slender majority that the fate of government bills was dependent on the votes of the CDU's refugee delegates. Linus Kather exploited this weakness and was able to extract important concessions from Adenauer regarding the Equalisation of Burdens legislation by warning that if his demands were not met he and his refugee colleagues in the CDU would resign the party whip and join the BHE.[93] To overcome this problem Adenauer, despite intense criticism from the CSU and refugee politicians in his own party, made overtures to the BHE's leaders to join the CDU/CSU-led coalition government after the 1953 Federal Election. In fact, the CDU even gave financial inducements to the BHE leadership in Bonn from 1953 onwards in order to retain its loyalty.

BHE politicians at state level also received 'donations' from the CDU and in December 1955 Asbach was offered 60,000 DM a year on condition that his party continued its coalition with the CDU in Schleswig-Holstein.[94] Even though these payments obviously remained confidential, Adenauer's negotiations with the BHE's leaders caused deep resentment among CDU refugee politicians and at a meeting of the party's Federal Expellee Committee in August 1953, Hermann Eplée expressed the view that 'we should have resigned from the CDU in 1947'.[95] Kather was equally exasperated and left the party in June 1954.[96] Despite this discord from within his own party, Adenauer's 'integration policy' towards the BHE turned out to be very successful. As well as the seven BHE *Bundestag* delegates who joined the CDU in July 1955, a number of their colleagues from Schleswig-Holstein and Baden-Württemberg followed the same path in the period 1955–60.[97] This process not only reduced the political threat that the BHE posed to the CDU but also contributed to the increased electoral support the party gained from refugee voters in the second half of the 1950s.

A key reason for the expellees' support for the CDU in the 1950s was that the party shared their intense hostility towards communism. In fact, under Adenauer's leadership, anti-communism became a unifying ideology in the FRG and the refugees and expellees proved especially receptive to one of the CDU's slogans at the *Bundestag* Election of 1953 which maintained that 'all roads [of Marxism] lead to Moscow'.[98] However, the most important explanation for the increasing identification of the refugees and expellees with the CDU was that they gave Federal Chancellor Adenauer and his Economics Minister Ludwig Erhard the credit for the improvement in their economic situation. The CDU's election slogan of 'no experiments' in 1957 struck a chord with refugees who were beginning to enjoy the benefits of West Germany's growing prosperity. The single most significant legislative measure was the Equalisation of Burdens Law, not just because of the long-term material benefits it promised to bring the newcomers but also because of its psychological importance in convincing them that Adenauer's government was taking their concerns seriously. In fact, Ulrike Haerendel has gone so far as to claim that this measure 'removed the expellees' main motivation to operate as an independent factor in West Germany's ... parliamentary system'.[99] It was therefore a key reason for the CDU/CSU's increased share of the refugee vote in the 1953 and 1957 Federal Elections at the expense of the BHE. However, it should be borne in mind that, despite this increased electoral support for the CDU/CSU among refugee voters during the 1950s, their identification with the party often remained weak. This was reflected in the refugees' marked underrepresentation among CDU members, especially in predominantly Catholic areas,[100] while in Bavaria relations between refugee and indigenous CSU members were still often characterised by friction and hostility in the mid-1950s.[101] Against this background, the Union parties' commanding lead over their rivals among refugee voters proved to be vulnerable during the 1960s.

The Refugees and Ostpolitik

During the 1960s the refugees became more firmly integrated in the established political parties, especially the CDU/CSU and SPD. At the same time, there were changes in the newcomers' voting patterns and in the first half of the 1960s the SPD eroded the dominant position the CDU/CSU had enjoyed among refugee voters at national level since 1953. From the mid-1960s *Ostpolitik* became a highly divisive issue in West German politics and this represented an important determinant of the refugees' voting behaviour.

The *Bundestag* Election held in September 1961, only a month after the construction of the Berlin Wall, saw a fall of 4.9 per cent in the CDU/CSU's share of the vote and corresponding gains of 4.4 per cent for the SPD and 5.1 per cent for the FDP. However, despite this setback, the CDU/CSU remained by far the largest party and renewed its coalition with the FDP. The impact of the refugees on the overall outcome is difficult to ascertain because of the shortage of statistical data on their voting behaviour. However, local studies and the voting returns in electoral districts made up almost exclusively of refugees indicate a significant swing to the Social Democrats after 1957, with the result that the CDU/CSU and SPD were running neck and neck.[102] For example, in Bavaria's refugee municipalities the SPD's share of the vote increased by 11.1 per cent on its performance at the 1957 Federal Election, while support for the CSU fell by 5.8 per cent. The FDP also recorded gains, but from a low base.[103] The increased support for the SPD among refugee voters was partly due to its more moderate image after its adoption of the Bad Godesberg programme in 1959. The contrast between Adenauer's failure to visit West Berlin until more than a week after the construction of the Berlin Wall on 13 August 1961 and the prompt and statesmanlike reaction to the crisis by Willy Brandt, the SPD's Chancellor Candidate, also contributed to its success. A further factor was the SPD's wide publicity of the closer relations it had developed with the expellee associations since 1959.[104] At the 1965 *Bundestag* Election the CDU/CSU retained its overall lead of some 8 per cent over the SPD but among the refugees both the SPD and CDU/CSU increased their share of the vote to the detriment of the FDP.[105] The point to stress, however, is that the overwhelming majority of refugee votes at both the 1961 and 1965 Federal Elections were cast for the three established political parties.

Up until 1965 all the main political parties had supported the refugees' right to return to their homelands (*Heimatrecht*) but this consensus gradually broke down during the second half of the 1960s. The initial impetus for change came from a memorandum issued by the Evangelical Church in October 1965 which called on the West German people to show their government that they would support steps 'in the spirit of reconciliation towards our eastern neighbours'.[106] At the same time, leading FDP and, in particular, SPD politicians began to advocate a more flexible and conciliatory approach to Eastern Europe. Amid a plethora of ambiguous and contradictory public pronouncements by leading Social Democrats between 1965 and 1968, it became clear that the party was no longer prepared to support the refugees' claims to their former homelands. This was confirmed when the SPD party conference in March 1968 accepted a motion to 'respect and recognise the existing European borders, especially Poland's current western boundary'.[107] The party conference held in April 1969 went one step further, endorsing a motion which described the Munich Agreement as 'unjust from inception'.[108] The CDU/CSU leadership, on the other hand, stressed its continuing commitment to the refugees' *Heimatrecht* and argued that no decision on the Polish–German border could be taken until a peace treaty had been signed. Against this background, the 1969 *Bundestag* Election represented a crucial barometer of expellee opinion on this contentious issue. The overall result saw an increase of 3.4 per cent in the SPD's share of the vote and a slight fall in support for the CDU/CSU. On the other hand, there was a shift towards the Union parties among the refugees and expellees. In fact, the CDU/CSU attracted the highest share of the expellee vote while the FDP lost further ground on its performance in 1965. However, in view of the SPD's avowed intention of renouncing West Germany's claim to the newcomers' homelands, the key point is that the party's share of the expellee vote at the 1969 *Bundestag* Election did not fall significantly and it retained the allegiance of a sizeable minority of the refugees and expellees.[109]

The outcome of the Federal Election in 1969 also assumed particular significance, because most refugee voters rejected the overtures of the National Democratic Party of Germany (*Nationaldemokratische Partei Deutschlands*, NPD). Founded in Hanover in November 1964, the NPD was a radical right-wing nationalist party which managed to overcome the 5 per cent hurdle in seven *Landtag* Elections held between 1966 and 1968. Its best result was recorded in Baden-Württemberg on 28 April 1968, when it won 9.8 per cent of the votes cast. The party directed its appeals particularly towards the refugees and expellees by vigorously supporting their right to return not just to the eastern territories but also to the Sudetenland and Danzig.[110] Its leaders included a number of refugees, notably the pugnacious Linus Kather who, at the age of 75, played a prominent part in the NPD's election campaign in Baden-Württemberg in 1968. However, at the 1969 *Bundestag* Election the party polled just 4.3 per cent and studies of the refugees' voting behaviour suggest that they were not substantially overrepresented among NPD voters.[111] It is clear, then, that the vast majority of the refugees rejected the revisionist slogans of the NPD and saw their future in the FRG rather than their former homelands.

The 1969 election marked the end of the CDU/CSU's domination of post-war West German politics and a coalition was formed between the SPD and FDP under the Chancellorship of Willy Brandt. For the refugee lobby the writing was on the wall when, within days of taking office, the new government abolished the Federal Ministry for Expellees and incorporated it in the Interior Ministry. Brandt's first term of office was largely devoted to *Ostpolitik*. Four treaties aimed at normalising the FRG's relations with Eastern Europe were negotiated and two of them, the Moscow and Warsaw Treaties, were ratified by the *Bundestag* in May 1972. However, Brandt, fearful that the *Bundestag* would reject the Basic Treaty between East and West Germany, contrived to lose a vote of confidence in order to bring about an early election in November 1972. The election, dominated by the *Ostpolitik* issue, resulted in a resounding endorsement of Brandt's foreign policy. In fact, the SPD won 45.8 per cent of the overall vote and for the first time became the largest party in the *Bundestag*. Significantly, the SPD attracted considerable support among the newcomers and in Bavaria's refugee municipalities gained its best-ever result.[112] The refugees and expellees turned out to be more willing to accept the territorial realities of the Second World War than many of their own politicians had predicted.

To sum up, the political integration of the refugees made great progress between 1949 and 1972. At the *Bundestag* Election in August 1949, a considerable number of expellees turned their backs on the SPD, CDU/CSU and FDP and voted instead for radical right-wing parties. The success the newly founded BHE achieved at State Elections in 1950–51 confirmed that many refugees had rejected the mainstream parties. Yet by 1961 support for right-wing splinter groups had virtually evaporated and the vast majority of refugee votes were cast for the SPD, CDU/CSU and FDP. This was due mainly to the steady improvement in the newcomers' economic and social position during the 1950s. However, it should also be borne in mind that the three mainstream parties gave radical right-wing groups little scope for making political capital out of the refugees' desire to return to their homelands since, prior to the mid-1960s, they had all consistently declared their support for the refugees' revisionist foreign policy demands. Even though many West German politicians admitted privately that there was little or no prospect of changing the post-war territorial status quo, they nevertheless underlined in public the refugees' *Heimatrecht*, focusing particularly on West Germany's claims to the area east of the Oder–Neisse rivers. Of course, this was due partly to electoral considerations but another important factor was the pressure exerted by the expellee associations and the next section will make a brief assessment of their role.

The influence of the expellee associations

Amid the plethora of expellee organisations which emerged in the late 1940s, the Central Association of German Expellees (*Zentralverband vertriebener Deutschen*, ZvD), founded in Frankfurt in April 1949, was one of the most important, having approximately a million members in the early 1950s.[113] It changed its name to League of

German Expellees (*Bund der vertriebenen Deutschen*, BvD) in 1954. The 20 Homeland Societies (*Landsmannschaften*) claimed to have 1,250,000 members in October 1949[114] and also formed an umbrella organisation, renamed Association of Homeland Societies (*Verband der Landsmannschaften*, VdL) in 1952. The main objective of the ZvD/BvD was to campaign for measures to relieve the refugees' material distress, while the dual remit of the *Landsmannschaften* was to foster and maintain the refugees' cultural heritage and proclaim their *Heimatrecht*.[115] After a brief and unsuccessful attempt to attract international support,[116] the expellee associations sought to gain their objectives by exerting pressure on the political parties and, in particular, the West German Government.

This strategy was based on the fact that a number of prominent figures in the expellee associations also enjoyed influence in the political parties and a few even held positions in government. These included Dr Hans Lukaschek, Federal Expellee Minister from 1949 to 1953, who was also a former President of the ZvD.[117] Lukaschek's successor as President of the ZvD was his CDU colleague Linus Kather, whose tireless work on behalf of the expellees won him the accolade of 'father' of the Equalisation of Burdens Law.[118] As a CDU delegate in the *Bundestag*, Kather was able to secure important amendments to this piece of legislation on behalf of the expellee associations because of the slim majority of the first Adenauer Government. In fact, the influence of the expellee associations on the West German Chancellor was so great that he even permitted them to choose Lukaschek's successor as Federal Expellee Minister in 1953, despite the fact that he had reservations about the National Socialist background of the candidate they suggested, Theodor Oberländer (BHE).[119]

However, it was in the sphere of foreign policy that the influence of the expellee associations was more controversial. Through speeches, memoranda and personal contact, they exerted constant pressure on the political parties to proclaim support for the refugees' *Heimatrecht* and their right of self-determination. While the expellee organisations publicly underlined their political neutrality, they did not hesitate to express their views during election campaigns and these often carried considerable weight with refugee voters. For example, their condemnation of SPD/FDP initiatives aimed at normalising West Germany's relationship with Eastern Europe contributed to the CDU/CSU's excellent result among refugee voters at the 1957 *Bundestag* Election.[120] While fear of losing the expellee vote prompted all three established parties to declare public support for the expellees' foreign policy aspirations up to 1965, the *Ostpolitik* adopted by the SPD and FDP in the second half of the 1960s indicated that the expellee associations had lost their veto on the Government's policy towards Eastern Europe. They were powerless to prevent the abolition of the Expellee Ministry in 1969 and the ratification of Brandt's Eastern Treaties. The outcome of the *Bundestag* Election of 1972 represented another blow to the expellee associations. Despite its outright rejection of Brandt's *Ostpolitik*, the SPD performed well among refugee voters, a clear sign that the expellee activists were out of touch with the views of the more moderate rank and file.

The expellee associations failed to learn the lessons from the events of 1969–72 and, despite the new climate of international detente, continued to enunciate the same revisionist demands they had been putting forward since the end of the Second World War. They pinned their hopes on reversing Brandt's *Ostpolitik* when the CDU/CSU returned to power and, during their period in opposition the Union parties and especially the CSU continued to curry favour with expellee associations.[121] However, after the CDU/CSU-led coalition assumed power in the autumn of 1982, the Silesian Homeland Society (*Landsmannschaft Schlesien*, LS) embroiled the new Chancellor, Helmut Kohl, in controversy. After Kohl had accepted an invitation to speak at its rally in Hanover on 17 June 1985, it announced that the event would be staged under the highly contentious slogan '40 years of expulsion. Silesia remains ours'.[122] Kohl also provoked deep concern at home and abroad in 1989–90 by initially refusing to confirm the Oder–Neisse line as Poland's western border for fear of losing the refugee vote in the forthcoming election.[123] Under intense pressure from the four wartime Allies, he eventually made concessions and the treaty between Poland and Germany to resolve the issue was finally ratified in October 1991. Kohl's prevarication on this issue in deference to the expellee lobby indicates that he overestimated their influence forty-five years after the end of the war since the overwhelming majority of the expellees had long since accepted the Oder–Neisse line as Poland's western border.

In some respects the expellee associations had a positive impact on the integration of the refugees and expellees in the FRG. In the early post-war years their very existence helped the uprooted, atomised and economically impoverished refugees to retain their identity and provide mutual support for one another. They also had some success in exerting pressure on the Adenauer Government to introduce legislative measures to improve the refugees' economic and social position. However, even at this stage their effectiveness was impaired by their disunity, epitomised by the often bitter conflicts between the ZvD/BvD and the VdL.[124] The failure of the expellee associations from the mid-1960s onwards to adapt to the new era of international detente had a negative effect on West German politics and made them increasingly out of touch with expellee opinion. In fact, just 1 per cent of the expellees belonged to one of the Homeland Societies in 1965[125] and these organisations were increasing dismissed as 'living in the past' (*Ewig-Gestrige*).[126] As Pertti Ahonen has argued, they would have been better served by paying less heed to the illusory *Heimatrecht* and devoting more attention to the maintenance of the expellees' cultural heritage.[127]

Social integration

While, as we have seen, the refugees' economic and political integration in the FRG was well advanced by the beginning of the 1960s, their integration into German society was a much longer and more difficult process. Case studies suggest that relations between the refugee and indigenous populations gradually improved in the 1950s, though tensions frequently persisted, especially in rural areas. Andreas Lüttig's study of the village of Wewelsburg in Westphalia concluded that, although the newcomers and local people cooperated more closely 'on purely practical' matters during the 1950s and there was also more social contact between the two groups, especially among younger people, 'differences and conflicts between natives and refugees [were] still clearly evident'.[128] This was also the case in some towns and cities. For example, Carl-Jochen Müller concluded that the implementation of the Equalisation of Burdens Law in Mannheim actually worsened refugee–native relations in the second half of the 1950s because the indigenous 'war victims' resented what they perceived to be the more generous treatment of the refugees and expellees.[129] Many elderly expellees continued to pin their hopes on a return to their homelands and, as Lüttig points out, often had mixed feelings about the increasing involvement of their children in village life. While expressing pride at the success of their offspring in integrating into the local community, they also regarded their children's actions in some respects as a betrayal of their roots.[130] This situation also took its toll on the refugees' children who were torn between loyalty to their parents and the desire to adapt to their new environment.[131] This sometimes provoked intergenerational conflict among refugee families and this can be illustrated by reference to marriage patterns between natives and newcomers.

The willingness of members of both the indigenous and refugee populations to enter into a 'mixed' marriage represents an important indicator of the newcomers' integration into their new homelands. Empirical studies undertaken in the early post-war years indicated that opposition to 'mixed marriages' was particularly pronounced among both refugees and natives located in small rural communities where, of course, relations between the two groups were particularly tense.[132] During the 1950s and 1960s there was a general increase in the incidence of 'mixed' marriages among the younger cohorts of newcomers[133] but in rural areas these often encountered opposition from their parents, parents-in-law and members of the local community.[134] For example, Rainer Schulze refers to a native farming family in the Rural District of Celle (Lower Saxony) where the eldest son's marriage to a refugee provoked such a serious family rift that his father disowned him and bequeathed the farm to the younger brother. More than forty years later the two brothers were still not on speaking terms, even though they lived in close proximity.[135]

Another important yardstick for measuring the refugees' integration into village life was their membership of local clubs and associations. In some places, the newcomers initially founded their own societies, while the native inhabitants responded by reviving their cultural traditions as a defence mechanism against the perceived threat to their own identity from the refugees.[136] Gradually, however, the native associations became less exclusive, though the extent and timing of this process varied widely. As a rule, young refugees were the most active participants in village societies and associations, often joining the local football or gymnastics club while still at school.[137] In fact, sport had an important 'integrative function' for refugees in rural communities, not only because it enabled them to establish contact with local people but also because of the opportunity it provided for them to gain acceptance and recognition among the native villagers through their sporting achievements.[138]

As organisations which, generally speaking, placed more emphasis on the performance of their members than their social background, sports clubs also afforded refugees the opportunity to occupy positions of authority and in 1951 they comprised 50 per cent of the executive committee of the Wewelsburg sports club.[139] Since many village clubs and associations admitted only men, choral societies often represented one of the few opportunities for refugee women to establish contact with local people and in Wewelsburg refugees made up some 40 per cent of the village choir in 1959.[140]

Several factors contributed to the easing of tensions between natives and refugees in rural areas of the FRG during the 1950s and 1960s. The indigenous population's fears that the newcomers represented a serious threat to their own identity gradually diminished as social contacts between the two groups increased. In addition, economic issues between the refugee and native populations became less divisive as unemployment began to fall in the first half of the 1950s and the Federal Government initiated major house building projects. Another crucial development was the arrival in rural areas of guest workers from Southern Europe during the 1960s. As a rule, the response of the refugees and native inhabitants was to form a common front against these foreign workers. It would appear that, to coin a phrase used by Marita Krauss, a system of 'competing dislikes' was in operation[141] – despite their misgivings about the refugees, the indigenous inhabitants considered them to be preferable to foreign workers, while the refugees themselves closed ranks with the native population, even though the problems facing the guest workers were similar to those they themselves had experienced some 15–20 years earlier.[142]

However, despite the improvement in relations between natives and refugees from the 1950s onwards, interviews carried out by Rainer Schulze with former refugees or expellees some 40–50 years after their flight or expulsion to Celle reveal that many never felt fully accepted by the native population. The refugees drew attention to the fact that 'admission to the natives' associations, in particular to the prestigious voluntary fire brigade associations, village church choirs, rifle associations and bowling clubs … was only granted hesitantly, and … in some places these traditional bastions of native rural elites often remained closed to them for decades'.[143] Schulze refers to an incident involving a refugee from East Brandenburg which took place at the rifle association's annual shooting competition in the 1980s. The refugee, who at the time was challenging for the lead, was approached by a local person he knew quite well and advised not to try too hard because it would be inappropriate for the winner to come from outside the village.[144] Other studies confirm that the refugees remained 'outsiders' long after their arrival in the West. In the mid-1960s they were frequently still underrepresented on the executive committee of clubs and societies.[145] Moreover, in some places, certain types of associations remained more or less a domain of the indigenous inhabitants until the 1960s or 1970s. In the small town of Weinheim, for example, just two refugees were members of the local history society (*Heimatverein*) as late as 1963 and both of them were married to a member of the indigenous inhabitants.[146]

It is then clear that, despite the refugees' post-war economic success, their integration into West German society was a much more problematic process. Prior to their flight or expulsion to the West, the refugees and expellees had, as a rule, had a strong regional identity; in fact, in many instances their families had lived in the same area for generations. However, the events of 1944–45 eroded these regional ties. Many became separated from family and friends during their flight or expulsion and even when individual communities did succeed in settling en masse in the Western Occupation Zones, the Occupying Authorities dispersed them because of fears that they would create 'minority cells' which might become a source of political instability.[147] As a result, they were deprived of the support networks they had relied on in their homeland. The extent to which the refugees and expellees were able to come to terms with this erosion of their old identity and develop a new identity in the West was partly determined by their personality and temperament. However, it also depended on a range of external factors including their response to the loss of their homeland, their experiences during their flight and expulsion and their relationship with the native population after their arrival in the West.[148]

Interviews carried out in the 1990s by Michael von Engelhardt in Bavaria and Rainer Schulze in the Rural District of Celle reveal that some 50 years after their flight or expulsion many refugees still identified closely with their former homelands. Engelhardt's study concluded that only 39.1 per cent of the interviewees regarded Bavaria as their first home, while 38.4 per cent viewed their former place of residence as their first but Bavaria as their second home. A sizeable minority (22.5 per cent) considered the village where they were brought up prior to their flight or expulsion to be their home.[149] Similarly, Schulze found that over 50 per cent of the refugees interviewed in Celle regarded their home as 'the place where they were born'.[150] Practically no one identified himself or herself without qualification as a native of Celle. All the refugees had clear memories of their original homeland and many still observed some of the customs and traditions associated with it. Some had retained their regional accent some 50 years later, while very few could converse in the local dialect of Celle. In short, many refugees still had close emotional ties with the place where they were born or grew up and these were reinforced by the visits they had undertaken to their former homeland since the 1970s.[151]

The integration of the refugees and expellees into German society was also impaired by their traumatic experiences during their flight or expulsion from their homelands. It was predominantly women, children and elderly people who were affected since most men were still fighting in the war. Most had suffered or witnessed terrible atrocities while many women had been raped by Soviet troops. Yet, after their arrival in the West they received little help in coming to terms with their suffering and trauma. While, in the context of the Cold War, the West German Government publicised the rape of refugee women by Soviet soldiers for propaganda purposes, it took little or no action to help the victims of such crimes on an individual basis.[152] As Michael Hughes put it, 'the experience of individual women ... [was] virtually obliterate[d] ... from social memory in a conspiracy of silence'.[153] Until recently, little research had been carried out on the impact of the expulsion on the refugees' long-term mental health but a major study by the Psychological Institute in Hamburg of 270 expellees, including 205 women, was completed in 1999. It revealed that some 54 years after the expulsion no fewer than 62 per cent showed 'trauma-related symptoms'; of these, 4.8 per cent were suffering from post-traumatic stress disorder while a further 25 per cent had some symptoms of this condition.[154]

The refugees' search for a new identity was also undermined by the fact that public attitudes to the key events in their lives oscillated in response to political considerations. During the 1950s the West German Government's policy of publicising the atrocities committed against the refugees and expellees during the course of their flight or expulsion from their homelands formed part of a strategy to portray the German people in collective memory not just as perpetrators but also as victims of the Second World War.[155] However, the political climate in the FRG began to change during the second half of the 1960s.[156] The extra-parliamentary opposition, with its slogan of 'do not trust anyone over the age of thirty', prompted young West Germans to question the role their own fathers had played in the war. Moreover, Willy Brandt's policy of reconciliation towards the East involved acknowledging and atoning for German war crimes committed under the National Socialist regime. In this climate, reference to the atrocities perpetrated by Soviet troops against the refugees was deemed politically unacceptable and the Brandt Government endorsed a proposal that the word 'expulsion' be replaced by the more neutral but misleading term 'population transfer' in school textbooks.[157] Those who dared to suggest that the refugees were also victims of the Second World War ran the risk of being dismissed as 'revanchist'. The outcome was, as Rainer Schulze put it, that 'once again the real memories of the refugees and expellees were subordinated to political considerations'.[158] This conclusion was even more applicable to the GDR where the Government's reference in September 1950 to 'former resettlers' indicated its view that a refugee problem no longer existed.[159]

However, the unification of Germany in October 1990 and the ratification of the German–Polish Border Treaty in 1991 paved the way for a more open discussion of the issue of German identity and collective memory, because the issue was no longer bedevilled by the tensions associated with the Cold War. In recent years television documentaries, films and books have focused renewed attention on the role of Germans as victims as well as perpetrators of the Second World War. Jörg Friedrich's book, published in 2002, entitled 'The Fire' (*Der Brand*), which examined the suffering inflicted on the civilian population of German cities by the Allied wartime bombing campaign, created enormous interest in Germany.[160] In addition, television programmes and literary publications about the flight and expulsion of the refugees and expellees have provoked a national debate which would have been inconceivable in the 1960s and 1970s. In 2001 a three part documentary entitled 'The Expellees: Hitler's last Victims' was screened on German television, as well as Guido Knopp's 'The Great Flight: The Fate of the Expellees'.[161] Of even greater significance was the publication in 2002 of a novel called 'Crabwalk' (*Im Krebsgang*) by the former Nobel prize winner,

Günter Grass.[162] The book deals with the fate of the more than 5,000 refugees on board the *Wilhelm Gustloff* when it was sunk by a Soviet submarine in January 1945. It constituted an important landmark in prompting public discussion about Germans as victims of the war and 'official' support for a public dialogue about flight and expulsion also came from the outgoing German President Dr Johannes Rau in a speech delivered to the League of Expellees in September 2003.[163]

In 1997 the late W. G. Sebald, referring to the wartime bombing of German cities, noted that 'those directly affected by the experience neither shared it with each other nor passed it on to the next generation'.[164] Yet exactly the same observation may be made about the flight and expulsion of the refugees and expellees. Many suppressed memories of the expulsion because the events they had witnessed or experienced were too painful to recall.[165] Married women who had been raped often kept the knowledge to themselves, fearing a negative reaction from their husband.[166] Moreover, as Schulze's study of Celle shows, few refugees recounted their experiences of flight and expulsion to the indigenous inhabitants, believing that the local people could not identify with and were not interested in their plight.[167] In fact, the apparent indifference of West German society to their fate made it all the more difficult for the refugees to come to terms with these events.

There were several other respects in which the attitude of the native population towards the refugees impeded the growth of a common identity between the two groups. While many refugees implicitly assumed that this identity would represent the synthesis of a two-way process combining the richest elements of both their and the 'native' culture, the indigenous inhabitants initially expected the newcomers to adopt their local customs. In Celle, for example, few of the native population attended events organised by the refugees to maintain their own cultural traditions.[168] A further problem was the widespread ignorance about the areas from which the refugees originated; many Germans do not know that, for example, the Polish industrial city of Wroclaw was once the German town of Breslau.[169]

To sum up, it is clear that some 60 years after their arrival in the West, many refugees and expellees still do not feel fully accepted by the native inhabitants. They still remember the hostile reception they received from the indigenous population in the early post-war years.[170] Similarly, many still bear the mental scars resulting from the traumatic experiences they suffered during their flight or expulsion and this problem has been aggravated by the fact that German society has only recently begun to address this issue. These events, as well as memories of their homelands, still help to shape the refugees' identities today. Yet, to quote Rainer Schulze, these experiences have not become part of 'the common German historical consciousness and collective memory'.[171] German collective memory today remains essentially that of the native inhabitants. The calls of Schulze and others for more discussion and research about the experiences and memories of the refugees and expellees have been supported by the *Bundestag*'s decision in July 2002 to establish a 'Centre against Expulsions' in memory not just of the expelled Germans but of other Europeans as well. According to Rau, one of its objectives is to provide 'a permanent memory to the individual suffering of the victims and the terrible fate of entire ethnic groups'.[172] At the same time, he stressed the importance of viewing the expulsion of the German refugees in its historical context and remembering that it took place in response to the atrocities committed in the name of National Socialism. However, the bitter debate which followed about whether the Centre should be based in Berlin or outside Germany showed that the flight and expulsion of German refugees and expellees remains a highly sensitive topic, especially in Poland and the Czech Republic.[173]

This chapter has shown that, while the integration of the refugees and expellees in the FRG has in many respects been very successful, the process has been less smooth than some German politicians are willing to acknowledge. However, seen from the perspective of the Allied and German political elites in the early post-war years, one of the most remarkable achievements was that the widely predicted political radicalisation of the refugees and expellees did not occur. Chapter 6 will assess the threat posed by the newcomers to the political stability of the Western Occupation Zones of Germany and discuss the reasons for the absence of large-scale unrest.

Notes

1 Führer, *Mieter, Hausbesitzer*, p. 43.
2 Frantzioch, *Die Vertriebenen*, p. 206
3 Führer, *Mieter, Hausbesitzer*, pp. 381–2.

4 F. J. Bauer, 'Zwischen "Wunder" und Strukturzwang. Zur Integration der Flüchtlinge und Vertriebenen in der Bundesrepublik Deutschland', *APZ*, B 32 (1987), p. 22.
5 Ellenrieder, 'Wohnverhältnisse von Flüchtlingen', p. 326.
6 Parisius, 'Flüchtlinge und Vertriebene in Osnabrück', p. 66.
7 Glensk, *Die Aufnahme und Eingliederung*, p. 265.
8 Nahm, ... *doch das leben ging weiter*, pp. 112–13.
9 U. Haerendel, 'Die Politik der "Eingliederung" in den Westzonen und der Bundesrepublik Deutschland: Das Flüchtlingsproblem zwischen Grundsatzentscheidungen und Verwaltungspraxis', in Hoffmann, Krauss and Schwartz (eds), *Vertriebene in Deutschland*, p. 123.
10 *Ibid.*, p. 124.
11 Ellenrieder, 'Wohnverhältnisse von Flüchtlingen', p. 374.
12 Haerendel, 'Die Politik der "Eingliederung"', pp. 122–3.
13 Frantzioch, *Die Vertriebenen*, p. 203.
14 Führer, *Mieter, Hausbesitzer*, p. 44
15 Rudolph, *Evangelische Kirche und Vertriebene*, Vol. 1, p. 129.
16 H. Oberpenning, *'Arbeit, Wohnung und eine neue Heimat ...': Espelkamp – Geschichte einer Idee* (Essen 2002), p. 96.
17 E. Püschel, *Die Hilfe der deutschen Caritas für Vertriebene und Flüchtlinge nach dem zweiten Weltkrieg* (Freiburg im Breisgau 1972), p. 101.
18 DCV, 371, Fasz. 8d, *Arbeitsbericht des Katholischen Siedlungsdienstes*, 16 November 1950, p. 3.
19 Führer, *Mieter, Hausbesitzer*, p. 43.
20 Schier, *Die Aufnahme und Eingliederung*, p. 242.
21 Quoted in Führer, *Mieter, Hausbesitzer*, p. 378.
22 *Die Neue Zeitung*, 6 March 1952, in ACDP, NL Nahm, 1–518–008/2 and Frantzioch, *Die Vertriebenen*, p. 205.
23 Frantzioch, *Die Vertriebenen*, p. 205.
24 Carstens, *Die Flüchtlingslager der Stadt Kiel*, p. 89.
25 Schier, *Die Aufnahme und Eingliederung*, pp. 243–4.
26 Frantzioch, *Die Vertriebenen*, p. 205.
27 Calculated from Ackermann, *Der "echte" Flüchtling*, pp. 288–91. The East German refugees were initially accommodated in camps for up to two years and then transferred to rented houses or flats.
28 LSH, Abt. 605, 996, Plaas (Ministry of Labour) to Minister-President's Office, 26 February 1952.
29 *Die Neue Zeitung*, 6 March 1952.
30 ACDP, NL Nahm, 1–518–002/2, Report of the Federal Commissioner for Resettlement, Dr Peter Paul Nahm, at a sitting of the *Deutscher Landkreistag*, 12 February 1952.
31 Quoted in Parisius, 'Flüchtlinge und Vertriebene in Osnabrück', p. 75.
32 See for example, LSH, Abt. 761, 4525, Interim Report of the Federal Commissioners for Resettlement, June 1952, p. 8. See also *ibid.*, p. 67.

33 Ellenrieder, 'Wohnverhältnisse von Flüchtlingen', p. 327.
34 According to Else Bohnsack, 'employment is ... the most important consideration influencing integration, not just economically but in other respects'. Quoted in Frantzioch, *Die Vertriebenen*, p. 213.
35 Roseman, 'The Uncontrolled Economy', p. 96.
36 Lüttinger, 'Der Mythos der schnellen Integration', p. 23.
37 Glensk, 'Großstädtischer Arbeitsmarkt und Vertriebenenintegration', p. 260.
38 *Ibid.*
39 In May 1955 newcomers comprised 35 per cent of those out of work in Lower Saxony and in September 1955, 38 per cent of the unemployed in Schleswig-Holstein. See Wennemann, 'Flüchtlinge und Vertriebene in Niedersachsen', p. 114 and Statistisches Landesamt Schleswig-Holstein (ed.), *Das Flüchtlingsgeschehen in Schleswig-Holstein*, p. 90.
40 Lüttinger, 'Der Mythos der schnellen Integration', p. 23.
41 Bauer, 'Zwischen "Wunder" und Strukturzwang', p. 23.
42 Lüttinger, 'Der Mythos der schnellen Integration', p. 24.
43 *Ibid.*, p. 35.
44 According to Handl, 'the integration of the refugees and expellees ... took place on a selective basis' and their disadvantaged position in relation to the indigenous inhabitants 'did not diminish until the second generation'. See J. Handl, 'War die schnelle Integration der Vertriebenen ein Mythos?', in Endres (ed.), *Bayerns vierter Stamm*, p. 210.
45 M. von Engelhardt, *Lebensgeschichte und Gesellschaftsgeschichte: Biographieverläufe von Heimatvertriebenen des Zweiten Weltkriegs* (Munich 2001), p. 159.
46 LSH, Abt. 761, 4525, Interim Report of the Federal Commissioners for Resettlement, June 1952, pp. 1–2.
47 Nahm, *... doch das Leben ging weiter*, p. 115.
48 See Schreyer, *Bayern – ein Industriestaat.*
49 Dusik, 'Die Gablonzer Schmuckwarenindustrie', p. 505.
50 Hughes, *Shouldering the Burdens of Defeat*, p. 158
51 Edding, *Die wirtschaftliche Eingliederung*, p. 87.
52 Messerschmidt, *Aufnahme und Integration*, p. 285.
53 *Ibid.*, p. 284.
54 *Ibid.*, p. 291.
55 *Ibid.*, pp. 289–90.
56 Schoenberg, *Germans from the East*, pp. 56 and 58.
57 StA, LRA 31620, *Das Flüchtlingssiedlungsgesetz vom 10. August 1949*, pp. 3–4.
58 StA, LRA 31620, *Das Flüchtlingssiedlungsgesetz vom 10. August 1949*, p. 7.
59 A. Bauerkämper, 'Die vorgetäuschte Integration: Die Auswirkungen der Bodenreform und Flüchtlingssiedlung auf die berufliche Eingliederung

von Vertriebenen in die Landwirtschaft in Deutschland 1945–1960', in Hoffmann and Schwartz (eds), *Geglückte Integration?*, p. 207.

60 *Ibid.*, 208.

61 In Schleswig-Holstein, for example, the British Military Government vetoed Erich Arp's Land Reform Bill, while in Bavaria the US Military Government's initial enthusiasm for dispossessing the large landowners soon waned. See Bauerkämper, 'Die vorgetäuschte Integration', p. 208 and G. Trittel, *Die Bodenreform in der Britischen Zone* (Stuttgart 1975), pp. 16–17.

62 U. Kleinert, 'Die Flüchtlinge als Arbeitskräfte – zur Eingliederung der Flüchtlinge in Nordrhein-Westfalen nach 1945', in K. J. Bade (ed.), *Neue Heimat im Westen: Vertriebene, Flüchtlinge, Aussiedler* (Münster 1990), pp. 50–1.

63 Nahm, ... *doch das Leben ging weiter*, p. 115.

64 J. Handl and C. Herrmann, 'Sozialstruktureller Wandel und Flüchtlingsintegration. Empirische Befunde zur beruflichen Integration der weiblichen Vertriebenen und Flüchtlinge des Zweiten Weltkrieges in Bayern', *Zeitschrift für Soziologie*, Vol. 22(2) (1993), p. 138.

65 Ó Dochartaigh, *Germany since 1945*, p. 42.

66 M. Balfour, *Germany: The Tides of Power* (London and New York 1992), pp. 109–10.

67 Ó Dochartaigh, *Germany since 1945*, p. 41.

68 R. Schulze, 'The Struggle of Past and Present in Individual Identities: The Case of German Refugees and Expellees from the East', in Rock and Wolff (eds), *Coming Home to Germany?*, p. 42.

69 *Ibid.*

70 W. Abelshauser, 'Schopenhauers Gesetz und die Währungsreform: Drei Anmerkungen zu einem methodischen Problem', *VfZ*, 33(1) (1985), p. 217.

71 Neumann, *Der Block der Heimatvertriebenen und Entrechteten*, pp. 500–2.

72 Hughes, *Shouldering the Burdens of Defeat*, p. 186.

73 Neumann, *Der Block der Heimatvertriebenen und Entrechteten*, pp. 347–51.

74 Wennemann, 'Flüchtlinge und Vertriebene in Niedersachsen', p. 102.

75 Neumann, *Der Block der Heimatvertriebenen und Entrechteten*, pp. 303–4.

76 *Ibid.*, p. 313.

77 *Ibid.*, p. 312.

78 F. Wiesemann, 'Erzwungene Heimat: Flüchtlinge in Nordrhein-Westfalen', in G. Brunn (ed.), *Neuland: Nordrhein-Westfalen und seine Anfänge nach 1945/46* (Essen 1986), p. 169.

79 Neumann, *Der Block der Heimatvertriebenen und Entrechteten*, p. 317.

80 *Ibid.*, pp. 309–10.
81 Quoted in D. Levy, 'Integrating Ethnic Germans in West Germany: The Early Postwar Period', in Rock and Wolff (eds), *Coming Home to Germany?*, p. 36.
82 Neumann, *Der Block der Heimatvertriebenen und Entrechteten*, pp. 72–3.
83 The agreement was rejected by the inhabitants of the Saar in October 1955 and the Saarland became part of the FRG on 1 January 1957.
84 Quoted in Ahonen, *After the Expulsion*, p. 106.
85 Quoted in Frantzioch-Immenkeppel, 'Die Vertriebenen in der Bundesrepublik Deutschland', p. 9.
86 Neumann, *Der Block der Heimatvertriebenen und Entrechteten*, p. 305.
87 J. Falter, 'Kontinuität und Neubeginn: Die Bundestagswahl 1949 zwischen Weimar und Bonn', *Politische Vierteljahresschrift* (*PV*), Vol. 22 (1981), p. 252.
88 Ahonen, *After the Expulsion*, p. 74. The FDP also acknowledged privately that most of the refugees who had defected from the BHE had voted for the CDU. See ADL, A13–3, Minutes of a meeting of the FDP's Expellee Committee, 19–20 June 1954, p. 2.
89 AdsD, SPD LV Bayern, 153, Report on the outcome of the 1953 *Bundestag* Election, September 1953. See also Bösch, 'Die politische Integration der Flüchtlinge', p. 122.
90 Ahonen, *After the Expulsion*, p. 144.
91 Bösch, 'Die politische Integration der Flüchtlinge', p. 116.
92 A. Grünbacher, 'The Chancellor's Forgotten Blunder: Konrad Adenauer's Foundation for Refugees and Expellees', *German Politics* (*GP*), Vol. 13(3) (2004), p. 483.
93 See Hughes, *Shouldering the Burdens of Defeat*, pp. 174–5 and Haerendel, 'Die Politik der "Eingliederung"', p. 119.
94 Bösch, 'Die politische Integration der Flüchtlinge', p. 119.
95 ACDP, 1–377–6/1, Kather and Eplée to Adenauer, 22 August 1953.
96 ACSP, NL Schütz, 2.2.3., Kather to Adenauer, 14 June 1954.
97 Bösch, 'Die politische Integration der Flüchtlinge', pp. 117–18.
98 P. Major, *The Death of the KPD: Communism and Anti-Communism in West Germany, 1945–1956* (Oxford 1997), p. 270.
99 Haerendel, 'Die Politik der "Eingliederung"', p. 118.
100 Bösch, 'Die politische Integration der Flüchtlinge', p. 120.
101 Mintzel, *Die CSU*, pp. 210, 443.
102 Ahonen, *After the Expulsion*, p. 163.
103 BSL (ed.), *Bundestagswahlergebnisse 1953 bis 1972 in Flüchtlingsgemeinden.*
104 For further details, see Ahonen, *After the Expulsion*, pp. 155–60.
105 *Ibid.*, p. 180.

106 Kirchenkanzlei der Evangelischen Kirche in Deutschland (ed.), *Die Lage der Vertriebenen und das Verhältnis des deutschen Volkes zu seinen östlichen Nachbarn* (Hanover 1965), p. 44.
107 Quoted in Ahonen, *After the Expulsion*, p. 232.
108 *Ibid.*
109 *Ibid.*, p. 242. Voting in Bavaria's *Flüchtlingsgemeinden* confirmed this general conclusion. The SPD vote fell from 37.6 to 35.8 per cent, while the CSU's share of the vote rose from 46.8 to 50.6 per cent. See BSL (ed.), *Bundestagswahlergebnisse 1953 bis 1972*.
110 R. Kühnl, R. Rilling and C. Sager, *Die NPD: Struktur, Ideologie und Funktion einer neofaschistischen Partei* (Frankfurt a. M. 1969), p. 160.
111 Ahonen, *After the Expulsion*, p. 242.
112 BSL (ed.), *Bundestagswahlergebnisse 1953 bis 1972*.
113 Precise figures are not available. See Ahonen, *After the Expulsion*, p. 29, and Schoenberg, *Germans from the East*, pp. 114–15.
114 Schoenberg, *Germans from the East*, pp. 114–15.
115 Wennemann, 'Flüchtlinge und Vertriebene in Niedersachsen', p. 99.
116 For details, see Ahonen, *After the Expulsion*, p. 50.
117 Frantzioch, *Die Vertriebenen*, p. 145.
118 S. Lee, 'CDU Refugee Policies and the Landesverband Oder/Neiße: Electoral Tool or Instrument of Integration?', *GP*, Vol. 8(1) (1999), p. 145.
119 Bösch, 'Die politische Integration der Flüchtlinge', pp. 121–2.
120 Ahonen, *After the Expulsion*, p. 144.
121 *Ibid.*, pp. 247–56 and Frantzioch, *Die Vertriebenen*, pp. 156–7.
122 D. Strothmann, '"Schlesien bleibt unser": Vertriebenenpolitiker und das Rad der Geschichte', in Benz (ed.), *Die Vertreibung der Deutschen aus dem Osten*, p. 209; and Frantzioch, *Die Vertriebenen*, pp. 157–8. The slogan was subsequently changed to the slightly less offensive '40 years of expulsion – Silesia remains our future in a Europe of free peoples'.
123 G. Hendriks, 'The Oder–Neiße Line Revisited: German Unification and Poland's Western Border', *Politics and Society in Germany, Austria and Switzerland*, Vol. 4(3) (1992), p. 10.
124 Lee, 'CDU Refugee Policies', p.135, and Ahonen, *After the Expulsion*, p. 145. For a more detailed discussion of the attempts to create a unified expellee association in the early 1950s, see Steinert, *Vertriebenenverbände*, pp. 151–67.
125 Hirsch, 'Flucht und Vertreibung', p. 21.
126 H.-W. Rautenberg, 'Die Wahrnehmung von Flucht und Vertreibung in der deutschen Nachkriegsgeschichte bis heute', *APZ*, B 53 (1997), p. 38.
127 Ahonen, *After the Expulsion*, p. 267.

128 Lüttig, *Fremde im Dorf*, p. 215.
129 C.-J. Müller, *Praxis und Probleme des Lastenausgleichs in Mannheim 1949–1959* (Mannheim 1997), pp. 359–63.
130 Lüttig, *Fremde im Dorf*, p. 217.
131 Hirsch, 'Flucht und Vertreibung', p. 22.
132 See for example, BSL (ed.), *Die Vertriebenen in Bayern*, p. 29.
133 J. Handl and C. Herrmann, *Soziale und berufliche Umschichtung der Bevölkerung in Bayern nach 1945: Eine Sekundäranalyse der Mikrozensus-Zusatzerhebung von 1971* (Munich 1994), p. 138.
134 Krauss, 'Die Integration Vertriebener am Beispiel Bayerns', p. 56.
135 Schulze, '"Wir leben ja nun hier"', pp. 81–2.
136 Erker, 'Revolution des Dorfes?', p. 404.
137 Exner, 'Integration oder Assimilation?', pp. 83–4.
138 *Ibid.*, p. 84, Lüttig, *Fremde im Dorf*, p. 193 and A. Lehmann, *Im Fremden ungewollt zuhaus: Flüchtlinge und Vertriebene in Westdeutschland 1945–1990*, 2nd edn (Munich 1993), p. 53.
139 Lüttig, *Fremde im Dorf*, p. 191.
140 *Ibid.*, p. 190.
141 Krauss, 'Die Integration Vertriebener am Beispiel Bayerns', p. 53.
142 R. Schulze, 'The German Refugees and Expellees from the East and the Creation of a Western German Identity after World War II', in Ther and Siljak (eds), *Redrawing Nations*, p. 317.
143 Schulze, 'The Struggle of Past and Present', p. 43.
144 *Ibid.*
145 Wennemann, 'Flüchtlinge und Vertriebene in Niedersachsen', p. 122.
146 H. Schmidt, *Das Vereinsleben der Stadt Weinheim an der Bergstraße* (Weinheim 1963), pp. 119–20. Quoted in Lehmann, *Im Fremden ungewollt zuhaus*, p. 54.
147 Grosser, 'Das Assimilationskonzept', p. 17.
148 The overall argument in this paragraph draws heavily on Schulze, 'The German Refugees and Expellees', pp. 317–19.
149 Von Engelhardt, 'Biographieverläufe', p. 73.
150 Schulze, 'The Struggle of Past and Present', p. 46.
151 This section is based on *ibid.*, pp. 45–8.
152 Lehmann, *Im Fremden ungewollt zuhaus*, pp. 151–2. See also M. L. Hughes, '"Through No Fault of Our Own": West Germans Remember Their War Losses', *GH*, Vol. 18(2) (2000), p. 197.
153 Hughes, '"Through No Fault of Our Own"', p. 197.
154 Hirsch, 'Flucht und Vertreibung', pp. 22–3. For an analysis of the long-term mental effects of expulsion and loss of homeland, see also A. von Friesen, *Der lange Abschied: Psychische Spätfolgen für die 2. Generation deutscher Vertriebener* (Gießen 2000).
155 On this issue, see, Moeller, 'War Stories', pp. 1023–4.
156 B. Faulenbach, 'Die Vertreibung der Deutschen aus den Gebieten

jenseits von Oder und Neiße: Zur wissenschaftlichen und öffentlichen Diskussion in Deutschland', *APZ*, B 51–2 (2002), p. 50.

157 Hirsch, 'Flucht und Vertreibung', p. 25.

158 Schulze, 'The Struggle of Past and Present', p. 52.

159 For a more detailed discussion, see Schwartz, 'Vertreibung und Vergangenheitspolitik', pp. 177–95.

160 J. Friedrich, *Der Brand: Deutschland im Bombenkrieg 1940–1945* (Munich 2002). Such was its popularity, that it sold 186,000 copies.

161 The accompanying books to the television series were K.E. Franzen, *Die Vertriebenen: Hitlers letzte Opfer: Mit einer Einführung von Hans Lemberg* (Berlin and Munich 2001) and G. Knopp, *Die große Flucht: Das Schicksal der Vertriebenen*, 3rd edn (Munich 2002).

162 G. Grass, *Im Krebsgang* (Göttingen 2002).

163 See www. tczew-witten.de/a040302.html, 'Auszüge aus der Rede von Bundespräsident Johannes Rau beim Tag der Heimat des Bundes der Vertriebenen … 7.9.2003' (accessed 11 April 2005).

164 Quoted in a review article by Christian Schütze for the *London Review of Books*. See books.guardian.co.uk/lrb/articles (accessed 11 April 2005).

165 Schulze, '"Wir leben ja nun hier"', p. 78.

166 Lehmann, *Im Fremden ungewollt zuhaus*, p. 152.

167 Schulze, '"Wir leben ja nun hier"', pp. 79–80.

168 Schulze, 'The Struggle of Past and Present', p. 51.

169 ‚Auszüge aus der Rede'.

170 Schulze, 'The Struggle of Past and Present', pp. 44–5 and Lehmann, *Im Fremden ungewollt zuhaus*, p. 32.

171 Schulze, 'The Struggle of Past and Present', p. 52.

172 'Auszüge aus der Rede'.

173 *Sunday Times*, 28 September 2003 and Hirsch, 'Flucht und Vertreibung', p. 26.

6

The issue of political radicalisation

Introduction

In the course of this book it has become evident that leading political figures in the Western Occupation Zones of Germany had deep fears that the 7.5 million German refugees and expellees from the East would represent a source of political radicalisation in the new West German state which was being founded under the guidance of the Western Allies. This view was based on the assumption that the severe economic deprivation the refugees were suffering would make them a fickle and volatile force vulnerable to the slogans of political agitators and demagogues. As Willibald Mücke, Co-Chair of the Main Committee of Refugees and Expellees in Bavaria, observed in the spring of 1948, 'people who have nothing to lose ... are a highly explosive source of tension in any human society'.[1] Leading political figures were particularly alarmed at the response of the refugee camp population to long-term material distress, arguing that the concentration of a large number of discontented people facilitated the task of irresponsible elements seeking to gain control over their fellow inmates. This argument sheds light on the attitude of the political elites to the so-called 'masses'. They did not consider the refugees to be independent, discerning individuals capable of making rational judgements but as helpless, gullible people who might support any party which promised to improve their material plight. In other words, leading politicians believed that, irrespective of their ideological views, the refugees and expellees might be attracted to the propaganda of both radical left-and right-wing parties.

As seen in chapter 4, the refugees' voting behaviour in the period 1945–50 indicated that the political elites were justified in regarding them as a source of discord in post-war German society.

The outcome of the first *Bundestag* Election in 1949 confirmed the expellees' vulnerability to the overtures of nationalist parties. On the other hand, the results of State, District and Federal Elections between 1946 and 1950 showed that the expellees were immune to the propaganda of the KPD irrespective of their acute economic misery. While the political elites undoubtedly misperceived the Communist threat, there is no doubt that they genuinely believed that the refugees might be attracted to communism.[2]

But how valid were the widespread fears expressed by leading politicians about unrest breaking out in refugee camps? To what extent did the refugees and expellees resort to extra-parliamentary activities to achieve their political demands? This chapter will seek to address these issues. It will show that protests and disturbances did occur in a number of refugee camps in 1948–49, as well as violent incidents at several election rallies. Brief reference will also be made to the activities of the trek associations established in Bavaria, Lower Saxony and Schleswig-Holstein in 1951–52 in protest at the slow progress of the Federal Government's refugee resettlement programme. However, these were isolated incidents and the widely feared mass radicalisation of the refugees and expellees did not occur. The main focus of the chapter therefore will be to examine the reasons for the absence of widespread unrest.

Hunger strikes and the trek associations

The mood of the refugees became increasingly volatile as a result of the further deterioration in their economic position following the Currency Reform of June 1948. As a result, the second half of 1948 witnessed protests, demonstrations and hunger strikes. Bavaria was the state worst affected. According to the US Military Government, as many as 35,000 refugees took part in demonstrations during October 1948, while the Bavarian Government received more than 500 protest resolutions from refugees in 1948–49.[3] Many of these resolutions called for the resignation of the Bavarian State Secretary for Refugees, Wolfgang Jaenicke.[4] Refugee camps in Southern Bavaria were the focal point of the protests. On 18 August 1948, Egon Herrmann, the leader of the 1,117 occupants of Dachau Camp, demanded increased food rations, repairs to the camp buildings and pocket money of 10 DM a month for each inmate.[5] State Secretary Jaenicke refused to meet these demands and, as a result, the refugees in Dachau and Munich-Allach transit camps began a hunger strike on 4 September. In the next few days, refugees in camps located in Rosenheim, Berchtesgaden and Augsburg followed their example[6] and no fewer than 72,000 refugee camp occupants joined the strike.[7] The action was called off on 10 September in response to wide-ranging concessions by the Bavarian Government. However, Herrmann continued to foment discord in Dachau Camp during the autumn of 1948. He also attempted to instigate unrest in refugee camps in the British Occupation Zone but his appeals met with little response.[8] On 27 November 1948 the disturbances in Dachau reached a climax when a mob of up to 150 refugees attacked a car carrying Bavarian Government officials who had been inspecting construction work at the camp.[9] Further unrest occurred during the summer of 1949 when refugees living in a number of camps in Franconia cooperated closely in opposing a decision to reduce their daily food allowance. In a protest resolution to the Bavarian Government, the inmates of Hammelburg Housing Camp (Lower Franconia) announced that they were 'determined to prevent ... the enforcement of.. [this] ministerial ruling',[10] while the occupants of a number of other camps in Franconia submitted similarly worded protest resolutions.[11]

Refugees were also involved in violent incidents in other parts of the Western Occupation Zones. For example, at an SPD election rally in Ludwigsburg in September 1948, the speaker, Karl Gerbrich, was assaulted and chased out of the hall by several hundred expellees.[12] Violence also broke out at an election meeting in North Rhine-Westphalia in the same month when expellees injured several policemen who were trying to arrest a prominent refugee 'for making a most outspoken speech against the Land authorities and Military Government'.[13]

The significant levels of support for the trek associations established in the three main refugee states in 1951–52 indicated the growing desperation of some of the most economically impoverished expellees more than six years after their flight or expulsion from their homelands. Frustration at the ineffectiveness of the Federal Government's resettlement programme prompted Reinhard Noback and Kurt Dahn to found the Schleswig-Holstein Trek Association in Süderbrarup (near Schleswig) on 29 October 1951. Noback announced plans to organise a march of refugee families to the south of Germany in the spring of 1952 to force the State

Governments to provide employment opportunities and housing facilities for them. The refugees and expellees reacted enthusiastically to the news and when membership lists closed in March 1952, 34,000 newcomers and their families had signed up for the trek.[14] It was estimated that some 80 per cent of those who joined were unemployed.[15] Similar organisations were established in the other two states most severely affected by the refugee influx. A Bavarian Trek Association was set up in Kulmbach (Franconia) by Herbert Brenske and Heinz Hanner in December 1951, while its counterpart in Lower Saxony was founded in Salzhausen (near Lüneburg) by Alf Kroll in January 1952. The prospect of treks was viewed with dread in governmental circles, in particular the spectre of clashes between refugee families and the police on West Germany's roads.[16] Although, much to the dismay of some of the local branches, the proposed treks from Schleswig-Holstein and Lower Saxony did not ultimately take place, a breakaway group of 55 unemployed refugees from Memmersdorf (near Bamberg, Upper Franconia) set out on 25 April 1952 for their destination of Reutlingen.[17]

The absence of widespread unrest

It is clear, then, that there was some evidence of radicalisation among the refugees and expellees, especially in the critical period after the Currency Reform. However, the unrest was largely confined to Bavaria and outbreaks of widespread radicalisation did not occur. Why was this? This chapter will assess the importance of the role played by the political and ecclesiastical elites, examining the importance of the legislative measures introduced by the Federal Government. It will also evaluate the mood of the refugees and expellees and suggest that the prevailing climate of anti-communism in the FRG in the 1950s acted as an important deterrent to political radicalism and served as a unifying ideology for both natives and refugees.

The Occupying Powers played a major role in averting widespread political radicalisation in the early post-war years. The American and British Military Governments took a number of measures designed to promote the integration of the newcomers into post-war German society and thwart the attempts of some groups of refugees to form a 'state within a state'.[18] To this end, the US Military Government stipulated that 'in order to prevent minority cells from developing …, expellees from one community abroad will be distributed and resettled among several German communities'.[19] This policy of splitting up refugee communities was aimed particularly at the *Volksdeutsche* since they were accustomed to living as minority groups in foreign countries. US Military Government officials were particularly concerned about the activities of the Sudeten Germans, who were reportedly planning to settle en masse in villages along Bavaria's border with Czechoslovakia.[20] As a result, the American Military Government banned the Sudeten German Relief Agency in April 1946.[21] Meanwhile, the British Military Government, also fearing the activities of minority groups, had decided as early as January 1946 to dissolve organisations representing the interests of one particular group of refugees.[22]

The decision of the Occupying Authorities to ban the formation of a refugee party was also of decisive importance in preventing the political radicalisation of the newcomers. A request in June 1946 by the Economic Party of Refugees in Mainburg to be registered as a political party in the Administrative Districts of Lower Bavaria and Upper Palatinate prompted the then US Deputy Military Governor, General Lucius Clay, to address this issue. He ordered the US Military Government in Bavaria in July 1946 to 'disapprove all applications to form political parties and political groups of expellees and refugees and ... dissolve any' already in existence.[23] This decision was based on several considerations. First, the establishment of a refugee party exclusively representing the interests of one section of the population contravened the US Military Government's aim of integrating the expellees into German society. It was also likely to lead to a further deterioration in relations between the newcomers and the indigenous inhabitants. Moreover, there was a real danger that 'such a party might ... become the focal point for irredentist movements which would again menace the peace of Central Europe'.[24] Interestingly, the British Military Government had already adopted the same policy as the Americans some six months earlier when in December 1945 it refused to grant a licence to a 'Reconstruction Party' (*Aufbaupartei*) established by refugees in the Rural District of Eiderstedt (Schleswig-Holstein).[25] Both the British and American Military Governments insisted that, as General Clay put it, 'expellees and refugees should express their political needs by joining the established political parties'.[26] This gave these mainstream parties the opportunity to integrate the newcomers into their ranks before they faced competition from an independent refugee party.

Even though the Western Allies maintained that the German authorities were exclusively responsible for solving the refugee problem, the British Military Government closely monitored the implementation of its policy decisions by the German state administrations, while the Americans were in practice more interventionist than they were prepared to concede publicly.[27] The key issue was accommodation. The Occupying Authorities, supported by the German political elites at regional level, were determined to avoid, wherever possible, the long-term accommodation of refugees in camps because, apart from humanitarian considerations, they believed that the presence of a large number of economically deprived people in a confined space provided the ideal conditions for outbreaks of political radicalisation. However, some local officials, under pressure from native householders who did not want to share their homes with refugees, opted to house the newcomers in camps, maintaining that no private accommodation was available. This situation led to Allied intervention in both the British and American Occupation Zones. In September 1946, the US Military Government ordered the Bavarian Minister-President, Wilhelm Hoegner, to 'take immediate action' to ensure that private accommodation was found for the refugees,[28] while in January 1947 the newly appointed British Officer in the *Regierungsbezirk* of Lüneburg (Lower Saxony) ordered the German authorities to eliminate within six weeks the huge disparity in the housing conditions of the native and refugee populations, paying particular attention to those living in camps.[29]

However, it should also be borne in mind that the mere presence of Allied troops on German soil helped to prevent outbreaks of unrest among the refugees and expellees. In Bavaria, for example, the US Military Government closely monitored the activities of Egon Herrmann and sent an observer to every meeting at which he spoke.[30] In addition, American representatives interviewed Herrmann on 8 August 1949, warning him that his outspoken remarks at public meetings contravened Military Government regulations.[31] Similarly, it was the US Military Police who came to the rescue of the SPD speaker attacked by refugees in Ludwigsburg in September 1948.[32] The Western Allies continued to monitor the security situation even after the establishment of the FRG and the head of the Displaced Persons Office of the United States High Commission liaised closely with the Federal Minister of the Interior, Dr Robert Lehr, concerning the activities of the Schleswig-Holstein Trek Association.[33] In fact,

Allied representatives kept Noback's house under observation.[34] It is clear, then, that, in the early post-war years, the Occupying Forces played a key role in neutralising the threat the refugees and expellees posed to public security in the Western Occupation Zones of Germany.

The German Federal and State Governments also responded swiftly to the first signs of unrest among the refugees. This is illustrated by the prompt reaction of the Bavarian authorities to the unrest in Dachau and Munich-Allach refugee camps. As soon as the hunger strikes began on 4 September 1948, the Government made a number of concessions. Even though the Bavarian Finance Minister had consistently maintained that there was no money to undertake repairs to refugee camps, Jaenicke declared shortly after the unrest broke out that 3 million DM would be made available to remedy the most serious shortcomings in the camps.[35] Significantly, practically half of this money was earmarked for Dachau and Allach.[36] In addition, a Government spokesman announced that refugee camp occupants in Bavaria would in future receive pocket money, while their daily food ration was to be increased from 1,850 to 2,150 calories.[37] When it later transpired that the disturbances in Dachau were politically motivated, the Bavarian Government adopted a tougher line with Herrmann and, following the violence against Government representatives at Dachau camp, he was arrested and subsequently received a suspended custodial sentence for a breach of the peace.[38]

The Federal Government also took seriously the threat posed by the trek associations. In fact, Federal Expellee Minister Lukaschek actually negotiated personally with Noback and Brenske in Bonn in January 1952. He undertook to speed up the resettlement process and shortly after the meeting the Federal cabinet – which had previously displayed little interest in this issue – endorsed the appointment of two commissioners to ensure that the states earmarked to receive the refugee resettlers fulfilled their legal obligations.[39] Lukaschek also promised to support the trek leaders' request to be involved in an advisory capacity in the process of selecting refugees for resettlement.[40] However, the Federal Government adopted an uncompromising position when the threat of treks became a reality. On 25 April 1952, the same day as the breakaway trek set out from Memmelsdorf, Lukaschek informed the trek leaders at a meeting in Bonn that he 'hoped to be able to prevent the trek without recourse to the police',[41] a clear threat to employ force against the refugees. To sum up, the political elites at both Federal and State level displayed a willingness to negotiate with and make concessions to the leaders of refugee groups which, in their view, posed a potential threat to public security, but were also prepared to adopt a harsher line if it proved necessary.

The Federal Government also sought to counteract the danger of political radicalisation by introducing legislation to improve the refugees' economic and social position. Franz Bauer has claimed that government policy towards the refugees after 1950 had minimal influence on their economic integration into West German society, but he underestimates its importance.[42] Although the Federal Government's efforts to resettle the refugees in areas which provided both employment opportunities and satisfactory accommodation were beset with difficulties, 915,000 refugees were ultimately relocated as a result of official schemes.[43] The Federal Government facilitated this process by directing a high proportion of public housing assistance to the industrial state of North Rhine-Westphalia, the most popular destination of refugee resettlers.[44] These population shifts also helped to reduce tension between the expellees and indigenous inhabitants in states such as Schleswig-Holstein which had been most severely affected by the influx of refugees.

The Immediate Aid Law of 8 August 1949 also played a key role in averting the feared radicalisation of the refugees. Under this measure the refugees and expellees received a payment of 70 DM a month. Even though this sum was not much more than their previous welfare benefits, it was important psychologically because the refugees no longer regarded themselves as welfare recipients.[45] They were also able to apply for financial assistance to purchase household equipment, although this often turned out to be a long and cumbersome bureaucratic process which for some ended in disappointment.[46] However, local reports from Southern Bavaria indicate that the majority of the refugees were initially satisfied with these provisions. The *Landrat* of Rosenheim reported in October 1949 that the payments had 'produced a high level of satisfaction among elderly refugees',[47] while his colleague in Bad Tölz noted in November 1949 that, as a result of this measure, 'the situation of many people has undoubtedly improved'.[48] The *Landräte* in other rural districts expressed similar sentiments.[49] It is clear, then, that, in the short term, the Immediate Aid Law helped to offset the radicalisation of the refugees following the Currency Reform, and Reinhold Schillinger has argued that it had a moderating effect on their voting behaviour at the first *Bundestag* Election held just six days after it came into force.[50] However, the Immediate Aid Law also provided funds for the construction of housing and creation of jobs – measures which in the long term proved to be of greater benefit to the newcomers than the direct financial payments they received. In fact, more than half of the 6 billion DM paid out to refugees and other war victims under the Immediate Aid Law up to August 1952 was to provide housing and jobs.[51]

The Equalisation of Burdens Law of August 1952, which replaced the Immediate Aid Law, was the single most important piece of legislation affecting the refugees and other groups of 'war victims'. Like the Immediate Aid Law, it had dual aims – to compensate the refugees for the loss of their homes, savings and other assets, as well as financing loans to promote their economic integration into the FRG. The money was to be raised by various taxes on assets over a 27 year period. This resulted in payments from the Equalisation of Burdens fund totalling 113.9 billion DM in the period 1949–79.[52] Admittedly, the application process for individual refugees seeking compensation was frequently long and unwieldy. Erker quotes the example of a refugee who applied in September 1952 for compensation for the 1,238 reichmarks in her savings account. She had to wait almost eight years to receive a payment of just 114.02 DM.[53] Of greater significance for the refugees' economic and social position was the financial credit available under the Equalisation of Burdens Law to establish business concerns, undertake housing construction and provide interest-free loans to enable independent refugee farmers to purchase or rent land. Although the refugees were disappointed with some aspects of the Equalisation of Burdens Law it was nonetheless a key factor in promoting their economic and social integration into West German society. Moreover, it was important from a psychological point of view because it convinced the refugees and expellees that the Federal Government was taking their concerns seriously.

Of course, any measure designed to redistribute wealth runs the risk of creating social conflict between the 'winners' and the 'losers'. Against this background, the success of the Equalisation of Burdens Law owes much to the sustained economic growth that the FRG experienced during the 1950s because the refugees and other 'war victims' were able to receive financial aid and compensation without the imposition of undue hardship on those required to pay additional taxes and levies. In fact, there is a very real sense in which West Germany's strong economic resurgence represented an antidote to political radicalism among the refugees. Brian Robertson, the British Military Governor, asserted in 1949 that 'if the economic integration [of the refugees] can be solved ... political ... considerations [will] lose much of their importance'[54] and subsequent developments bear out the validity of this statement. The crucial role played by economic factors in influencing the integration of the refugees is illustrated by a public opinion poll conducted in Schleswig-Holstein in 1953. It revealed that only some 40 per cent of those in work still regarded themselves as 'refugees', as opposed to 70 per cent of those who were unemployed.[55] Bearing in mind that leading political figures expressed deep concern about the vulnerability of economically deprived young people to political radicalism, it was important for the political stability of the FRG that most young newcomers obtained a job as the economy began to expand in the early 1950s. By the end of the decade, the refugees and expellees enjoyed virtually full employment and the majority were benefiting from the increasing prosperity, even if their standard of living was still below that of the indigenous population.

The role played by the churches in averting the feared mass radicalisation of the refugees should not be underestimated. As the only institution in the early post-war years within which large numbers of refugees could congregate, the church was in a position to exert a moderating influence over the newcomers. In fact, ecclesiastical organisations such as the *Kirchliche Hilfsstelle* were established with the explicit aim of counteracting the danger of political radicalisation by gaining control of the 'rootless refugee masses' through personal contact at local level.[56] These ecclesiastical welfare bodies did not just give the refugees spiritual and moral support but also attempted to meet their material needs. They mounted a campaign to draw the attention of the international community to the plight of the refugees. Their efforts elicited a good response and by March 1947 the EHW had received 12.4 million kg of food to distribute to the refugees, mainly from the United States, Switzerland and South America.[57] The German Caritas Association and the EHW also worked closely with the *Länder* governments to prevent outbreaks of unrest in refugee camps. In fact, in January 1947 the

Bavarian Government accepted an offer by Caritas officials to assume responsibility for administering as many as 41 camps.[58] By the spring of 1948 most of the larger camps in the Western Occupation Zones of Germany had their own Catholic priest, while the remainder received frequent visits from the local clergyman.

Ecclesiastical welfare associations also played a key role in neutralising the threat emanating from the trek associations. The EHW led the way. At the beginning of 1952, Dr Hermann Maurer, the head of its refugee department, visited Noback in Süderbrarup. The meeting went well and the EHW adopted a strategy of co-operating closely with the trek associations in an attempt to gain control over them, even suggesting that they establish an office in Stuttgart, where the EHW was based.[59] In April 1952, Dr Paul Collmer, head of the EHW's socio-political department, invited Noback and Kroll to Frankfurt to discuss the demands they would put forward in their forthcoming meeting with Federal Minister Lukaschek.[60] In a further attempt to avert the proposed trek, the EHW and Caritas jointly established interdenominational Ecclesiastical Resettlement Offices in Kiel and Regensburg in May 1952. By the time of its closure in May 1954, the office in Kiel had resettled more than 5,300 refugees.[61] Although this was a modest figure in relation to those relocated as part of the official government programme, the leaders of the Ecclesiastical Resettlement Office considered the organisation to be a resounding success because 'it had managed to restrain the trek movement'.[62] The validity of this claim is supported by the trek leaders themselves who in August 1952 explained their decision to postpone their proposed trek by referring to the involvement of ecclesiastical agencies in the resettlement issue.[63]

The extent to which West Germany's political parties can take credit for the absence of widespread political radicalisation is more difficult to assess. The decision of the Western Allies to ban the formation of a refugee party compelled the newcomers to join the established political parties if they wished to influence the political process. The SPD, CDU/CSU and FDP gave public declarations of support for the refugees, especially during election campaigns, but in practice often adopted an ambivalent attitude towards them. In his empirical study of the expellee problem, the academic Julius Isaac reported in July 1949 that 'the refugees complain that the existing political parties have paid only lip service to their needs'[64] and it is certainly true that any party which gave priority to the expellees' interests was likely to be punished at election time by the more numerous indigenous voters. On the other hand, all the mainstream political parties in principle supported the main legislative measures introduced by the Federal and State Governments to facilitate the integration of the refugees into post-war Germany. For example while, as seen above, there were disagreements between and within the SPD, CDU/CSU and FDP about the terms of the Immediate Aid Law and the Equalisation of Burdens Law, all political parties accepted the need for legislation to assist and compensate the 'war-damaged'.[65] However, despite the widespread fears about the emergence of a refugee party, the electoral successes of the BHE in 1950–51 can in retrospect be seen to have reduced rather than increased the likelihood of radicalisation among the expellees. Its establishment gave hope to impoverished refugees who had lost trust in the mainstream parties; at the same time, the rise of the BHE prompted the CDU/CSU, SPD and FDP to pay more attention to the refugee issue because Waldemar Kraft, its Federal Chairman from 1951 to 1957, was prepared to form a coalition with any party which promised to promote the refugees' economic and social interests.

The consensus among all political parties except the KPD to uphold the refugees' right to return to their homelands undoubtedly contributed to the absence of large-scale radicalism in the early post-war years because it gave impoverished and desperate people some hope of finding a way out of their misery. According to a survey carried out by the Bavarian Statistical Office in 1950, almost 58 per cent of refugees believed that the solution to their economic predicament was to return home.[66] This view was even more pronounced (63.6 per cent) in small rural communities of fewer than 2,000 people where a high proportion of the newcomers were out of work.[67] Some were in such despair that, as the international situation deteriorated in 1947–48, they hoped for a war between the United States and the Soviet Union because it might enable them to regain their homelands since, they argued, the West was likely to prevail in any military conflict.[68] Many members of the native population, especially in rural areas, also encouraged the refugees to return home because this would reduce the competition for jobs and housing. To sum up, the declarations of support from the political parties for the refugees' claim to their homelands undoubtedly helped to avert large-scale political radicalisation in the early post-war years.

Even though German political leaders feared that the expellee associations might become vehicles for nationalism and irredentism[69] they in fact proved to be an antidote to political radicalism in the late 1940s and early 1950s. They boosted the refugees' hopes of a return to their homelands by exerting relentless and, until the mid-1960s, successful pressure on the main political parties to resist any temptation to adopt a more flexible approach towards Eastern Europe. They also helped the expellees to retain some sense of identity in the early post-war years when they were most susceptible to political radicalism. Moreover, the expellee associations were able to promote the economic and social integration of their followers by helping to shape legislation affecting the refugees, especially during the first Adenauer Government of 1949–53. This was achieved partly through their party political representatives such as Linus Kather but the expellee associations also employed extra-parliamentary pressure to good effect, organising a demonstration of 60,000 refugees in Bonn in February 1951 in protest at the original version of the 'Law relating to the Assessment of Damage resulting from Expulsion and the War' (*Schadensfeststellungsgesetz*)[70] and another equally large demonstration in May 1952 against the proposed terms of the Equalisation of Burdens Law.[71] It is thus clear that the expellee associations did not create but actually helped to prevent radicalism among the refugees and expellees in the early post-war years.[72]

While the absence of mass radicalisation can be partly attributed to the policies of the political elites, the mood of the refugees themselves must also be examined. On 5 August 1950, the leaders of the expellee associations announced the Charter of German Expellees at a mass rally in Stuttgart. This document, in which the expellees renounced any thought of 'revenge or retribution' for the loss of their homelands,[73] has been widely regarded as evidence of their moderation and restraint. However, this conclusion requires qualification because the unrest in parts of Bavaria in 1948–49 indicates that there was certainly the potential for widespread radicalisation among the refugees and expellees. That this did not happen was due partly to their lack of unity. Although the pressure exerted by the trek associations prompted the Federal and *Länder* Governments to give a higher priority to the refugee resettlement programme, co-operation between the Bavarian Trek Association and its counterparts in Schleswig-Holstein and Lower Saxony broke down in March 1952.[74] However, this disunity was not confined to the refugees' 'elite groups' and some local reports suggest that it was only divisions among the rank and file which prevented mass unrest. For example, the *Landrat* of Erding (Upper Bavaria) observed in July 1949: 'That an explosion has not yet occurred is due solely to the simply appalling disunity of the refugees.'[75]

One of the most important reasons for these divisions among the refugees and expellees was that, as Chistoph Kleßman put it, they lacked a 'distinctive class or homogeneous group consciousness'.[76] This was mainly the result of their divergent geographical origins. While the 'National Germans' came from areas which had formed part of Germany on 31 December 1937, the 'Ethnic Germans' had lived as minorities in no fewer than nine different foreign countries. While all these groups wanted to return home, they disagreed fundamentally about the best tactics to achieve this aim.[77] The divisions based on country of origin were exacerbated by differences in religion, social class and political affiliation.[78] A charismatic leader was required to overcome these deep splits among the refugees and expellees. In fact, the *Landrat* of Erding argued in July 1949 that 'a catastrophe is bound to occur when a really capable and gifted personality succeeds in unifying the refugees'[79] and independent observers such as the British academic C. A. Macartney reached the same conclusion.[80] This view is reinforced by Egon Herrmann's initial success in organising hunger strikes in refugee camps in Southern Bavaria, and his support did not begin to erode until it became clear that he was working on behalf of the KPD. To sum up, the absence of outbreaks of mass radicalisation among the refugees was due less to their inherent moderation than to their disunity.

The deep-seated anti-communism of the refugees and expellees was also an important factor in explaining the absence of widespread unrest and radicalism in the early post-war years because they feared that if, in the tense international climate prevailing during the Cold War, they succeeded in bringing down the West German State, it might well be replaced by a communist regime. The refugees' hostility to communism had its roots in long-standing anti-Soviet prejudices, intensified by Nazi propaganda. These preconceptions were reinforced by the traumatic experiences they had suffered during their flight or expulsion from their homelands as the Red Army moved westwards during 1944–45. They blamed the Soviet Union and its communist satellite states in Eastern Europe for the loss of their homes, tending to forget that the actions of Soviet troops and indigenous populations were in response to the atrocities committed by the National Socialists during the Second World War. The arrival in the West from 1946 onwards of refugees fleeing from the SBZ for economic and political reasons reinforced the expellees' hatred of communism.[81] The onset of the Cold War further intensified this antipathy, as is graphically illustrated by events following the outbreak of the Korean War. Refugees living in villages in the Harz mountains and other areas close to the East German border were so fearful of an invasion by East German and Soviet troops that they had their most precious possessions packed in readiness for an evacuation. There was also widespread panic buying and in Bavaria supplies of winter clothes and sugar sold out completely.[82] In fact, anti-communism became an important unifying factor in West German society in the 1950s because the overwhelming majority of both the refugee and native populations identified closely with it, irrespective of their religion, social class or party political loyalties.[83] The fact that refugees and natives alike shared this anti-communist ideology provided a measure of political consensus and, along with growing prosperity, represented the key factor for the gradual development of loyalty to the FRG during the 1950s.

In conclusion, it is clear that the absence of mass radicalisation among the German refugees and expellees can be attributed to a wide range of different factors. While hostility to communism and the improvement in the refugees' material position amid the resurgence in the West German economy were the most important long-term factors, the 'preventative' measures undertaken by the Western Allies and German State Governments in the early post-war years also played an important part in averting widespread unrest in 1948–49. At the same time, the importance of the Federal Government's legislative measures should not be underestimated. While the Equalisation of Burdens Law was the most important piece of legislation in the long term, the Immediate Aid Law was of crucial significance because of its timing. Introduced just before the first *Bundestag* Election, at a time when the economic situation of many refugees had reached a critical level, it gave them renewed hope.

While this book has so far concentrated on the refugee problem in the Western Occupation Zones of Germany/FRG, the final chapter will focus on the refugees and expellees in the SBZ/GDR. Much less attention has been paid to the refugee question in the SBZ/

GDR than in the western part of Germany; in fact, serious research on this topic did not begin until after the unification of Germany in October 1990. However, since that time a number of regional studies and collections of documents have been published, as well as a monumental work by Michael Schwartz focusing on the policy of the authorities in the SBZ/GDR towards the refugees and expellees.[84] Against this background, chapter 7 will examine the refugee problem in the SBZ/GDR in the early post-war years, drawing comparisons and contrasts with the situation in the Western Occupation Zones of Germany. It will also evaluate the policy of the Soviet and East German authorities towards these new population elements.

Notes

1 W. Mücke, *Drei Jahre deutsches Flüchtlingsproblem* (unpublished ms 1948), p.8, in BHStA, MArb 8005a 1752.

2 In his study of Hesse, Rolf Messerschmidt argues that Peter Paul Nahm, who was appointed in August 1946 as the Hesse Government's Special Representative for Refugee Affairs, deliberately overestimated the threat of radicalisation for political purposes. See Messerschmidt, *Aufnahme und Integration*, pp. 139–46. However, this argument is certainly not valid for Bavaria, where the fears of radicalism expressed by the political elites closely reflected the reports they were receiving from local level.

3 Erker, *Vom Heimatvertriebenen zum Neubürger*, p. 64.

4 See for example, BA, NL Jaenicke, Spokesman for Refugees in Brückenau (Lower Franconia) to Jaenicke, 5 August 1948 and BHStA, MArb 822, Spokesman for Refugees in the District Council of Schrobenhausen (Upper Bavaria) to Ehard, 11 September 1948.

5 IfZ, RG 260 OMGUS, 1948/145/5, Van Wagoner (Head of OMGB) to Clay (OMGUS), 7 September 1948.

6 *Süddeutsche Zeitung*, 7 September 1948, in KA, Bayerische Innenpolitik, 1948/22a.

7 B. Melendy, 'Expellees on Strike: Competing Victimization Discourses and the Dachau Refugee Camp Protest Movement, 1948–1949', *German Studies Review*, Vol. 28 (2005), p. 114.

8 PRO, FO 1013/774, Dr Hubert Kehren (Head of the State Refugee Office in North Rhine-Westphalia) to Mr. Young (Headquarters of Manpower Housing of GB Military Government), 12 October 1948.

9 Melendy, 'Expellees on Strike', pp. 118–19.

10 BLA, Hammelburg camp committee to Bavarian State Chancellery, 26 June 1949.

11 For further details, see I. Connor, 'The Bavarian Government and the Refugee Problem 1945–1950', *European History Quarterly* (*EHQ*), Vol. 16(2) (April 1986), pp. 142–3.
12 ADL, FDP Britische Zone, 8, Dr Fritz Oellers to Dr Franz Blücher, 13 September 1948.
13 PRO, FO 1013/368, Matheson (Regional Governmental Officer) to Chief Manpower Officer, 27 September 1948.
14 BA, B125, 11, Noback to Dr Otto Lenz (State Secretary of the Federal Chancellor's Office), 28 January 1953.
15 AdsD, SPD Parteivorstand, 828, undated memorandum by SPD member.
16 For further details, see I. Connor, 'German Refugees and the Bonn Government's Resettlement Programme: The Role of the Trek Association in Schleswig-Holstein, 1951–3', *GH*, Vol. 18(3) (2000), pp. 354–5.
17 *Die Welt*, 30 April 1952, in AdsD, SPD Parteivorstand, 828.
18 This issue was less acute in the French Occupation Zone because it accommodated far fewer refugees. For a study of the refugee problem in one of the *Länder* in the French Occupation Zone, see A. Kühne, *Entstehung, Aufbau und Funktion der Flüchtlingsverwaltung in Württemberg-Hohenzollern 1945–1952: Flüchtlingspolitik im Spannungsfeld deutscher und französischer Interessen* (Sigmaringen 1999).
19 Quoted in S. Schraut, 'Die westlichen Besatzungsmächte und die deutschen Flüchtlinge', in Hoffmann and Schwartz (eds), *Geglückte Integration?*, p. 35.
20 BHStA, MArb, II/3a, 1857/II, General Morale Report from Josef Lindemann (External Commissioner), 12 February 1946.
21 BA, Z18, 24, *Tätigkeitsbericht des Hauptausschusses der Flüchtlinge und Ausgewiesenen in Bayern, 1947* (Munich 1947), p. 3.
22 This proposal originated from a meeting of leading German politicians in the British Occupation Zone held in Oldenburg on 25 January 1946. See J.-D. Steinert, 'Organisierte Flüchtlingsinteressen und parlamentarische Demokratie: Westdeutschland 1945–1949', in Bade (ed.), *Neue Heimat im Westen*, p. 66.
23 IfZ, RG 260 OMGUS, 3/175–3/15, Clay to OMGB, 9 July 1946.
24 Quoted in Grosser, 'Das Assimilationskonzept der amerikanischen Flüchtlingspolitik', p. 23.
25 For further details, see Rogers, *Politics after Hitler*, p. 110.
26 IfZ, RG 260 OMGUS, 3/175–3/15, Clay to OMGB, 9 July 1946.
27 Schraut, 'Die westlichen Besatzungsmächte', pp. 41–4.
28 Haerendel, 'Die Politik der "Eingliederung"', p. 113.
29 Brosius, 'Zur Lage der Flüchtlinge im Regierungsbezirk Lüneburg', p. 14.
30 For example, the local Military Governor was in attendance when

Herrmann delivered a speech to some 800 refugees in Weiden (Upper Palatinate) on 27 March 1949. See *Der Neue Tag*, 31 March 1949, in KA, Innenpolitik 1949/50.

31 IfZ, RG 260 OMGUS, 7/34–1/6, Donald T. Shea (Director of Intelligence Division of OMGB) to Director of Intelligence (OMGUS), 9 August 1949.

32 ADL, FDP Britische Zone, 8, Dr Fritz Oellers to Franz Blücher, 13 September 1948.

33 LSH, Abt. 761, 4524, Bruns (Representative of the Scheswig-Holstein Government for Resettlement Projects in Württemberg-Baden, Hesse and Rhineland-Palatinate) to Ministry of Labour in Kiel, 7 March 1952.

34 A. Noback, *Initiative von unten: Geschichte der Treck-Bewegung* (unpublished ms, 1959), p. 31, in BA, B125, 5.

35 BLA, Committee for Refugee Questions, Minutes of Meeting of 20 September 1948, p. 37.

36 *Ibid.*, p. 30.

37 IfZ, RG 260 OMGUS, 1948/145/5, Murray van Wagoner (Land Director of OMBG) to Clay, 7 September 1948 and BLA, Committee for Refugee Questions, Minutes of Meeting of 9 November 1948, pp. 11–12.

38 E. Pscheidt, 'Die Flüchtlingslager', in Prinz (ed.), *Integration und Neubeginn*, Vol. 1, pp. 267–8.

39 BA, B150, 6551B, Final Report of the Federal Commissioners for Resettlement, 11 August 1953, p. 1.

40 BA, B125, 9, Press Release by the Federal Government Press and Information Office, 30 January 1952.

41 BA, B125, 10, Summary of the discussions between Lukaschek and the trek leaders on 25 and 26 April 1952.

42 Bauer, 'Zwischen "Wunder" und Strukturzwang', p. 31.

43 Nahm, ... *doch das Leben ging weiter*, p. 115.

44 Haerendel, 'Die Politik der "Eingliederung"', pp. 132–3.

45 R. Schillinger, *Der Entscheidungsprozess beim Lastenausgleich 1945–1952* (St Katharinen 1985), p. 144.

46 BHStA, MInn 80303, Headquarters of the Bavarian Rural Police to the Bavarian Minister of the Interior, 14 June 1952. The report on the security situation in May 1952 noted the concern of some refugees 'that they would come away empty handed [in the Equalisation of Burdens Law] just as they had done with regard to household goods under the Immediate Aid Law'. See also Erker, *Vom Heimatvertriebenen zum Neubürger*, pp. 67–72.

47 StA, LRA 57249, Monthly Report of *Landrat* of Rosenheim to Government of Upper Bavaria, October 1949.

48 StA, LRA 134069, Monthly Report of *Landrat* of Bad Tölz to Government of Upper Bavaria, November 1949.

49 For example, the *Landrat* of Erding observed that the payments resulting from the Immediate Aid Law were 'in many instances able to relieve severe distress'. See LRA Erding, File 16/4, Monthly Report of *Landrat* to the Government of Upper Bavaria, November 1949.
50 Schillinger, *Der Entscheidungsprozess*, p.144.
51 *Ibid.*, p. 288.
52 *Ibid.*, p. 289.
53 Erker, *Vom Heimatvertriebenen zum Neubürger*, p.73.
54 Quoted in Schulze, 'The Struggle of Past and Present', p. 40.
55 Calculated from Neumann, *Der Block der Heimatvertriebenen und Entrechteten*, p. 7.
56 BA, Z18, 116, *Die kirchliche Betreuung der ausgewiesenen Volksgruppen*, p. 1.
57 EZA, 2/210, Report compiled by EHW entitled, 'Relief Work in Germany', August 1947, p. 2.
58 DCV, 374.025, Fasz. 1, *Flüchtlingsfürsorge der Caritas in Bayern nach dem Stande vom 1. Januar 1947*, compiled by DCV Munich, 1 March 1947.
59 ADW, ZB, 914, Collmer to Maurer, 14 February 1952.
60 ADW, ZB, 914, Collmer to Maurer, 12 April 1952.
61 Noback, *Initiative von unten*, p. 25.
62 ADW, ZB, 903, Minutes of a meeting of the Ecclesiastical Resettlement Office, 15–16 October 1953.
63 BA, B125, 10, Alf Kroll to Noback, 13 August 1952.
64 J. Isaac, 'German Refugees in the U.S. Zone 1948/1949', p. 11, in IfZ, RG 260 OMGUS, 3/165 – 1/15.
65 See pp. 102, 110, 119.
66 BSL (ed.), *Die Vertriebenen in Bayern*, p. 42.
67 *Ibid.*, pp. 14, 30.
68 For example, the Mayor of a parish in the Rural District of Altötting (Upper Bavaria) reported that, although the communist putsch in Czechoslovakia had led to a deterioration in the mood of the indigenous inhabitants, 'the refugees hope ... that it will enable them to return home sooner'. See StA, LRA 65849, Weekly Report of the Mayor of Reischach to the Police in Altötting, 15 March 1948. Similarly, the refugee spokesman in the parish of Dorfen (Rural District of Erding, Upper Bavaria) warned that 'very many [refugees] – and there are a number of educated people among them – want another war'. See BHStA, MArb 822, Refugee spokesman of Dorfen to Erding District Commissioner for Refugee Affairs, 4 August 1948. Helmut Grieser also found evidence of the same attitude among refugees in Kiel. See Grieser, *Die ausgebliebene Radikalisierung*, p. 166.
69 See for example, a memorandum produced by the Catholic *Kirchliche Hilfsstelle* which asserted that 'the Homeland Societies are endangered

by right-wing radicalism which ... in certain circumstances might form a tactical alliance with Moscow in order to win back their lost homeland'. See BA, Z18, *Um die Zukunft der kirchlichen Volksgruppenarbeit in München*, nd, p. 2.

70 Haerendel, 'Die Politik der "Eingliederung"', p. 119.

71 Buscher, 'The Great Fear', p. 219.

72 This argument is put forward by Ahonen, *After the Expulsion*, p. 271. See also Neumann, *Der Block der Heimatvertriebenen und Entrechteten*, p. 12.

73 www.pommersche-landmannschaft.de/body_charta.htm (accessed 9 May 2005).

74 See for example, BA, B125, 9, Brenske and Hanner (Treck-Vereiningung Landesverband Bayern) to Noback (Treck-Vereiningung Schleswig-Holstein), 12 March 1952 and Noback to Brenske and Hanner, 17 March 1952.

75 LRA Erding, File 16/4, Monthly Report of *Landrat* to the Government of Upper Bavaria, July 1949.

76 C. Kleßmann, *Die doppelte Staatsgründung: Deutsche Geschichte 1945–1955* (Göttingen 1982), p. 243.

77 J. Carey, 'Political Organization of the Refugees and Expellees in West Germany', *Political Science Quarterly* (*PSQ*), Vol. 66 (1951), p. 194.

78 See for example, Stadtarchiv München (StD), Flüchtlingsamt Nr. 7: Flüchtlingswesen, *Auszug aus dem Ost-West Kurier*, 4 February 1951. This article, based on a conversation with a refugee spokesman, concluded that the expellees in Munich were 'torn apart and divided in parties, denominations, homeland societies and other smaller interest groups'.

79 LRA Erding, File 16/4, Monthly Report of *Landrat* to the Government of Upper Bavaria, July 1949.

80 GStA, MA 130674, Macartney, *Das Flüchtlingsproblem in der amerikanischen Zone Deutschlands*.

81 For a detailed study of the motives of refugees and expellees from the GDR, see Ackermann, *Der "echte" Flüchtling*.

82 BA, NL Schlange-Schöningen, 11, unpublished essay by Schlange-Schöningen, nd but from the context it was probably written in the autumn of 1950.

83 For a fuller discussion of this issue, see Major, *The Death of the KPD*, pp. 257–9.

84 Schwartz, *Vertriebene und "Umsiedlerpolitik"*.

7

Refugees in the Soviet Occupation Zone/German Democratic Republic

Introduction

While chapter 2 examined the enormous difficulties resulting from the influx of almost 7.9 million refugees and expellees into the Western Occupation Zones of Germany, the problems facing the German and Allied authorities in the SBZ were in some respects even more formidable. According to the provisional census carried out in December 1945, some 2.5 million refugees were located in the SBZ[1] and by April 1949 the figure exceeded 4.3 million (see Table 7.1). At that time, refugees and expellees comprised 24.2 per cent of the population in the SBZ, well above the figure of 15.8 per cent in the Western Occupation Zones of Germany.[2] The SBZ was hardest hit by the refugee influx as a result of its geographical position. In fact, three of its five states – Saxony, Brandenburg and Mecklenburg-West Pomerania – directly bordered the eastern territories from which millions of Germans fled or were expelled. While many of these refugees and expellees were in transit to the Western Occupation Zones of Germany, a large number settled in the SBZ. According to the census of 1946, the most numerous groups of *Reichsdeutsche* in the SBZ were the Silesians (1,048,678), East Prussians (490,710), Pomeranians (504,471) and East Brandenburgers (229,611), while the Sudeten Germans (840,843) were by far the largest group of *Volksdeutsche*.[3]

The Soviet authorities were simply overwhelmed by this huge flood of refugees and expellees and it was not until July 1945 that the Soviet Military Administration in Germany (*Sowjetische Militäradministration in Deutschland*, SMAD) attempted to instil some order into the chaos which prevailed. On 19 July Marshal Schukow instructed that the *Reichsdeutsche* should be directed to Mecklenburg and the eastern parts of Brandenburg, while the

Sudeten Germans were to be located in the area which in 1947 became the state of Saxony-Anhalt.[4] Saxony was not to receive any more expellees in recognition of its acute housing shortage, a decision which remained in force until March 1946.[5] However, the Saxon Government took this as a pretext to transport to other states a large number of the refugees already residing within its borders.[6] It was not until the establishment in September 1945 of the Central Agency for German Resettlers (*Zentralverwaltung für deutsche Umsiedler*, ZVU) that the German authorities began to come to terms with the expellee problem. Reception camps were set up where the expellees were registered and given a medical examination. By the beginning of 1946 more than 350 of these camps were in operation[7] but the conditions were invariably deplorable. Most refugees spent several weeks in a reception camp before being sent to a more permanent place of residence.

The distribution of these new population elements among the states in the SBZ was very uneven. As Table 7.1 shows, Mecklenburg-West Pomerania bore the brunt of the expellee influx, while in Saxony resettlers comprised a modest 17.2 per cent of the inhabitants in the spring of 1949. As in the Western Occupation Zones, these wide variations can be attributed primarily to the availability of housing for the newcomers. In Saxony, the most industrialised state, the housing shortage was particularly acute since its towns and cities had suffered heavy bombing. On the other hand, the state of Mecklenburg-West Pomerania was predominantly agricultural,

Table 7.1 Refugees in the SBZ, 19 April 1949

State	*Total population*	*Total refugees*	*% of refugees in population*
Brandenburg	2,646,991	655,466	24.8
Mecklenburg–West Pomerania	2,126,790	922,088	43.3
Saxony	5,798,990	997,798	17.2
Saxony-Anhalt	4,303,441	1,051,024	24.4
Thuringia	2,988,288	685,913	23.0
Totals	17,864,500	4,312,289	24.1

Source: Adapted from Bundesarchiv Berlin (BArch), DO 2/49, p. 146. Reproduced in Wille, 'Compelling the Assimilation', p. 266.

recorded a food surplus in the pre-war years and was the most sparsely populated state in the SBZ.[8] Yet even within the individual states the scale of the refugee influx varied enormously; as a rule, the border regions were worst affected as the expellees gathered in large numbers in the expectation that they would soon be able to return to their former homelands.[9] The point to emphasise, however, is that the expellee problem in the SBZ, as in the Western Occupation Zones, was essentially a rural phenomenon and in 1949, 47 per cent of the expellees were still located in villages with a population of fewer than 2,000.[10]

Brief reference should be made to the issue of terminology. As noted in chapter 2, the wartime Allies did not employ uniform nomenclature in describing the Germans who fled or were expelled into Germany in 1944–45 from their homelands in Eastern and Central Europe. Political considerations influenced the choice of terminology. In particular, the Soviet Union vigorously rejected the term 'expellee' because it implied that the Germans from the East had been forcefully removed from their homes by or with the encouragement of Soviet troops. The Soviet authorities therefore euphemistically referred to the refugees and expellees who flooded into their Occupation Zone as 'resettlers' and, as seen above, the refugee administration they created in September 1945 was called the 'Central Agency for German Resettlers'. The term 'resettlers' was also intended to underline to these new population groups that they had been directed to the SBZ as part of a planned and legal resettlement process and there was no possibility of them being allowed to return home.[11]

The economic position of the refugees

Loss of personal belongings

One of the most pressing problems for the expellees after their arrival in the SBZ was their lack of material possessions. While the amount of luggage they had been permitted to bring varied, many had been able to retrieve only their most cherished personal belongings. The expellees' predicament was epitomised by a report from a parish in the District of Dippoldiswalde (Saxony) in November 1947: 'The economic situation of the new arrivals is catastrophic. There is a shortage of clothing, shoes and, above all, household goods. (Many families do not have a saucepan.)'[12]

The SED took a number of measures to overcome this problem, but with little success. The State Government of Thuringia introduced a law in November 1946 which allowed for the confiscation of unused household equipment for the benefit of 'newcomers and bomb victims'. While this operated effectively in some places, there were others such as the town of Jena where it was not enforced.[13] Efforts to increase furniture production to supply needy refugees were thwarted by a shortage of wood and tools, as well as the demands of SMAD.[14] From 1946 onwards the SED also made regular appeals to the indigenous inhabitants to donate to the refugees items of clothing and furniture they did not need, arguing that 'the whole of the German people were responsible for the war'.[15] In 1948, 'resettler-weeks' were held throughout the SBZ during which collections were made on behalf of the new population groups. However, the results were extremely disappointing. For example, in Saxony, a state of some 5.8 million people, just 15,842 pieces of furniture and 32,438 pairs of shoes were donated.[16] The poor response was partly due to 'collection fatigue' since the National Socialists had made frequent appeals for donations for the wartime evacuees.[17] The success of the 'resettler-weeks' was also undermined by the SED's decision to restrict the role played by ecclesiastical welfare organisations.[18] As a result, the refugees and expellees still lacked many essential items of daily life some three years after their arrival in the SBZ. According to figures produced by the ZVU, some 696,000 beds, 242,000 tables, 846,000 chairs, 272,000 kitchen cupboards and 334,000 wardrobes were still needed in March 1948.[19] Even though production of these items increased after the Currency Reform introduced in June 1948, most resettlers could not afford to buy them. The much vaunted Resettler Law of September 1950 which provided for expellees to receive an interest-free loan of 1,000 marks to purchase furniture and other household goods promised more than it delivered. Deluged with far more applications than it had expected, the SED introduced restrictions in December 1950 on those resettlers who could apply for credit and even then the funds proved insufficient to meet the demand.[20]

Food

The refugees and expellees in the SBZ were also affected more severely than the indigenous inhabitants by the post-war food shortage. Although official statistics indicate that the food situation in the SBZ in mid-1946 was better than in either the British or French Occupation Zone,[21] the average calorie intake of the population totalled only 55 per cent of the figure in 1936.[22] The Soviet authorities retained the system of food rationing which had operated during the war and consumers were divided into six different categories. Workers undertaking hard manual labour received the most generous rations and, as a result, refugees were willing to work in the uranium mines in the *Erzgebirge* from 1948 onwards.[23] At the other end of the scale, pensioners, housewives and the unemployed had to survive on very low daily rations which in Leipzig amounted to just 200g of bread, 300g of potatoes, 15g of sugar and 7g of cereals in November 1945.[24] Generally speaking, the food crisis was less acute in the countryside than in urban areas and the prospect of supplementing their food supplies prompted many resettlers to work on the land in the early post-war years. In fact, they made up no fewer than 40.7 per cent of agricultural labourers in the SBZ in April 1946, well above their proportion of the population.[25]

On the other hand, refugees and expellees in the towns and cities were hit with particular severity by the food shortage. Soup kitchens were opened in Neubrandenburg in the autumn of 1945 to provide resettlers with a daily hot meal,[26] while in Rostock provision was made for them to purchase hot soup in local restaurants at a price of 30 or 60 pfennigs.[27] However, the situation remained acute and in Neubrandenburg the soup kitchens had to be closed in March 1946 due to the shortage of food. In urban areas the refugees were especially prone to malnutrition and hunger because, in contrast to the native inhabitants, they lacked the 'connections' required to participate in the thriving black market and had few possessions they could barter for food. In desperation, many made trips into the countryside to beg or forage for food and reports from the town of Görlitz in the summer of 1945 referred to the 'constant flood of people from dawn until dusk heading for the surrounding villages, sometimes more than 30 kilometres away, in order to obtain potatoes'.[28]

Some of the causes of the food shortage in the SBZ have been discussed in detail in chapter two since they also affected the Western Occupation Zones of Germany. The influx of resettlers and loss of the eastern territories to Poland and the Soviet Union in the post-war territorial settlement were important factors, as well as a succession of poor harvests in the early post-war years. The fruit harvest in the SBZ in 1946 yielded only half that of 1938,[29] while the harvest in 1947 produced little more than half the projected amount in some parts of Saxony.[30] In addition, damage to the transportation system disrupted the distribution of food from the countryside to the towns. A further problem was that many farmers in the SBZ, as in the Western Occupation Zones, sold some of their produce on the black market.[31]

However, there were other factors which contributed significantly to the food crisis in the SBZ. War damage reduced the quantity of land available for cultivation. While agricultural land in Saxony and Thuringia remained largely untouched by the war, the eastern areas of Brandenburg – especially around Berlin – and parts of Mecklenburg suffered heavy damage.[32] The shortage of livestock was a major problem. In comparison to 1938, the number of cattle had fallen by 38 per cent, chickens by 48 per cent, sheep by 56.4 per cent and pigs by 72.9 per cent.[33] This was partly due to war damage, especially in the northern and eastern areas of the SBZ; in addition, the flight of farmers to the West as Soviet troops advanced in 1944–45 depleted supplies of livestock since they invariably took their animals with them.[34] Soviet troops exacerbated the problem by confiscating large numbers of cattle and horses, especially from Mecklenburg-West Pomerania.[35] They also removed agricultural machinery and fertilisers as reparations.[36] Soviet policy worsened the food shortage in several other respects. In particular, the decision to expropriate the Junkers and large estate owners and divide up their land among resettlers and native agricultural labourers led to a fall in food production. To sum up, the post-war food shortage in the SBZ was not a short-term phenomenon. The situation did not improve significantly until the autumn of 1948 and even then less quickly than in the Western Occupation Zones.[37]

Housing

The need to provide adequate housing for the expellees was one of the most pressing problems facing the Soviet authorities in Germany after the Second World War. However, the prerequisites could scarcely have been less favourable. As Karl Christian Führer has argued, Germany's housing shortage, which dated from the First World War, had represented 'one of the major social problems of the Third Reich'[38] and this shortfall was exacerbated by the Allied wartime bombing of urban and industrial centres such as Dresden,

Chemnitz, Plauen and Leipzig. In Leipzig, for example, 54.8 per cent of the pre-war housing had been damaged or totally destroyed.[39] Some rural areas which were the scene of heavy fighting as Soviet troops advanced at the end of the war also suffered severe damage. One of the worst affected was the Rural District of Lebus (Brandenburg), where 32 per cent of the housing stock was totally destroyed and a further 39.7 partly damaged.[40] However, it should be borne in mind that, as a rule, the impact of wartime bombing was less severe in the SBZ than the Western Occupation Zones. While 17.6 per cent of housing in the American Occupation Zone was totally destroyed and 27.2 per cent in the British Occupation Zone,[41] the figure in the SBZ totalled only 10 per cent.[42]

In the SBZ, as in the Western Occupation Zones, it was the housing issue which dictated that the resettler problem was in essence a rural phenomenon. Country districts had generally suffered much less wartime damage than urban areas and were therefore better equipped to provide accommodation for the refugees and expellees. The underlying maxim of Soviet housing policy was that the resettlers should not be accommodated in camps except as a short-term emergency measure.[43] On the contrary, they were to be billeted with private householders, a principle reinforced by the Housing Law issued by the Allied Control Council in March 1946. The effectiveness of this policy depended on the impartiality and moral courage of the native elites at local level whose task was to assign expellees to indigenous householders. However, in small rural parishes, the mayor, determined to protect the interests of his own community,

Table 7.2 'Living space' of SBZ population (m^2), 31 March 1949

State	*Native population*	*Expellees*
Brandenburg	10.5	4.6
Mecklenburg–West Pomerania	10.7	3.9
Saxony	9.2	5.6
Saxony-Anhalt	9.5	6.2
Thuringia	10.9	5.7
SBZ	10.2	5.2

Source: BArch, DO 2/49, p.153. Reproduced in Wille, 'Compelling the Assimilation ', p. 273.

tended to ignore or only half-heartedly implement the instructions of his superiors. While the SED required local officials to identify homes with space to accommodate expellees, a survey carried out in Brandenburg revealed that just 25,000 of the state's 600,000 houses had been inspected by 1948.[44]

As Table 7.2 shows, wide regional variations in expellee housing existed. Overcrowding among resettlers was most acute in the predominantly rural state of Mecklenburg-West Pomerania, where the discrepancy between the amount of 'living space' enjoyed by the native and expellee populations was also more pronounced than elsewhere. But even in Saxony-Anhalt, the state with the best record for expellee housing, there were examples of resettlers having to endure extremely cramped living conditions as late as August 1949. In fact, in the Rural District of Jerichow I, no fewer than 115 refugee families with five or more members had just one room at their disposal.[45] Expellees accommodated on farms often had to endure particularly squalid conditions. Many lived for several years in attics, stables or farm outbuildings which had never been intended to serve as anything other than temporary emergency accommodation. In fact, an investigation ordered by the Soviet Control Commission in 1950 into expellee housing in Mecklenburg-West Pomerania revealed that more than 4,600 resettlers were living in 'barns, stables and halls'.[46]

Housing conditions in towns and cities in the SBZ were also often deplorable in the early post-war years. Empirical surveys revealed that the majority of expellees lived in cramped conditions, while reports and complaints to housing officials highlighted particularly bad examples of overcrowding. In September 1949, a representative of the Public Health Office in Leipzig referred to expellee families where 'the parents and three grown-up daughters sleep together in one room, which also serves as their living quarters and kitchen'.[47] The vast majority of resettlers living in urban areas were billeted with members of the indigenous inhabitants. For example, in Chemnitz (Saxony), 81 per cent of expellees were subtenants and in the nearby small town of Glauchau the figure was even higher.[48] Relations with the native householder were often tense and most resettlers longed to rent their own flat, however modest it might be, because it would give them independence. However, many did not achieve this goal until the 1960s.[49]

The only lasting solution to the housing shortage was to construct new dwellings but practically no progress was made in the early post-war years. In fact, a report drawn up in mid-1947 by the ZVU admitted that 'the only housing units that have been built are in the imagination of our statisticians'.[50] Construction work was severely hampered by the scarcity of building materials, a problem which was exacerbated by the Soviet decision to dismantle cement and glass factories, as well as brickworks.[51] It should also be pointed out that, at a time of general financial stringency, the SED did not regard house building as a priority, except for farmers who received plots as a result of the Land Reform. Another key factor was that, unlike the Western Occupation Zones of Germany, the SBZ did not benefit from Marshall Aid monies. This contributed to the huge discrepancy in housing construction in 1949; as many as 185,000 new dwellings were built in FRG, while the corresponding figure in the GDR was just 15,320.[52]

Despite the misgivings of the Soviet authorities, refugee camps were set up at the outset of the Occupation in the expectation that their inmates would soon be able to return to their homelands. Some of these camps were former military establishments while others had served as forced labour camps during the Third Reich. While the existence of the camps was, generally speaking, as a result of the housing shortage, local officials sometimes established them in order to protect the native inhabitants from having to share their homes with the resettlers.[53] SMAD ordered that the camps should be closed down as soon as possible and official statistics would suggest that it achieved a high measure of success. However, such claims must be viewed with caution since local and State officials often disguised the true picture. For example, according to the Government in Mecklenburg-West Pomerania, only 4,500 resettlers were still resident in camps in July 1947.[54] However, this figure referred only to the refugees in reception camps; the housing camps were omitted because they had been taken over by the local authorities or administered by the factory or firm which employed the expellees. There is also evidence that local officials falsified the statistics by re-designating refugee camps as 'apartment complexes'.[55] It also emerged that the statisticians who undertook the first national survey of expellee housing in April 1950 'forgot' to include a number of refugee camps. However, even though the survey's finding that only 43,085 resettlers in the GDR were living in camps represented an underestimate,[56] the real figure was nonetheless well below the

306,000 refugees residing in camps or other forms of mass accommodation in the FRG in September 1950.[57]

It is clear, then, that many expellees continued to live in overcrowded, squalid conditions in the early 1950s. In Mecklenburg-West Pomerania, some 10,000 expellees were still residing in camps in 1951.[58] An inspection carried out in rural districts of Saxony in 1952 concluded that a significant disparity was beginning to emerge between different social groups and drew particular attention to the deplorable conditions in which elderly people and single mothers were living.[59] The 1950s and 1960s witnessed a gradual, though sporadic, improvement in expellee housing, but this occurred despite rather than because of the SED's housing policy. It allowed much of the existing housing stock to stagnate and afforded less priority to house construction than industrial growth.[60] As a result, just 504,953 new flats were built in the GDR between 1950 and 1961.[61] This amounted to just 8.8 per cent of the dwellings constructed in West Germany (5,763,020) during the same period.[62] Yet the housing situation nonetheless improved because the exodus of 2.6 million GDR citizens to West Germany in the period 1949–61 relieved the pressure on accommodation for those who remained.[63]

Employment

The integration of the refugees into the labour market in the SBZ was also beset with difficulties. At first sight their employment prospects appeared promising since the number of indigenous males registered for work in October 1946 was 1.8 million lower than in 1939.[64] However, despite the availability of jobs, just 1.4 million of the 3.6 million expellees living in the GDR in October 1946 were gainfully employed.[65] In terms of occupational structure, no fewer than 43.8 per cent of expellees in work in April 1947 had found employment in agriculture or forestry, mostly as agricultural labourers.[66] Expellees were also overrepresented in the civil service where they replaced native civil servants or employees who had lost their jobs because of their connections with the Nazis.[67] In fact, almost a third of teachers in the GDR in 1950 were expellees, well above their proportion of the population.[68] On the other hand, the expellees were at first underrepresented among industrial workers and in April 1947 just 2.5 per cent of them worked as coal miners or in the steel industry.[69] Similarly, the number of refugee craftsmen was very small and even the Sudeten Germans from Gablonz who already enjoyed a world-wide reputation for jewellery and glass making encountered enormous difficulties in re-establishing themselves in Saxony-Anhalt and Thuringia.[70]

As the Occupation progressed, the expellees' employment situation deteriorated. In April 1949 the number of gainfully employed expellees remained static at 1.4 million in spite of the influx of some 700,000 new arrivals since October 1946.[71] While this can be partly attributed to the flight of expellees to the West, it also reflected a sharp rise in refugee unemployment because of increased competition from returning prisoners-of-war and the negative effects of the Currency Reform. In Saxony, for example, 26.8 per cent of the expellees registered for work were unemployed in December 1947, and by March 1949 this figure had risen to 35.9 per cent.[72] Moreover, even expellees who succeeded in finding work often accepted a job for which they had not been trained.[73]

How can we explain the difficulties in integrating the expellees into the labour market? A fundamental problem was that many of them were not available for employment. In fact, just 41.6 per cent of the refugees in the SBZ were fit to work in December 1946, as opposed to 60.1 per cent among the native inhabitants.[74] The small number of male expellees in the 21–49 age group was particularly striking. On the other hand, the expellees who arrived in the SBZ included a higher proportion of women than in any of the states in the Western Occupation Zones except Schleswig-Holstein.[75] In fact, 507,000 of the 714,000 expellees recorded as unemployed in April 1949 were women who were in many cases unable to accept work because they were looking after small children or lacked the necessary qualifications.[76]

The failure of many refugees to obtain employment commensurate with their training and qualifications was mainly a result of the inability of the Soviet authorities to distribute them according to their occupational structure. In the SBZ, as in the Western Occupation Zones, the refugees and expellees were directed to rural areas because of the acute housing shortage in the towns and cities. While the ship building yards in Rostock and Wismar (Mecklenburg-West Pomerania), as well as Saxony's textile mills and its uranium and coal mining industries experienced serious labour shortages in the early post-war years, expellee shipbuilders and miners were working as agricultural labourers in the countryside.[77] At the same time, the random distribution of the refugees meant that the majority of those located in the industrial city of Leipzig had worked in agriculture prior to their flight or expulsion.[78] Efforts by the Soviet authorities to resettle the expellees enjoyed only limited success. The widespread protests at the forced resettlement of 2,000 people from the port of Wismar to make way for badly needed expellee ship builders from Stettin deterred SMAD from repeating this experiment.[79] Instead it tried to overcome the housing shortage in urban areas by giving up military establishments to accommodate key expellee workers and authorising the conversion of housing camps located on the outskirts of naval towns to 'workers' dwellings'.[80] But efforts to resettle the expellees were often thwarted by disagreements between the ZVU and other government agencies, as well as the reluctance of the expellees themselves to move away from villages or hamlets which at least provided adequate food provisions.[81]

The economic policies of the Soviet Union towards its occupation zone exacerbated the difficulties the expellees encountered on the labour market. While economic recovery in the Western Occupation Zones was stimulated by Marshall Aid monies from mid-1948 onwards, post-war reconstruction in the SBZ was severely hampered by the Soviet Union's exploitation of its economic resources. In fact, Norman Naimark has estimated that the removal of industrial plant and machinery, agricultural equipment and raw materials by the Soviet authorities after the Second World War amounted to approximately a third of the SBZ's 'productive capacity of industry'.[82] The Soviet Union also extracted 3.3 billion marks worth of goods from current production in the SBZ in 1946, almost 60 per cent of the total value.[83] In addition, the Soviet policy of concentrating scarce economic resources on the 'new farmer' programme had a harsh impact on industrial concerns and, in particular, the new private commercial undertakings established by the expellees. The requirement under SMAD Order 209, announced on 9 September 1947, to construct 37,000 houses for new farmers by the end of the following year exhausted practically all the funds set aside for house construction and, as a result, building projects in the towns and cities were delayed or abandoned.[84] This policy was not reversed until 1949–50.

Refugee craftsmen experienced particular difficulties in re-establishing themselves in the SBZ. They often suffered discrimination from the local Chambers of Crafts (*Handwerkskammern*), organisations dominated by local craftsmen who feared the competition the newcomers would provide.[85] A further issue was the refusal of the authorities in the SBZ to recognise the qualifications gained by Ethnic Germans, while in Saxony-Anhalt even National Germans who were able to provide evidence of their qualifications had to re-sit the examinations.[86] A more fundamental problem was the SED's growing opposition to private industry and this influenced its refusal to provide much-needed credit for independent expellee craftsmen and other commercial enterprises in the precarious financial climate after the Currency Reform. As a result, many expellee businesses collapsed and in Saxony-Anhalt almost half of the independent expellee craftsmen operating in September 1948 had lost their livelihood by March 1949.[87]

In the GDR, as in the FRG, the 1950s witnessed a population exodus from the countryside into the towns and cities. This was particularly true of the resettlers, who displayed greater flexibility and mobility than their native counterparts. By 1952 almost 500,000 resettlers were working in the industrial sector as opposed to just 250,000 in agriculture.[88] Industrial firms such as the Wismut uranium mining company recruited large numbers of expellees who in some pits comprised up to 80 per cent of the work force.[89] The other major influence on expellee employment patterns in the 1950s was the continuing exodus of GDR citizens to West Germany. Expellees themselves were significantly overrepresented among those who fled, comprising 34.5 per cent of 'GDR refugees' in 1950 and 32.7 per cent in 1951, well above their proportion of the population.[90] While this development helped to reduce expellee unemployment in some areas, it also had negative long-term consequences since many of those who left were skilled workers or young people who would have promoted economic reconstruction. Nevertheless, the GDR economy expanded during the 1950s and young expellees enjoyed good job prospects in the steel, chemical and coal mining industries, while their older counterparts only rarely reached the very top of their profession, mainly because of their often uneasy relationship with the SED.[91]

Relations between the refugee and native populations

Relatively little research has so far been undertaken on refugee–native relations in the SBZ but initial studies suggest that there were striking similarities with the situation in the Western Occupation

Zones. It is clear, for example, that in the SBZ, as in the British and American Occupation Zones, the refugees encountered less hostility in urban than rural areas. A spokesman for the provincial administration in Brandenburg noted in 1946 that 'in the cities, assimilation into the indigenous population [has occurred] considerably faster than in the countryside'[92] and research conducted in the early 1950s indicated that this conclusion was also valid for other parts of the SBZ/GDR.[93] It should be stressed, however, that even in towns and cities the native inhabitants sometimes adopted a negative attitude to the expellees. According to a report from the industrial centre of Zwickau (Saxony) in 1947, the majority of the indigenous population had little sympathy for the plight of the refugees,[94] while similar observations were made in the industrial area of Bitterfeld.[95] On the other hand, expellees assigned to rural districts invariably experienced an even more unfriendly reception from the local people. For example, Ute Schmidt's empirical study of the integration of Bessarabian Germans in rural Mecklenburg concluded that 'the relationship between the natives and immigrants was initially extremely tense'.[96] This was particularly true of parishes with a large Sorb[97] population and there were reports of refugees who arrived in these villages being pelted with stones.[98]

The conflict between the indigenous and expellee populations was a source of deep concern to the Occupying forces[99] who repeatedly had to remind the German State and Local Governments of their obligations towards the refugees.[100] In fact, SMAD introduced harsh penalties in an attempt to eradicate discrimination against these new population groups. While the ZVU claimed that this helped to bring about an improvement in expellee–native relations, a survey conducted in a number of parishes in Brandenburg in April 1947 revealed that the situation had deteriorated significantly since December 1946.[101] In fact, the Soviet Military Administration in Brandenburg issued a directive in March 1947 criticising the 'inadequate efforts to counteract the resentful mood of the indigenous inhabitants towards the resettlers'.[102] The indifferent or even hostile attitude of the native population to the expellees was also reflected in its often lukewarm response to the SED's appeals for donations to help the expellees and during the so-called 'resettler-weeks' in 1948 the 2.3 million indigenous inhabitants of Thuringia contributed the grand total of '110 pairs of shoes, 132 saucepans and 10 big cookers'.[103]

In the SBZ, as in the Western Occupation Zones of Germany, the indigenous political elites at local level often practised discrimination against the refugees and expellees. The failure of the Land Reform to meet the expectations of expellee farmers was due partly to the failure of indigenous land commissioners to treat them equitably in the distribution of land, agricultural machinery and livestock.[104] Similarly, the discriminatory practices of local housing officials provoked great resentment among the expellees and contributed to their poor relations with the native population.

While there were many underlying causes of the tense relations between the native and expellee populations, most of the conflicts which developed were of an economic nature. Housing proved to be the most explosive issue. Native householders deeply resented having to share their homes with impoverished expellees and some newcomers required the assistance of the police to gain access to their lodgings. One lady urged the expellees assigned to her 'to go back to where you came from, you Polish pigs', adding, 'if the Poles had killed you, I would still have my home'.[105] An analysis of the expellees' complaints in 1946–47 about their housing situation in the industrial town of Werdau (Saxony) provides an excellent insight into the type of issues which arose. It concluded that 'the communal use of the kitchen and bathroom or toilet frequently caused friction'[106] and there were also disputes about gas, electricity and water bills. Some indigenous householders denied 'their' expellees access to furniture or refused to give them a key to the washroom or cellar. Rent levels also proved to be a common source of acrimony and in her study of Thuringia Steffi Kaltenborn found evidence of native householders grossly overcharging the expellees with whom they shared their homes.[107] High rents were a particularly divisive issue in areas heavily dependent on tourism. For example, the influx of expellees on the island of Rügen forced the local authorities to accommodate some of them in hotels and guest houses in the seaside resorts of Sellin and Binz. The resulting fall in the number of available beds for visitors led to a slump in the tourist trade. Faced with the possible collapse of their livelihood, hoteliers retaliated by raising rents to levels far beyond what the expellees could afford.[108]

Farmers in the SBZ, as in the Western Occupation Zones, invariably adopted a hostile attitude towards the refugees and expellees. Initially they viewed the newcomers as a potential asset who would replace prisoners-of-war who had not yet been released and the forced labourers on whom they had relied during the war. However, problems soon developed. The farmers expected the expellees to work for board and lodging while some of the expellees demanded financial remuneration as well.[109] A further issue from the farmers' perspective was that 'the expellees did not disappear when harvest time was over and they were no longer needed'.[110] Kaltenborn's study of Thuringia concluded that the large, wealthy landowners who had emerged largely unscathed from the war invariably displayed scant sympathy for the expellees. In one farmhouse in the District of Langensalza an expellee family of eight was allocated a room of 14 m^2, while the farmer used three larger, furnished rooms for storage purposes.[111]

Employment issues also contributed to the bad blood which developed between the refugee and native populations. While expellee farmers and craftsmen suffered discrimination from local indigenous elites, the native inhabitants maintained with considerable justification that they were disadvantaged on the employment market by the SED's inability or unwillingness to implement the denazification procedure against resettlers applying for posts in the public sector. This was extremely galling for the indigenous population, many of whom viewed the newcomers as unrepentant National Socialists who could have no complaints about being expelled from their homeland.[112] While the failure to denazify the expellees can be attributed mainly to the lack of documentary evidence against them, there is some evidence to suggest that it was also motivated by the SED's desire to secure their political support [113] The native inhabitants particularly resented the preferential treatment enjoyed by the small number of Sudeten German resettlers who had formerly belonged to the Communist Party in Czechoslovakia, while the so-called 'anti-fascist resettlers' were themselves bitterly disappointed at the failure of the local authorities to meet their material expectations, especially with regard to accommodation.[114]

As in the Western Occupation Zones, there were important underlying causes of the negative reaction of the indigenous inhabitants in rural parts of the SBZ to the influx of refugees and expellees. Local reports indicate that the native population in tight-knit village communities frequently viewed the newcomers as 'foreigners' who posed a threat to traditional rural life as they knew it. For example, an expellee from Neumark who was relocated to a village near Bernau (Brandenburg) complained in the autumn of 1948 that he

' was perceived and treated ... like an unwanted intruder and alien element'.[115] The native population's prejudice against the expellees was exacerbated by the fact that some of the new arrivals spoke Slavonic languages and were able to communicate with members of the Occupation forces in their own language.[116] These perceived Slavonic associations reinforced the view among the indigenous inhabitants that the expellees were racially inferior and had much in common with the foreigners from Eastern Europe who had been forced to work in Germany as agricultural labourers during the Second World War.

In the early post-war years, religion was an important source of conflict, especially in the countryside. Large numbers of Catholic refugees – mainly Sudeten Germans and Silesians – settled in the SBZ, an area which had been almost exclusively Protestant since the sixteenth century. Religious prejudice was widespread and Christopeit's study of the overwhelmingly Protestant province of Mark Brandenburg concluded that the local people equated Catholicism with 'insincerity or deceitfulness'.[117] Priests in Thuringia complained bitterly that Catholic expellees were afraid to attend mass in case the Protestant farmer with whom they were billeted withheld their food provisions or demanded that they leave altogether.[118]

Relations between the expellee and indigenous inhabitants in the GDR undoubtedly improved during the 1950s. This was particularly true of the towns and cities and Lutz Niethammer's empirical study concluded that by this stage discrimination against expellees in industrial areas was a thing of the past.[119] Similarly, a study of Schwerin which revealed that no fewer than 30 per cent of marriages in the period 1947–54 were between members of the expellee and indigenous communities suggests that relations between the two groups were good in urban areas.[120] But even in the countryside significant progress was made. This was partly due to the general improvement in the economic situation during the 1950s but an equally important factor was that the disparity in the economic and social position of the two groups narrowed.[121] In addition, the SED inadvertently brought the expellees and natives closer together through their mutual hostility to the far-reaching economic, social and political changes it introduced at the behest of the Soviet Union, a country many Germans regarded as their arch enemy. In particular, the suppression of the uprising of 17 June 1953 by Soviet and East German troops increased solidarity between the resettlers and the indigenous inhabitants.[122] Several other aspects of the SED's repressive policies promoted expellee–native relations by ensuring that both groups came into contact with each other. While it banned the formation of refugee organisations and dissolved native associations such as rifle clubs which had constituted an integral part of rural life for generations, it exerted pressure on both groups to join mass organisations such as the Free German Youth (*Freie Deutsche Jugend*, FDJ) which were controlled by the regime.[123]

The SED and the refugees: aspects of economic and social policy

Social welfare measures

In an article published in 1997, Michael Schwartz argued that the SMAD provided generous material aid for the resettlers in the SBZ/GDR in the period 1945–52 and this compared favourably with the economic and social measures introduced to help the refugees and expellees in the Western Occupation Zones/FRG during the same period.[124] One of the most important measures introduced in the SBZ to alleviate the resettlers' material predicament was SMAD Order 304, announced on 15 October 1946. It promised a payment of 300 marks to expellees who were unfit to work and an additional 100 marks for each of their dependents under the age of 14.[125] However, in Brandenburg the slow and often grudging implementation of this directive by indigenous bureaucrats aroused anger among the expellees,[126] while in Thuringia and Mecklenburg-West Pomerania the money ran out in July and November 1947 respectively.[127] Despite these difficulties, 1,199,669 adults and 763,664 children had benefited from this measure by the end of 1948, some 45 per cent of the expellee population, and payments totalled no fewer than 401 million marks.[128] While the importance of this directive should not be exaggerated, it undoubtedly gave some help to those resettlers most in need.

Although the SED claimed as early as 1948 that the expellee problem had been solved, SMAD instructed the new GDR regime in 1950 to introduce legislation to 'further improve the position of the former resettlers in the GDR'. Significantly, the law was announced on 8 September, shortly before the elections to the People's Chamber on 15 October. Its provisions focused on three main areas. It granted expellees an interest-free loan of up to 1,000 marks per family to buy furniture and other household goods; it also gave financially needy expellee craftsmen and new farmers interest-free credit of up to 5,000 marks to construct houses or business premises; finally, it provided scholarships for gifted expellee children to attend universities and vocational colleges and promoted the education of the children of impoverished resettlers by giving them 25 marks a month to stay on at school.[129]

While the expellees initially greeted the Resettler Law enthusiastically, this optimism gave way to disappointment since the supply of consumer goods soon began to run out due to the huge demand. Moreover, the applications for credit far exceeded the funds at the disposal of the GDR Government in Berlin. For example, the 80,000 marks it transferred to the District of Hoyerswerda (Saxony) constituted just 7 per cent of the total amount for which the expellees had applied.[130] As a result, restrictions were imposed on the number of resettlers who could submit applications. As early as December 1950, the SED announced that the monthly income of resettlers eligible to apply for credit to purchase furniture and other household goods should not exceed 250 marks for those living in urban areas and 200 marks for those located in rural communities. An important long-term issue was that the financial aid the resettlers received took the form of loans rather than payments. As one expellee put it in a letter to GDR President Wilhelm Pieck in May 1951: 'There is no comparison between granting interest free loans to resettlers ... and Equalisation of Burdens legislation because the loans have to be paid back.'[131] It is clear that, for pensioners in particular, the repayments often caused very real hardship.[132] Despite these shortcomings, some 660,000 families, more than half of the expellee population, had received loans to purchase consumer goods by the end of 1952.[133]

It is clear, then, that the expellees in the SBZ/GDR received more financial help in the early post-war years than their counterparts in the Western Occupation Zones/FRG. SMAD Order 304, as we have seen, ultimately provided payments for some 45 per cent of the expellees in the SBZ, while more than half of them took advantage of the loans available under the Resettler Law of September 1950. By contrast, the Immediate Aid Law was not introduced in the Western Occupation Zones until 8 August 1949. In the long run, however, expellees in West Germany received higher payments than their compatriots in the GDR as a result of the Equalisation of Burdens Law of August 1952. While the SED declined to introduce a similar measure, expellees who had settled in the GDR did receive a lump sum of 4,000 DM from the German Government after the unification of Germany in 1990.[134]

Land reform and the new farmers' programme

The Soviet leadership viewed the implementation of land reform as a key objective not just in the SBZ/GDR but also in the other parts of Eastern Europe under its occupation. In the SBZ the political elites aimed to eliminate the power of the Prussian Junkers and large landowners, whom they regarded as enthusiastic militarists and supporters of National Socialism, by confiscating their estates and dividing them up among the agricultural labourers. The aim of the policy was, as Wilhelm Pieck put it, to transfer land from the Junkers to the farmers ('*Junkerland in Bauerhand*').[135] In the event, however, the Junkers no longer posed a threat by May 1945. In fact, Norman Naimark quotes one study which shows that no fewer than 6,448 of a group of 8,827 Prussian aristocrats had perished during the war.[136] That the Soviet authorities nonetheless introduced the Land Reform was a result of political considerations. They were determined to establish political control in rural areas and win for the KPD the loyalty of agricultural labourers by giving them land. The need to integrate the millions of dispossessed resettlers living in the countryside thus remained of secondary importance in the eyes of the Soviet elites.[137]

Details of the Land Reform were announced by Wilhelm Pieck on 2 September 1945. Estates of over 100 ha would be confiscated without compensation, divided up and distributed in plots of 5–10 ha. According to Pieck, the beneficiaries were to be 'farmers with little or no land, small tenant farmers, agricultural labourers and also resettlers'.[138] The impact of this measure on the expellees has been the subject of some debate. Michael Schwartz has argued that it led to 'limited integration' for those resettlers who benefited from it and enabled the former independent refugee farmers (*Landwirte*) to retain their social position in their new homeland.[139] Arnd Bauerkämper, on the other hand, maintains that the 'professional integration [of the resettlers] in the countryside was to a large extent a myth',[140] while Philipp Ther concluded that the 'land reform ended in disaster, especially for the expellees'.[141]

The response of the resettlers to Pieck's announcement was mixed. Some, especially former *Landwirte*, were reluctant to apply for land because their only concern was to return home,[142] while others feared that it would prove inefficient to farm plots of fewer than 10 ha. However, the majority of the resettlers initially responded enthusiastically to the prospect of receiving land. One refugee based in Crossen (Saxony) recalled that all he wanted in September 1945 was 'to settle down ... nothing brought me more joy than the news of the land reform ... my dream became reality'.[143] It should be underlined that, in purely numerical terms, the expellees benefited disproportionately from the Land Reform and no fewer than 91,155 of them had received a farmstead by March 1950.[144] This represented 43.3 per cent of the recipients, well above their proportion of the population (24.2 per cent in April 1949).[145] At the same time, the Land Reform project was fraught with difficulties and Wolfgang Meinicke has estimated that only 15 per cent of the new expellee farms proved to be economically viable.[146] For some resettlers the situation was so bleak that they gave back their plots of land. In Brandenburg, for example, 2,944 expellees had abandoned their farms by the end of 1947, 12 per cent of those who had received land.[147] This trend continued and it was estimated that by 1952 more than 80,000 new farmers had returned their land, including large numbers of expellees. This represented 38.4 per cent of the new farms established as a result of the Land Reform.[148] Many of those who retained their farmsteads continued to suffer severe economic deprivation, while resettlers who succeeded in making their enterprises profitable were bitterly disappointed by the SED's decision to collectivise agriculture. Significantly, the introduction of collectivisation coincided with a sharp rise in the number of farmers who fled to the West.

Some of the problems facing the resettlers who took advantage of the Land Reform were a legacy of the Second World War. As noted above, agricultural land in some parts of Brandenburg and Mecklenburg suffered severe war damage, while the sharp fall in the number of livestock was partly the result of farmers fleeing with their animals as Soviet troops advanced westwards in 1944–45. However, Soviet policy towards its occupation zone undoubtedly worsened the post-war crisis in agriculture. The removal of livestock, agricultural machinery and fertilisers as reparations reduced productivity, while the excessive food quotas introduced by the Soviet authorities, and the punishments if farmers failed to meet them, led to widespread despair.[149]

The failure of most resettlers to make their farms profitable was also partly due to the discrimination they suffered from the indigenous rural elites. The land commissioners appointed to implement the Land Reform were generally controlled by members of the indigenous population: in January 1946, for example, just 800 of more than 10,000 commissioners in Saxony were expellees,[150] while in Saxony-Anhalt there were just 784 newcomers among the 10,723 members of the commissions in November 1945.[151] Some land commissioners discriminated against the resettlers in the allocation of land. Up to March 1946, only 78 per cent of expellee applicants in Saxony were successful, as opposed to 84 per cent of landless indigenous farmers, 86 per cent of indigenous agricultural labourers and 95 per cent of indigenous farmers with a little land.[152] Meanwhile, the land commissioners in Brandenburg as a rule allocated the best farmland to native applicants and also gave them more grazing land than the resettlers.[153]

The land commissioners also discriminated against expellees in the allocation of agricultural machinery and equipment, livestock and accommodation, all of which were in very short supply. In Brandenburg, for example, new expellee farmers had on average just four pigs, four cows, three horses and two chickens in December 1947. Only 32 per cent of them had a horse drawn plough and 25 per cent a harrow.[154] Moreover, expellee farmers in Brandenburg had been allocated just 28 per cent of the available residential accommodation up to July 1949, while the indigenous landless farmers had received 37 per cent.[155] The Association for Mutual Farmers' Assistance (*Vereinigung der gegenseitigen Bauernhilfe*, VdgB), which was responsible for loaning to new farmers the agricultural equipment and machinery confiscated from the estates of large landowners, also failed to prevent discrimination against resettler farmers because its local branches were invariably dominated by the native elites.[156]

As noted above, the housing conditions of many resettlers located in rural areas were deplorable and in October 1947 just 28 per cent of new expellee farmers in the SBZ had their own residential accommodation.[157] Many of the others lived in barns, stables, farm outbuildings or attics. On 9 September 1947, SMAD reacted to the housing crisis in the countryside by announcing Order 209, the so-called 'new farmers' programme'. It ordered the construction of 37,000 homes for new farmers by the end of the following year. This measure was intended to benefit the expellees in particular; no fewer than 12,000 of these new homes were to be built in Mecklenburg-West Pomerania, where expellees made up more than 43 per cent of the population,[158] and the supplementary regulations published in 1949 stipulated that resettlers should be given priority in the construction of residential housing.[159]

However, the house building programme for new farmers failed to meet the high expectations it raised. Although it improved the conditions of some resettler farmers, some 45 per cent still did not have their own home in October 1950.[160] This was caused primarily by the serious shortage of building materials. In Brandenburg, for example, only half of the required building stones and 10 per cent of the roof tiles were available in the spring of 1948, while supplies of cement, lime and nails had been completely exhausted.[161] Financial issues also contributed to the failure of the house construction programme for new farmers. Government funds for 1949 ran out as early as July and all building work had to be postponed until 1950. In addition, some resettlers were deterred from taking part in the programme since they had to contribute 15 per cent of the cost of the project, while others found themselves so heavily in debt that they gave up their farms altogether.[162]

To sum up, the results of the Land Reform were disappointing for the resettlers. The SED recognised from the outset that the transition from large estates to small holdings would prove difficult. Moreover, it was unable to prevent the native elites in small rural communities from discriminating against the expellees in the allocation of land and the resources they needed to farm it effectively. Financial factors were also of crucial importance. Although the SED devoted a high proportion of its scarce resources to the new farmers, its inability to provide sufficient funds undoubtedly contributed to the failure of the programme. It should be added that the decision to concentrate building resources in the countryside also had serious repercussions for the towns and cities, where post-war reconstruction practically came to a halt in 1948.[163]

The SED and the refugees: the quest for political loyalty

The Local and State Elections of 1946

The Soviet authorities, like the Western Allies, expressed apprehension that the refugees and expellees would represent a source of political radicalisation in the early post-war years. Although these fears were based partly on the material distress the newcomers were experiencing, the most important consideration was a recognition that the expellees held the Soviet Union responsible for the loss of their homelands and the atrocities committed against them during their flight or expulsion.[164] SMAD sought to avert this perceived danger of political radicalisation by a policy of ideological re-education which was to begin in the reception camps where the expellees were accommodated after their arrival in the SBZ. They were classified as 'reactionary', 'reliable' or 'indifferent'.[165] 'Reactionary' expellees – including active Nazi supporters and large estate owners – were sent to detention centres. Those deemed to be politically 'reliable' – antifascist elements such as former KPD members and other opponents of National Socialism – were given responsibility for exerting political influence over their fellow expellees in return for special privileges. They were regarded as an elite group whose task was to win the support of the politically 'indifferent' for the SED regime by influencing their political outlook through personal contact. In Saxony-Anhalt the SED organised meetings in refugee camps at which its representatives addressed controversial issues – arguing, for example, that the expellees' loss of their homelands was solely due to National Socialist policies.[166] It also sought to influence the political outlook of camp inmates through newspapers, books and films. However, the SED elites recognised that they would be unable to gain the support of the expellees without meeting their material needs and during the Local and State Election campaigns in 1946 underlined the benefits expellee farmers had derived from the Land Reform and outlined plans to improve the housing and employment position of other expellees, as well as providing them with clothing, furniture and other essential items.[167]

The Local Elections held in September 1946 represented the first indicator of the political attitudes of the expellees in the SBZ even though by no means all of them were eligible to vote because they had not been resident in the constituency for the necessary three months. It should be borne in mind that SMAD discriminated against both the CDU and the LDPD. In Saxony, for example, SMAD refused to allow either the CDU or the LDPD to organise at parish level and it also restricted their ability to produce election literature by withholding paper supplies.[168] Nonetheless, it is possible to draw some conclusions about the expellees' voting behaviour. The SED gained no fewer than 57.1 per cent of the vote in the SBZ.[169] Studies of the results in Mecklenburg-West Pomerania, Saxony-Anhalt and Saxony show that the party achieved particularly good results in areas where expellee farmers had benefited from the Land Reform legislation.[170] This pattern was particularly striking in Mecklenburg-West Pomerania, a predominantly agricultural state heavily populated with refugees where the SED won no less than 69.6 per cent of the vote.[171] At the same time, SMAD's own analysis of the expellees' voting behaviour revealed considerable disquiet. It concluded that the SED had failed to gain the majority of expellee votes in the SBZ as a result of shortcomings in its electoral campaign, especially in relation to the issue of Poland's western border, and the expellees' continuing material deprivation.[172] For example, in Saxony, where the CDU polled heavily among Catholic Silesian resettlers and also benefited from the preponderance of women among these newcomers,[173] the SED's Regional Association admitted on 20 September 1946 that it had 'paid insufficient attention to the expellees and refugees'.[174]

At the *Landtag* Election held on 20 October 1946, the SED gained 46.7 per cent of the overall votes cast, 9.5 per cent lower than at the Local Elections the previous month. SED analysts attributed this fall in support partly to the influence of the expellees and this view is confirmed by studies showing that a majority of the newcomers in both Saxony and Saxony-Anhalt voted for either the CDU or LDPD.[175] The sharp increase in the CDU's share of the vote in Mecklenburg-West Pomerania was also attributed to the influence of the refugees and expellees.[176] The loss of support for the SED among the expellees was mainly due to the Polish border question. While, for tactical reasons, the party softened its stance on this issue during the election campaign, it acknowledged after the election that the strident demands of the CDU in particular for a revision of the Oder–Neisse line had cost it expellee votes.[177] As the election campaign progressed, the SED placed greater emphasis on improving the expellees' material position and, as we have seen, SMAD Order 304 was published shortly before polling day, promising financial help to disabled expellees and their dependents under the age of 14.[178] But this electoral strategy did not reap dividends. While many expellee farmers continued to vote for the SED because they had benefited personally from the party's policies, the majority of economically destitute refugees had little faith in its promises. This interpretation is supported by the critical comments made on the extraordinarily high number of spoilt ballot papers – 9.5 per cent of the votes cast at the Local Elections and 5.6 per cent at the *Landtag*

Election.[179] While the majority of spoilt ballot papers at the *Landtag* Election demanded an improvement in the food, housing or employment situation, others called on the Soviet authorities to allow the expellees to return home.[180] 'Our future is in our homeland' and 'give us our homeland back' were typical of the remarks made on this subject.[181]

The policy of 'forced integration'[182]

While electoral considerations prompted the SED to pay close attention to the refugees and expellees during the summer and autumn of 1946, its attitude towards the new population elements underwent a significant change in 1947–48. As Philipp Ther has argued, the SED increasingly displayed a 'tendency not to solve but to suppress expellee problems'.[183] Symptomatic of this change in attitude was the decision to close down the ZVU on 1 July 1948.[184] The transfer of responsibility for expellee affairs from an autonomous body such as the ZVU to a Department for Resettlers within the Ministry of the Interior was a clear sign of the declining importance of the resettler issue in SED eyes. This was confirmed by the suggestion of a leading SED official in 1948 that the term 'resettler' should no longer be used since the process of integrating these new population elements was already well advanced.[185] In the spring of 1949 the resettler advisory committees were dissolved and the expellee periodical *Die neue Heimat* ceased publication.[186] According to the SED, the 'resettler problem' had been solved, even though the available statistical evidence indicated that this was by no means the case. Moreover, the SED leaders ordered repressive measures to be taken against those expellees who refused to give up their cultural and regional identity.

With the onset of the Cold War, the Soviet Union exerted pressure on the SED to adopt a tougher stance on the issue of Germany's border with Poland and eradicate the expellees' hopes of returning to their former homelands. In response, Paul Merker, the Head of the SED's Department for Resettlers, published a pamphlet in 1947 in which he urged the expellees not to become preoccupied with returning home because it would prevent them from integrating fully into their new homeland.[187] This new hard-line policy was stated more explicitly by Walter Ulbricht at a press conference held in Warsaw in October 1948: 'The Oder–Neisse line is the final peace border between Germany and Poland. A change in this border is out of the question. Anyone who raises this issue will only be continuing the old campaign of hostility towards Poland.'[188] The Görlitz Treaty signed by Poland and the GDR on 6 July 1950 formally confirmed the Oder–Neisse line as Poland's western border.[189] Recognising the expellees' anger at the loss of the eastern territories, the SED's leaders underlined at every opportunity that it was the National Socialists rather than the Russians who were to blame.[190] At the same time, they dealt harshly with any dissent and expellees who mentioned their former homeland in public were liable to prosecution.[191]

The SED's policy of 'forced integration' found expression in several other respects. It outlawed the establishment of expellee associations and interest groups, as well as expellee homeland societies (*Landsmannschaften*) on the grounds that attempts to preserve the resettlers' historical or cultural heritage would hinder their integration in the SBZ/GDR. For example, in October 1947 the police in Bitterfeld (Saxony-Anhalt) dissolved a Resettler Refugee Association founded a few months earlier.[192] The SED also closely monitored the activities of the Churches in relation to the expellees, believing that they were acting as cover organisations for regional expellee associations.[193] In the months leading up to the signing of the Görlitz Treaty the SED regime monitored expellee activities particularly closely, breaking up organised and even informal meetings.[194] Harsh penalties were often imposed against those taking part and in Neuruppin (District of Züllichau, Brandenburg) two expellees who regularly met up with their fellow countrymen in a restaurant received prison sentences of 10 and 15 years respectively, to be served in the former concentration camp in Sachsenhausen, for breaking the law prohibiting the right to assemble.[195]

To sum up, the policies of the SED towards the refugees and expellees began to diverge sharply from those of the Western Allies in 1948–49. While the British and American Military Governments gradually relaxed the restrictions on the formation of expellee interest groups and *Landsmannschaften*, the Soviet authorities adopted a harsh policy, outlawing all expressions of the expellees' cultural identity and imposing draconian penalties on those who failed to comply.

Refugee attitudes towards the SED, 1947–53

The efforts of the SED to win the political support of the resettlers achieved little success. Although the party's public statements gave the impression that the majority of the refugees identified with the newly established regime they were heavily underrepresented among the elected delegates of the political parties. In Saxony-Anhalt, for example, resettlers comprised some 25 per cent of the population in 1949 but only 8 per cent of *Landtag* delegates, 12 per cent of district assembly representatives and 13 per cent of town councillors.[196] In Brandenburg and Saxony the figures were even lower.[197] The SED's strategy of using 'antifascist' resettlers to influence the political outlook of their compatriots backfired because the expellees resented the privileges they enjoyed and regarded them as government spies.[198]

The most divisive issue between the refugees and the SED regime concerned the Oder–Neisse frontier. Ulbricht's announcement in October 1948 that this represented the permanent 'peace border' between Germany and Poland provoked fury among many expellees and there was even dissent within the ranks of the SED itself.[199] A report compiled by the Brandenburg Government expressed disquiet that the expellees' preoccupation with a return to their homelands was jeopardising the success of the new farmers' programme.[200] Opposition to Ulbricht's ruling was especially widespread among resettlers located in areas adjoining the Polish frontier and at the elections to the People's Congress in May 1949 no fewer than 45.2 per cent of voters rejected the SED in the border constituency of Görlitz.[201] The GDR regime responded by ordering the CDU and LDPD to remove party members who had spoken out against the 'peace border'.[202] After the Görlitz Treaty had been signed, the Government suppressed any outward signs of opposition to the agreement. However, many expellees remained deeply hostile to the SED and their anger came to the surface during the uprising of 17 June 1953 when they took part in demonstrations against the regime, denouncing the 'peace border' and demanding the right to be able to return to their homelands.[203]

The continuing hostility of many refugees towards the SED can also be attributed to the party's failure to meet their material aspirations. The SED elites attempted to convince the expellees in the SBZ that their economic position was superior to that of their compatriots in the Western Occupation Zones.[204] Letters from resettlers appeared in the press extolling the success of the SED's policy to promote their economic integration in the SBZ/GDR.[205] But for most expellees, the reality was quite different. As seen above, many were still desperately short of personal possessions in the early 1950s and continued to live in cramped and often squalid accommodation. Moreover, the expellees' employment situation actually deteriorated in 1948–49. Even the new expellee farmers who had generally supported the SED in the 1946 elections turned against the party in 1947–48 as the high expectations raised by the Land Reform failed to materialise.[206] As noted above, the Resettler Law of September 1950, introduced shortly before the elections to the People's Chamber held on 15 October, at first received a positive response from the expellees, but this soon changed when it became clear that the SED had once again promised more than it was able to deliver.[207]

To sum up, only a minority of the expellees identified with the SBZ/GDR regime after the Second World War. Some who owed their professional success to the measures introduced by the SED supported the party,[208] while young expellees generally had a more positive attitude to the regime than older age groups.[209] However, the majority of the resettlers had an uneasy or hostile relationship with the SED. For many it represented the 'Russian party' and was therefore implicated in the brutal treatment they had received during their flight or expulsion from their homelands.[210] Some of these expellees attempted to withdraw from any political involvement and concentrated instead on building up their professional career.[211] A minority actively opposed the regime by participating in the uprising of 17 June 1953. In addition, some 800,000 fled to the FRG for economic or political reasons in the period 1949–61.[212] This represented about a third of those who left the GDR for the West during this period, well above the expellees' proportion of the population.

Conclusion

In the early post-war years the Soviet authorities displayed a greater willingness than the Western Allies to promote the integration of the expellees at the expense of the indigenous population. As a result of the heavy pressure SMAD exerted on local authorities to billet the resettlers with native householders, it was able to close down the refugee camps more quickly in the SBZ/GDR than was the case in the FRG.[213] Moreover, SMAD Order 304, issued in October 1946, gave financial assistance to expellees who were unfit to work, while the Resettler Law of September 1950 provided loans for expellees to purchase consumer goods and construct residential housing and business premises. It also offered scholarships for gifted expellee children to follow courses in higher education. In addition, one of the aims of the Land Reform was to promote the economic integration of the expellees and they received preferential treatment in the new farmers' programme of September 1947.

However, the success of these measures was limited. It is true that the Land Reform gave expellee *Landwirte* in the SBZ better opportunities to resume their former profession than their counterparts in the Western Occupation Zones. Moreover, the financial aid the expellees in the SBZ/GDR received was greater than that granted to their counterparts in West Germany up to the Equalisation of Burdens Law of August 1952. Yet the initial enthusiasm of the resettlers in the SBZ/GDR for these measures soon turned to disappointment because the SED had raised expectations it was unable to fulfil. This was partly due to the opposition of the indigenous elites at local level, but the most important reason was that the SBZ/GDR lacked the financial resources to honour the pledges it had made to the resettlers. A further complaint was that the assistance the expellees received from the new farmers' programme and the Resettler Law took the form of loans rather than payments. Despite much debate among SED functionaries up to October 1948, there was no Equalisation of Burdens Law in the GDR.[214] By the time this piece of legislation was introduced in the FRG in 1952, the GDR was already phasing out its special measures to promote the economic integration of the resettlers, a process which was completed in 1953. Yet at this stage much still remained to be done and many resettlers continued to live in squalid conditions.

Although SMAD recognised that the heavy investment it had made in expellees living in the countryside had not brought about their swift economic integration in the SBZ, it was unwilling to accept the implications of these findings. As a result, SED leaders began to argue publicly from 1948 onwards that the resettlers were no longer an issue because they had been successfully integrated. This tendency to suppress the expellee problem was reinforced by the SED's insistence that the new population groups give up their regional and cultural identity. It also expected them to abandon all hopes of returning home. Moreover, all expellee organisations were outlawed and, as time progressed, the regime responded increasingly harshly to resettlers who dared even to refer in public to their former homeland. This was in marked contrast to the FRG, where expellee associations exerted considerable influence on West Germany's foreign policy up to 1990, a 'Refugee Party' formed part of the Federal Government from 1953 to 1957 and a Federal Ministry for Expellees existed until 1969. In the GDR, on the other hand, public discussion of the expellee problem was suppressed until the fall of the Berlin Wall in November 1989 and the reunification of the two German states in October 1990. This repression made it all the harder for expellees in the GDR to come to terms with the loss of their homeland, and this was illustrated by the enthusiasm with which they attended meetings of the expellee associations in the period following the fall of the Berlin Wall.[215]

Notes

1 D. Hoffmann, 'Vertriebenenintegration durch Arbeitsmarktlenkung? Zur Beschäftigungspolitik der SBZ/DDR (1945–1950)', in Hoffmann and Schwartz (eds), *Geglückte Integration?*, p. 176.

2 BHStA, MArb 27, *Statistischer Informationsdienst*, No. 110. This percentage relates to July 1949.

3 Quoted in M. Wille, 'Compelling the Assimilation of Expellees in the Soviet Zone of Occupation and the GDR', in Ther and Siljak (eds), *Redrawing Nations*, p. 267.

4 P. Ther, 'Expellee Policy in the Soviet-occupied Zone and the GDR: 1945–1953', in Rock and Wolff (eds), *Coming home to Germany?*, p. 59.

5 *Ibid.*

6 Hoffmann, 'Vertriebenenintegration', p. 175.

7 Ther, 'Expellee Policy', p. 60.

8 M. Rusche, 'Die Eingliederung der Vertriebenen in Mecklenburg-Vorpommern, dargestellt unter besonderer Berücksichtigung der Wohnraumproblematik', in M. Wille, J. Hoffmann and W. Meinicke (eds), *Sie hatten alles verloren: Flüchtlinge und Vertriebene in der sowjetischen Besatzungszone Deutschlands* (Wiesbaden 1993), pp. 133–4.

9 P. Pape, 'Flüchtlinge und Vertriebene in der Provinz Mark Brandenburg', in Wille, Hoffmann and Meinicke (eds), *Sie hatten alles verloren*, p. 115.

10 Schwartz, *Vertriebene und 'Umsiedlerpolitik'*, p. 637.

11 Ther, 'Expellee Policy', p. 60.

12 Quoted in Schrammek, *Alltag und Selbstbild*, p. 158.

13 S. Kaltenborn, 'Wohn- und Lebensverhältnisse von Vertriebenen 1948 in

Thüringen', in Hoffmann and Schwartz (eds), *Geglückte Integration?*, p. 286.
14 Wille (ed.), *Die Vertriebenen*, Vol. 2, pp. 267–8.
15 Quoted in Ther, *Deutsche und polnische Vertriebene*, p. 161.
16 *Ibid.*, p. 162.
17 G. Christopeit, 'Die Herkunft und Verteilung der Evakuierten, Flüchtlinge und Vertriebenen in der Provinz Mark Brandenburg und ihr Verhältnis zu der einheimischen Bevölkerung', in Wille, Hoffmann and Meinicke (eds), *Sie hatten alles verloren*, p. 101.
18 Ther, *Deutsche und polnische Vertriebene*, p. 162.
19 Wille (ed.), *Die Vertriebenen*, Vol. 2, p. 271.
20 Ther, 'Expellee Policy', pp. 71–2 and Schrammek, *Alltag und Selbstbild*, pp. 216–17.
21 Kleßmann, *Die doppelte Staatsgründung*, pp. 47–8.
22 J. Roesler, 'The Black Market in Post-war Berlin and the Methods Used to Counteract it', *GH*, Vol. 7(1) (1989), p. 93.
23 J. Roesler, 'The Refugee Problem in the SBZ 1945–1949', *GDR Monitor*, No. 21 (Summer 1989), pp. 11–12.
24 I. Schwab, *"Neue Heimat – Neues Leben"? Flüchtlinge und Vertriebene in Leipzig 1945 bis zum Beginn der 50er Jahre* (Leipzig 1999), p. 25.
25 Bauerkämper, 'Die vorgetäuschte Integration', p. 198.
26 W. Rothe, *Vertrieben und angekommen: Flüchtlinge und Umsiedler in Neubrandenburg: Dokumente und Berichte aus den Jahren 1945 bis 1948* (Neubrandenburg 1996), p. 71.
27 C. Krause, 'Flüchtlinge und Vertriebene in Rostock – Versuch einer Situationsbeschreibung für die Zeit vom Mai bis August 1945', in Wille, Hoffmann and Meinicke (eds), *Sie hatten alles verloren*, p. 158.
28 Quoted in Schrammek, *Alltag und Selbstbild*, p. 151.
29 W. Meinicke, 'Die Bodenreform und die Vertriebenen in der SBZ und in den Anfangsjahren der DDR', in Wille, Hoffmann and Meinicke (eds), *Sie hatten alles verloren*, p. 56.
30 C. Kurzweg, *Die Vertriebenenpolitik der Liberal-Demokratischen Partei Deutschlands: Das Beispiel Sachsen 1945–1950* (Hamburg 2004), p. 269.
31 Mehlhase, *Flüchtlinge und Vertriebene*, p. 118.
32 Meinicke, 'Die Bodenreform', p. 55.
33 *Ibid.*
34 *Ibid.*, p. 56.
35 M. Holz, *Evakuierte, Flüchtlinge und Vertriebene auf der Insel Rügen 1943–1961* (Cologne 2003), p. 457.
36 N. Naimark, *The Russians in Germany: A History of the Soviet Zone of Occupation, 1945–1949* (Cambridge, Mass. and London 1995), p. 154.
37 Mehlhase, *Flüchtlinge und Vertriebene*, p. 125.
38 K.C. Führer, 'Managing Scarcity: The German Housing Shortage and

the Controlled Economy 1914–1990', *GH*, Vol. 13(3) (1995), p. 337.
39 Calculated from Schwab, *"Neue Heimat – Neues Leben"?*, p. 70.
40 Wille (ed.), *Die Vertriebenen*, Vol. 2, p. 194.
41 Schraut, *Flüchtlingsaufnahme in Württemberg-Baden*, p. 229.
42 Wille, 'Compelling the Assimilation', p. 272.
43 Schrammek, *Alltag und Selbstbild*, p. 159.
44 Ther, 'Expellee Policy', p. 63.
45 Mehlhase, *Flüchtlinge und Vertriebene*, p. 112.
46 Rusche, 'Die Eingliederung', p. 142.
47 Quoted in Schrammek, *Alltag und Selbstbild*, p. 159.
48 *Ibid.*, p. 160.
49 *Ibid.*, p. 166.
50 Quoted in Wille, 'Compelling the Assimilation', p. 273.
51 Mehlhase, *Flüchtlinge und Vertriebene*, p. 108.
52 Führer, 'Managing Scarcity', pp. 343 and 347.
53 Rusche, 'Die Eingliederung', p. 139.
54 *Ibid.*, p. 140.
55 Wille, 'Compelling the Assimilation', p. 273.
56 Ther, *Deutsche und polnische Vertriebene*, pp. 209–10.
57 Führer, *Mieter, Hausbesitzer*, p. 369.
58 Rusche, 'Die Eingliederung', p. 142.
59 Schrammek, *Alltag und Selbstbild*, pp. 199–200.
60 Führer, 'Managing Scarcity', p. 342.
61 Calculated from *ibid.*, p. 343.
62 Calculated from *ibid.*, p. 347.
63 Calculated from Ackermann, *Der "echte" Flüchtling*, pp. 288–91.
64 Hoffmann, 'Vertriebenenintegration', p. 179.
65 *Ibid.*, p. 183.
66 Wille, 'Compelling the Assimilation', p. 275.
67 For details, see D. van Melis, '"Angabe nicht möglich" – Integration statt Entnazifizierung der Flüchtlinge in Mecklenburg-Vorpommern', in Hoffmann and Schwartz (eds), *Geglückte Integration?*, p. 166.
68 Ther, *Deutsche und polnische Vertriebene*, p. 268.
69 Wille, 'Compelling the Assimilation', p. 275.
70 Mehlhase, *Flüchtlinge und Vertriebene*, pp. 168–78.
71 Hoffmann, 'Vertriebenenintegration', p. 183.
72 Donth, *Vertriebene und Flüchtlinge*, pp. 423–4.
73 Ther, *Deutsche und polnische Vertriebene*, p. 268.
74 Hoffmann, 'Vertriebenenintegration', p. 179.
75 Wille, 'Compelling the Assimilation', p. 268.
76 *Ibid.*, p. 276.
77 Donth, *Vertriebene und Flüchtlinge*, p. 162 and Rusche, 'Die Eingliederung', pp. 142–3.
78 Schwab, *"Neue Heimat – Neues Leben"?*, p. 104.

79 Rusche, 'Die Eingliederung', p. 143.
80 *Ibid.*
81 Hoffmann, 'Vertriebenenintegration', p. 189.
82 Naimark, *The Russians in Germany*, p. 169.
83 *Ibid.*
84 Ther, 'Expellee Policy', p. 65.
85 Hoffmann, 'Vertriebenenintegration', p. 181.
86 Mehlhase, *Flüchtlinge und Vertriebene*, p. 168.
87 *Ibid.*, p. 169.
88 Ther, *Deutsche und polnische Vertriebene*, p. 270.
89 P. Hübner, 'Industriearbeit als Faktor der Vertriebenenintegration in der SBZ/DDR', in Hoffmann, Krauss and Schwartz (eds), *Vertriebene in Deutschland*, p. 301.
90 *Ibid.*, p. 303.
91 A. von Plato, 'Vergangene Perspektiven? Schwerpunkte, Fragen und Probleme der Flüchtlingsforschung vor und nach der Wende', in Hoffmann, Krauss and Schwartz (eds), *Vertriebene in Deutschland*, p. 103 and Ther, *Deutsche und polnische Vertriebene*, p. 271.
92 Quoted in Bauerkämper, 'Social Conflict', p. 295.
93 See for example, P.-H. Seraphim, *Die Heimatvertriebenen in der Sowjetzone* (Berlin 1954), p. 180.
94 Schrammek, *Alltag und Selbstbild*, p. 248.
95 Quoted in M. Schwartz, '"Zwangsheimat Deutschland": Vertriebene und Kernbevölkerung zwischen Gesellschaftskonflikt und Integrationspolitik', in K. Naumann (ed.), *Nachkrieg in Deutschland* (Hamburg 2001), pp. 124–5.
96 U. Schmidt, '"Drei- oder viermal im Leben neu anfangen zu müssen ..." – Beobachtungen zur ländlichen Vertriebenenintegration in mecklenburgischen "Bessarabier-Dörfern"', in Hoffmann and Schwartz (eds), *Geglückte Integration?*, p. 299.
97 Sorbs were of Slavonic origin and most were located in the south eastern areas of the SBZ.
98 Ther, *Deutsche und polnische Vertriebene*, p. 289.
99 Quoted in Rothe, *Vertrieben und angekommen*, p. 24.
100 For example, see Schwartz, '"Zwangsheimat Deutschland"', pp. 126–7.
101 Ther, *Deutsche und polnische Vertriebene*, p. 287.
102 Christopeit, 'Die Herkunft und Verteilung', p. 104.
103 Ther, 'Expellee Policy', p. 62.
104 Bauerkämper, 'Social Conflict', pp. 288–9.
105 Quoted in Ther, *Deutsche und polnische Vertriebene*, p. 286.
106 Schrammek, *Alltag und Selbstbild*, p. 161.
107 Kaltenborn, 'Wohn- und Lebensverhältnisse', p. 285.
108 Holz, *Evakuierte, Flüchtlinge*, pp. 224–49.
109 Christopeit, 'Die Herkunft und Verteilung', p. 98.

110 *Ibid.*, p. 99.
111 Kaltenborn, 'Wohn- und Lebensverhältnisse', p. 283.
112 Christopeit, 'Die Herkunft und Verteilung', p. 100.
113 Van Melis, '"Angabe nicht möglich"', pp. 166–7.
114 M. Grottendieck, 'Zwischen Integration und Abstoßung: Probleme der Eingliederung von Vertriebenen im münsterländischen Greven sowie von "antifaschistischen Umsiedlern" im mecklenburgischen Ludwigslust im Vergleich', in Hoffmann and Schwartz (eds), *Geglückte Integration?*, pp. 247–71.
115 Quoted in Bauerkämper, 'Social Conflict', p. 285.
116 Christopeit, 'Die Herkunft und Verteilung', p. 100.
117 *Ibid.*, p. 106.
118 Quoted in Schwartz, '"Zwangsheimat Deutschland"', p. 131.
119 Quoted in Ther, *Deutsche und polnische Vertriebene*, pp. 292–3.
120 *Ibid.*, p. 338.
121 *Ibid.*, p. 292.
122 A. von Plato, 'Vergangene Perspektiven?', p. 105.
123 Schrammek, *Alltag und Selbstbild* , pp. 248–9.
124 Schwartz, 'Vertreibung und Vergangenheitspolitik', p. 179.
125 Wille (ed.), *Die Vertriebenen*, Vol. 3, p. 192.
126 See for example, Pape, 'Flüchtlinge und Vertriebene', p. 130.
127 Wille (ed.), *Die Vertriebenen*, Vol. 3, p. 158.
128 *Ibid.*, p. 159.
129 *Ibid.*, p. 423.
130 Ther, 'Expellee Policy', p. 72.
131 Schwartz, 'Vertreibung und Vergangenheitspolitik', p. 181.
132 See for example, Schrammek, *Alltag und Selbstbild* , pp. 218–19.
133 Wille (ed.), *Die Vertriebenen*, Vol. 3, p. 458.
134 Hirsch, 'Flucht und Vertreibung', p. 19.
135 Naimark, *The Russians in Germany*, p. 143.
136 *Ibid.*, p. 142.
137 *Ibid.*, p.144; Donth, *Vertriebene und Flüchtlinge*, pp.169–70; Bauerkämper, 'Social Conflict', pp. 287–8.
138 Quoted in Schrammek, *Alltag und Selbstbild*, p. 236.
139 Schwartz, 'Vertreibung und Vergangenheitspolitik', p. 180.
140 Bauerkämper, 'Die vorgetäuschte Integration', p. 211.
141 Ther, 'The Integration of Expellees', p. 794.
142 Bauerkämper, 'Die vorgetäuschte Integration', p. 202; see also Mehlhase, *Flüchtlinge und Vertriebene*, p. 153.
143 Quoted in Naimark, *The Russians in Germany*, p. 157.
144 Bauerkämper, 'Die vorgetäuschte Integration', p. 211.
145 Ther, 'Expellee Policy', p. 64.
146 Quoted in Ther, 'The Integration of Expellees', pp. 794–5.
147 Bauerkämper, 'Die vorgetäuschte Integration', p. 203.

148 Von Plato, 'Vergangene Perspektiven?', p. 87.
149 Naimark, *The Russians in Germany*, pp. 158–61.
150 Donth, *Vertriebene und Flüchtlinge*, p. 171.
151 Mehlhase, *Flüchtlinge und Vertriebene*, p. 152.
152 Donth, *Vertriebene und Flüchtlinge*, p. 171.
153 Bauerkämper, 'Social Conflict', p. 288.
154 Bauerkämper, 'Die vorgetäuschte Integration', p. 202.
155 Bauerkämper, 'Social Conflict', pp. 289–90.
156 *Ibid.*, p. 290; Meinicke, 'Die Bodenreform', p. 67.
157 Meinicke, 'Die Bodenreform', p. 74.
158 *Ibid.*, p. 73.
159 Ther, 'Expellee Policy', p. 65.
160 Wille (ed.), *Die Vertriebenen*, Vol. 2, p. 292.
161 Ther, 'Expellee Policy', p. 65.
162 Mehlhase, *Flüchtlinge und Vertriebene*, pp. 159–60.
163 Ther, 'Expellee Policy', p. 66.
164 M. Wille, 'Die Vertriebenen und das politisch-staatliche System der SBZ/DDR', in Hoffmann, Krauss and Schwartz (eds), *Vertriebene in Deutschland*, p. 203. See also T. Mehlhase, 'Die SED und die Vertriebenen. Versuche der politischen Einflußnahme und der "Umerziehung" in den ersten Nachkriegsjahren in Sachsen-Anhalt', in Wille, Hoffmann and Meinicke (eds), *Sie hatten alles verloren*, pp. 159–60.
165 Wille, 'Die Vertriebenen und das politisch-staatliche System', pp. 203–4.
166 Mehlhase, 'Die SED und die Vertriebenen', p. 160.
167 *Ibid.*, p. 161.
168 See for example, Donth, *Vertriebene und Flüchtlinge*, p. 179.
169 K.-H. Hajna, *Die Landtagswahlen 1946 in der SBZ: eine Untersuchung der Begleitumstände der Wahl* (Frankfurt a. M. 2000), p. 195.
170 Donth, *Vertriebene und Flüchtlinge*, p. 211 and Mehlhase, 'Die SED und die Vertriebenen', p. 166.
171 This is based on J. Falter and C. Weins, 'Die Wahlen in der Sowjetisch Besetzten Zone von 1946: Eine wahlhistorische Analyse', in H. Mehringer, M. Schwartz and H. Wentker (eds), *Erobert oder befreit? Deutschland im internationalen Kräftefeld und die Sowjetische Besatzungszone (1945/46)* (Munich 1999), pp. 215–33. For a one-sided account of the expellees' voting behaviour in the local and state elections in Mecklenburg-West Pomerania in 1946, see Roesler, 'The Refugee Problem', pp. 19–20.
172 Donth, *Vertriebene und Flüchtlinge*, pp. 211–12.
173 *Ibid.*, pp. 210–11.
174 Kurzweg, *Die Vertriebenenpolitik*, p. 159
175 Donth, *Vertriebene und Flüchtlinge*, p. 231 and Mehlhase, 'Die SED und die Vertriebenen', p. 168.
176 Hajna, *Die Landtagswahlen 1946*, p. 207.

177 *Ibid.*, pp. 199–200.
178 Donth, *Vertriebene und Flüchtlinge*, p. 226.
179 Hajna, *Die Landtagswahlen 1946*, p. 181.
180 *Ibid.*, pp. 191–3.
181 *Ibid.*, p. 193.
182 This term has been borrowed from Mehlhase, 'Die SED und die Vertriebenen', p. 169.
183 Ther, 'Expellee Policy', p. 68.
184 *Ibid.*, p. 69.
185 *Ibid.*
186 Wille, 'Compelling the Assimilation', p. 277.
187 Mehlhase, 'Die SED und die Vertriebenen', p. 169.
188 Quoted in Wille, 'Die Vertriebenen und das politisch-staatliche System', p. 213.
189 Ther, *Deutsche und polnische Vertriebene*, p. 345.
190 Naimark, *The Russians in Germany*, pp. 149–50.
191 Wille, 'Compelling the Assimilation', p. 271.
192 Mehlhase, 'Die SED und die Vertriebenen', pp. 172–3.
193 Ther, 'Expellee Policy', pp. 70–1. For a more detailed discussion, see Schwartz, *Vertriebene und "Umsiedlerpolitik"*, pp. 544–72.
194 Ther, 'Expellee Policy', p. 71.
195 Christopeit, 'Die Herkunft und Verteilung', p. 105.
196 Mehlhase, 'Die SED und die Vertriebenen', p. 176.
197 Ther, 'Expellee Policy', p. 67.
198 Mehlhase, 'Die SED und die Vertriebenen', p. 164.
199 Wille, 'Die Vertriebenen und das politisch-staatliche System', pp. 213–14.
200 *Ibid.*, p. 214.
201 Kurzweg, *Die Vertriebenenpolitik*, p. 313.
202 *Ibid.*, p. 315 and Wille, 'Die Vertriebenen und das politisch-staatliche System', p. 214.
203 Wille, 'Die Vertriebenen und das politisch-staatliche System', p. 217.
204 *Ibid.*, p. 207.
205 Mehlhase, 'Die SED und die Vertriebenen', p. 173.
206 Donth, *Vertriebene und Flüchtlinge*, pp. 347–8.
207 Schwartz, 'Vertreibung und Vergangenheitspolitik', p. 181.
208 *Ibid.*, p. 192.
209 Wille, 'Compelling the Assimilation', p. 276.
210 Wille, 'Die Vertriebenen und das politisch-staatliche System', p. 204.
211 *Ibid.*, p. 210.
212 Ther, 'The Integration of Expellees', p. 800.
213 Ther, 'Expellee Policy', p. 73.
214 M. Schwartz, '"Ablenkungsmanöver der Reaktion": Der verhinderte Lastenausgleich in der SBZ/DDR', *DA*, 32 (1999), pp. 401–6.
215 Hirsch, 'Flucht und Vertreibung', p. 20.

Conclusion

When the Western Allies and the Soviet Union assumed control of Germany at the end of the Second World War, one of their most daunting tasks was to integrate the millions of dispossessed refugees and expellees who were flooding into a country ravaged by the effects of the war. In fact, the Bavarian State Secretary for Refugees, Wolfgang Jaenicke, described the refugees 'as one of the gravest problems ... to confront Bavaria in its history spanning 1400 years'.[1] In the early post-war years, the political elites in the Western Occupation Zones of Germany regarded these new population groups as a huge economic burden whose poverty and material deprivation made them a dangerous and fickle force, capable of destabilising the new political state which was being established. Jaenicke expressed his concern in June 1947 that the refugees would become 'an asocial and potentially revolutionary element in our country' if they were not integrated into the Western Occupation Zones of Germany.[2] Allied and German politicians voiced fears that the newcomers' extreme economic hardship would make them vulnerable to the overtures of both radical right-wing groups and the KPD.

However, an analysis of the refugees' voting behaviour indicates that leading politicians misperceived the nature of the political threat emanating from these new population groups. The outcome of *Landtag* elections between 1946 and 1950 and the first *Bundestag* Election in August 1949 demonstrated unequivocally the refugees' emphatic rejection of communism. Memories of their treatment by Soviet troops during their flight or expulsion from their homelands were sufficient to make the refugees and expellees immune to the overtures of the KPD. On the other hand, radical right-wing groups did gain significant electoral support from the newcomers in Bavaria and parts of Lower Saxony at the first *Bundestag* Election.

Meanwhile, the triumph of the newly established BHE at *Landtag* Elections in Bavaria, Lower Saxony and Schleswig-Holstein in 1950–51 indicated that many refugees and expellees had become alienated from the mainstream political parties.

Yet, the electoral fortunes of the BHE declined steadily during the 1950s and by the end of the decade its support was largely confined to older refugees who continued to harbour hopes of being able to return to their homelands and those who had not established themselves economically. In the *Bundestag* Elections of 1953 – and, in particular – 1957, the majority of refugee voters supported the CDU/CSU in recognition of the material benefits they were beginning to enjoy as a result of West Germany's economic resurgence. While the CDU/CSU lost ground to the SPD among expellee voters during the 1960s, the point to stress is that the vast majority continued to support the mainstream parties and were by this stage rightly viewed as a source of political stability. Similarly, fears of unrest breaking out among the refugees had evaporated by the mid-1950s. While the hunger strikes in a number of refugee camps in Bavaria in the autumn of 1948 and the outbreak of violence at Dachau Camp on 28 November 1948 had a profound effect on Bavarian Government ministers, the situation improved after the arrest of the instigator of the protests, Egon Herrmann. Although the Federal Government was deeply alarmed at the activities of the Trek Associations established in Bavaria, Lower Saxony and Schleswig-Holstein in late 1951 and early 1952, the prospect of treks being undertaken had already receded by 1953. The absence of large-scale unrest was due to several factors. While the 'preventative' measures of the political and ecclesiastical elites were important in the early post-war years, the expellees' hostility to communism and their improving economic position during the 1950s, partly due to government measures such as the Equalisation of Burdens Law, gradually promoted a degree of loyalty to the FRG.

But how swiftly did the economic integration of the refugees and expellees proceed after the establishment of the FRG? The census of 1960 revealed that, while their housing conditions had improved significantly since 1950, they remained less good than those of the indigenous inhabitants. Similarly, the refugees and expellees had more or less achieved full employment by 1961 but continued to lag behind the native population in terms of occupational structure. Paul Lüttinger's pioneering empirical study showed that this was still the case in 1971 and that on average the refugees also had lower pensions than their indigenous counterparts.[3] Lüttinger's and other regional studies concluded that it was only the second generation of refugees and expellees who achieved full economic integration.[4]

Conclusions about the economic and political integration of the 'resettlers' in the SBZ/GDR are more tentative since serious research on these issues did not begin until after the collapse of the Berlin Wall. However, it is clear that the SED's policy of concentrating its scarce resources in the countryside failed, while its social welfare measures promised more than they delivered. The fact that 'resettlers' made up an above-average proportion of the 2.6 million who fled to the West between 1949 and 1961 suggests that they integrated less well than their counterparts in the FRG. At the same time, this flood of refugees to the West made the housing shortage less acute because it increased the available space for those who remained. The exodus of GDR citizens to the West also contributed to the improvement in the employment prospects of the resettlers during the same period, but a more important factor was their willingness to migrate from the countryside to urban and industrial centres in search of jobs. On a political level, the majority of resettlers had little time for the SED; the minority who identified with the regime tended to be young people or those who attributed their professional success to the party. In response to the SED's increasingly harsh treatment of dissent from 1950 onwards, many resettlers fled to the FRG, while others took part in the East German uprising in June 1953.

The integration of the refugees and expellees into (West) German society has proved to be a much more protracted process than their economic and political integration. While relations between the refugee and native populations in rural parts of West Germany generally improved during the 1950s, newcomers continued to be 'outsiders' and only gradually secured access to clubs and associations which had traditionally been the preserve of the indigenous villagers. While the arrival of guest workers from Southern Europe in rural communities during the 1960s often brought the refugees closer to the native population, they still did not feel completely accepted in their new homeland. In fact, interviews with former refugees conducted by Rainer Schulze and Michael von Engelhardt in the 1990s revealed that many still retained strong emotional ties with their former homeland.[5] Their integration into German society was also impeded by the fact that they had never been afforded the opportunity to discuss and come to terms with the atrocities they had witnessed or suffered during their flight or expulsion. This applied to an even greater extent to refugees located in the SBZ/GDR.

Since 1990 the flight and expulsion of the refugees and expellees from their homelands has formed an important part of a wider public debate about the role of Germans as victims as well as perpetrators of the Second World War. The debate was stimulated by events in the FRG to mark the fortieth anniversary of the end of the Second World War, in particular a controversial visit on 5 May 1985 by Chancellor Kohl and US President Ronald Reagan to a cemetery in Bitburg where SS troops were buried. This prompted the 'historians' dispute' (*Historikerstreit*), a debate among prominent West German historians about whether the Holocaust can be regarded as a unique phenomenon. Significantly, Ernst Nolte, one of the main protagonists in the debate, drew parallels between the victims of the Holocaust and the German expellees, maintaining that both groups were deserving of sympathy, an argument his critics saw as an attempt to relativise Nazi war crimes.[6]

The collapse of the communist regimes in Eastern Europe in 1989–90 and, in particular, Chancellor Kohl's formal recognition of the Oder–Neisse line as the German–Polish border, laid the foundations for a more open and measured discussion of the flight and expulsion of the refugees and expellees from their homelands, not just in academic circles[7] but also in the public domain. Public debate about the role of Germans as victims of the Second World War has been prompted by the publication of books such as Knopp's *The Great Flight* (*Die große Flucht: Das Schicksal der Vertriebenen*), while Grass' novel *Crabwalk* (*Im Krebsgang*) on the sinking of the *Wilhelm Gustloff* caught the public imagination to such an extent that it was Germany's best-selling book in 2002. This is perhaps a first step in the creation of a common collective memory for the German people, embodying not just the experiences of the native population but also the refugees and expellees.

Notes

1 BLA, Committee for Refugee Questions, minutes of the meeting of 11 June 1947, p. 7.

2 Bundesarchiv and Institut für Zeitgeschichte (eds), *Akten zur Vorgeschichte der Bundesrepublik Deutschland 1945–1949*, Vol. 2 (Munich 1979), p. 557.

3 Lüttinger, 'Der Mythos der schnellen Integration', p. 24.
4 *Ibid.*, p. 35 and Handl, 'War die schnelle Integration der Vertriebenen ein Mythos?', p. 210.
5 Von Engelhardt, 'Biographieverläufe', p. 73 and Schulze, 'The Struggle of Past and Present', p. 46.
6 For a clear summary of the arguments in the debate, see B. Heuser, 'The *Historikerstreit:* Uniqueness and Comparability of the Holocaust', *GH*, Vol. 6(1) (1988), pp. 69–78.
7 See for example, M. Schwartz, 'Dürfen Vertriebene Opfer sein? Zeitgeschichtliche Überlegungen zu einem Problem deutscher und europäischer Identität', *DA*, 38 (2005), pp. 494–505.

References

Archival sources

Archiv für Christlich-Demokratische Politik, Sankt-Augustin (ACDP)

Nachlaß Linus Kather (01–377)
Nachlaß Peter Paul Nahm (01–518)

Archiv für Christlich-Soziale Politik der Hanns-Seidel-Stiftung, Munich (ACSP)

Nachlaß Ernst Glaser
Nachlaß Hans Schütz

Archiv des Deutschen Caritasverbandes, Freiburg im Breisgau (DCV)

Kriegsfolgenhilfe (Signatur 371)
Vertriebenenhilfe (Signatur 374)

Archiv des Deutschen Liberalismus der Friedrich-Naumann-Stiftung, Gummersbach (ADL)

FDP Britische Zone
FDP Bundesparteitage (A 1)
Bundesvertriebenenausschuß der FDP 1950–65 (A 13)

Archiv des Diakonischen Werkes der Evangelischen Kirche in Deutschland, Berlin (ADW)

Zentralbüro des Hilfswerks, Stuttgart (ZB)

Archiv der Hansestadt Lübeck (AHL)

SPD-Kreisverband Lübeck

Archiv der sozialen Demokratie der Friedrich-Ebert-Stiftung, Bonn (AdsD)

SPD Landesverband Baden-Württemberg
SPD Landesverband Bayern

SPD Landesverband Schleswig-Holstein (LV S-H)
SPD-Parteivorstand
Protokolle des Parteivorstands 1946–59
Nachlaß Heinrich Albertz
Nachlaß Franz Osterroth

Bayerisches Hauptstaatsarchiv, Munich. Abt. 1: Allgemeines Staatsarchiv (BHStA)

Bayerisches Arbeitsministerium (MArb)
Bayerisches Innenministerium (MInn)
Bayerisches Wirtschaftsministerium (MWi)

Bayerisches Hauptstaatsarchiv, Munich. Abt. II: Geheimes Staatsarchiv (GStA)

Der Bayerische Bevollmächtigte beim Länderrat (Bev. Stuttgart)

Bayerisches Hauptstaatsarchiv, Munich. Abt. IV: Kriegsarchiv (KA)

Zeitgeschichtliche Sammlung

Bayerisches Landtagsarchiv, Munich (BLA)

Verhandlungen des Bayerischen Ausschusses für Flüchtlingsfragen, 1. Wahlperiode. Stenographische Berichte.
Eingaben an den Bayerischen Landtag

Bundesarchiv, Koblenz (BA)

Kirchliche Hilfsstelle (Z18)
Zentralamt für Arbeit in der Britischen Zone (Z40)
Treckvereinigung Schleswig-Holstein (B125)
Bundesministerium für Vertriebene (B150)
Nachlaß Hans Schlange-Schöningen (NL 71)
Nachlaß Wolfgang Jaenicke (NL 135)

Evangelisches Zentralarchiv in Berlin (EZA)

Bestand 2: Kirchenamt der EKD, 1929–86

Institut für Zeitgeschichte, Munich (IfZ)

RG 260 OMGUS
Nachlaß Wilhelm Hoegner (Ed 120)

Landesarchiv Schleswig-Holstein, Schleswig (LSH)

Abteilung 605, Staatskanzlei
Abteilung 761: Sozialministerium

Landeskirchliches Archiv, Nuremberg (LKA)

Landeskirchenrat (LKR)

Landratsamt Erding (LRA Erding)

16/4 Berichte an die Regierung von Oberbayern

National Archives (formerly known as Public Record Office), Kew (PRO)

FO 944: Control Office for Germany and Austria (COGA), Finance Department

FO 1005: CCG, Records Library 1943–59

FO 1006: CCG, Schleswig-Holstein 1945–55

FO 1013 CCG, North Rhine-Westphalia 1944–55

FO 1014: CCG, Hansestadt Hamburg 1945–54

Niedersächsisches Hauptstaatsarchiv, Hanover (NHStA)

Nds 50 Staatskanzlei

Nds 120 Regierungspräsident Lüneburg

Nds 200 Finanzministerium

Nds 380 Ministerium für Bundesangelegenheiten

Nordrhein-Westfälisches Hauptstaatsarchiv, Düsseldorf (HStA)

Regierungsbezirk Düsseldorf

Staatsarchiv München (StA)

Wochen- und Monatsberichte der Landratsämter an die Militärregierung und die Regierung von Oberbayern, 1945–52: Altötting, Bad Aibling, Bad Tölz, Berchtesgaden, Rosenheim, Traunstein

Stadtarchiv München (StD)

Bürgermeister und Rat

Flüchtlingsrat

Published sources

Bayerisches Staatsministerium für Arbeit und Sozialordnung (ed.), *30 Jahre Flüchtlingsverwaltung in Bayern* (Munich 1975)

Bayerisches Statistisches Landesamt (ed.), *Bayern in Zahlen: Monatshefte des Bayerischen Statistischen Landesamtes*, No.4 (April 1947)

Bayerisches Statistisches Landesamt (ed.), *Die Wahlen in den Gemeinden und Kreisen Bayerns 1946 und 1948*, Beiträge zur Statistik Bayerns, No. 147 (Munich 1949)

Bayerisches Statistisches Landesamt (ed.), *Die erste Bundestagswahl in Bayern am 14. August 1949*, Beiträge zur Statistik Bayerns, No. 150 (Munich 1950)

Bayerisches Statistisches Landesamt (ed.), *Die Vertriebenen in Bayern: Ihre berufliche und soziale Eingliederung bis Anfang 1950*, Beiträge zur Statistik Bayerns, No. 151 (Munich 1950)

Bayerisches Statistisches Landesamt (ed.), *Wahl zum Bayerischen Landtag am 26. November 1950*, Beiträge zur Statistik Bayerns, No. 163 (Munich 1951)

Bayerisches Statistisches Landesamt (ed.), *Volk- und Berufszählung am 13. September 1950 in Bayern: Volkszählung 1. Teil Gliederung der Wohnbevölkerung*, Beiträge zur Statistik Bayerns, No. 171 (Munich 1952)

Bundesarchiv and Institut für Zeitgeschichte (eds), *Akten zur Vorgeschichte der Bundesrepublik Deutschland 1945–1949*, Vol. 2 (Munich 1979)

Bundesministerium für Arbeit (ed.), *Entwicklung und Ursachen der Arbeitslosigkeit in der Bundesrepublik Deutschland 1946–1950* (Bonn 1950)

Bundesministerium für Vertriebene (ed.), *Vertriebene und Flüchtlinge volksdeutschen Ursprungs: Bericht eines Sonder-Unterkomitees des Rechtausschusses des Abgeordnetenhauses …* (Bonn 1950)

Das Flüchtlingsproblem in der amerikanischen Besatzungszone: Ein Bericht des Länderrates an General Clay (Stuttgart 1948)

Die Umsiedlung der Heimatvertriebenen in der Bundesrepublik Deutschland: Gutachten des Instituts für Raumforschung Bonn in Verbindung mit dem Soziographischen Institut an der Universität Frankfurt am Main (Bonn 1951)

Forschungsinstitut der Konrad-Adenauer-Stiftung (ed.), *Wahlergebnisse in der Bundesrepublik Deutschland und in den Bundesländern 1946–1988* (Sankt Augustin 1988)

Statistisches Landesamt Schleswig-Holstein (ed.), *Das Flüchtlingsgeschehen in Schleswig-Holstein infolge des 2. Weltkriegs im Spiegel der amtlichen Statistik* (Kiel 1974)

Secondary literature

Abelshauser, W., 'Schopenhauers Gesetz und die Währungsreform: Drei Anmerkungen zu einem methodischen Problem', *VfZ*, Vol. 33(1) (1985), pp. 214–18.

Ackermann, V., *Der "echte" Flüchtling: Deutsche Vertriebene und Flüchtlinge aus der DDR 1945–1961* (Osnabrück 1995).

Ahonen. P., *After the Expulsion: West Germany and Eastern Europe 1945–1990* (Oxford 2003).

Ahonen, P., 'Collective Action and Expellee Integration: West Germany, East Germany and Finland after the Second World War', *Annali dell'Istituto storico italo-germanico in Trento*, XXIX (2003), pp. 617–38.

Ahonen, P., 'The Impact of Distorted Memory: Historical Narratives and Expellee Integration in West Germany 1945–1970', in R. Ohliger, K. Schönwälder and T. Triadafilopoulos (eds), *European Encounters:*

Migrants, Migration and European Societies since 1945 (London 2003), pp. 238–56.

Albrecht W. (ed.), *Kurt Schumacher: Reden – Schriften – Korrespondenzen 1945–1952* (Bonn 1985).

Bade, K. J. (ed.), *Neue Heimat im Westen: Vertriebene, Flüchtlinge, Aussiedler* (Münster 1990).

Bade, K. J. (ed.), *Fremde im Land: Zuwanderung und Eingliederung im Raum Niedersachsen seit dem Zweiten Weltkrieg* (Osnabrück 1997).

Bade, K. J. and J. Oltmer (eds), *Zuwanderung und Integration in Niedersachsen seit dem Zweiten Weltkrieg* (Osnabrück 2002).

Balfour, M., *Germany: The Tides of Power* (London and New York 1992).

Bauer, F. J., *Flüchtlinge und Flüchtlingspolitik in Bayern 1945–1950* (Stuttgart 1982).

Bauer, F. J., 'Der Bayerische Bauernverband, die Bodenreform und das Flüchtlingsproblem 1945–1951', *VfZ*, Vol. 31(3) (1983), pp. 443–82.

Bauer, F. J., 'Zwischen "Wunder" und Strukturzwang: Zur Integration der Flüchtlinge und Vertriebenen in der Bundesrepublik Deutschland', *APZ*, B 32 (1987), pp. 21–33.

Bauerkämper, A., 'Die vorgetäuschte Integration: Die Auswirkungen der Bodenreform und Flüchtlingssiedlung auf die berufliche Eingliederung von Vertriebenen in die Landwirtschaft in Deutschland 1945–1960', in D. Hoffmann and M. Schwartz (eds), *Geglückte Integration? Spezifika und Vergleichbarkeiten der Vertriebenen-Eingliederung in der SBZ/DDR* (Munich 1999), pp. 193–214.

Bauerkämper, A., 'Social Conflict and Social Transformation in the Integration of Expellees in Rural Brandenburg, 1945–1952', in P. Ther and A. Siljak (eds), *Redrawing Nations: Ethnic Cleansing in East-Central Europe, 1944–1948* (Lanham, Boulder, New York and Oxford 2001), pp. 285–305.

Beckmann, T., '*Alle wollen in die Stadt*: Pendlertradition und Eingliederung der Vertriebenen im Altkreis Leonberg', in M. Beer (ed.), *Zur Integration der Flüchtlinge und Vertriebenen im deutschen Südwesten nach 1945: Ergebnisse der Tagung vom 11. und 12. November 1993 in Tübingen* (Sigmaringen 1994), pp. 129–46.

Beer, M., 'Flüchtlinge – Ausgewiesene – Neubürger – Heimatvertriebene. Flüchtlingspolitik und Flüchtlingsintegration in Deutschland nach 1945, begriffsgeschichtlich betrachtet', in M. Beer, M. Kintzinger and M. Krauss (eds), *Migration und Integration: Aufnahme und Eingliederung im historischen Wandel* (Stuttgart 1997).

Benz, W. (ed.), *Die Vertreibung der Deutschen aus dem Osten: Ursachen, Ereignisse, Folgen* (Frankfurt a. M. 1985).

Böberach, H. (ed.), *Meldungen aus dem Reich: Auswahl aus den geheimen Lageberichten des Sicherheitsdienstes der SS 1939–44*, 2nd edn (Munich 1968).

Böhm, M. H., 'Gruppenbildung und Organisationswesen', in E. Lemberg and F. Edding (eds), *Die Vertriebenen in Westdeutschland: Ihre Eingliederung und ihr Einfluß auf Gesellschaft, Wirtschaft, Politik und Geistesleben*, Vol. 1 (Kiel 1959), pp. 521–605.

Bösch, F., 'Die politische Integration der Flüchtlinge und Vertriebenen und ihre Einbindung in die CDU', in R. Schulze, R. Rohde and R. Voss (eds), *Zwischen Heimat und Zuhause: Deutsche Flüchtlinge und Vertriebene in (West-) Deutschland 1945–2000* (Osnabrück 2001), pp. 107–25.

Brandes, D., *Der Weg zur Vertreibung 1938–1945: Pläne und Entscheidungen zum 'Transfer' der Deutschen aus der Tschechoslowakei und aus Polen* (Munich 2001).

Braun, H., 'Demographische Umschichtungen im deutschen Katholizismus nach 1945', in A. Rauscher (ed.), *Kirche und Katholizismus 1945–1949* (Paderborn 1977), pp. 9–25.

Brelie-Lewien, D. von der, *"Dann kamen die Flüchtlinge": Der Wandel des Landkreises Fallingbostel vom Rüstungszentrum im "Dritten Reich" zur Flüchtlingshochburg nach dem Zweiten Weltkrieg* (Hildesheim 1990).

Brelie-Lewien, D. von der, 'Flüchtlinge in einer ländlichen Region – Aspekte des Strukturwandels zwischen "Drittem Reich" und Nachkriegszeit', in D. von der Brelie-Lewien, H. Grebing, A. Hohenstein, D. von Reeken, H. Rinklake und G. J. Trittel, *Niedersachsen nach 1945: Gesellschaftliche Umbrüche, Reorganisationsprozesse, sozialer und ökonomischer Strukturwandel* (Hanover 1995), pp. 110–51.

Brelie-Lewien, D. von der and H. Grebing, 'Flüchtlinge in Niedersachsen', in B. U. Hucker, E. Schubert and B. Weisbrod (eds), *Niedersächsische Geschichte* (Göttingen 1997), pp. 619–34.

Brosius, D., 'Zur Lage der Flüchtlinge im Regierungsbezirk Lüneburg zwischen Kriegsende und Währungsreform', in D. Brosius and A. Hohenstein, *Flüchtlinge im nordöstlichen Niedersachsen 1945–1948* (Hildesheim 1985), pp. 3–86.

Brosius, D. and A. Hohenstein, *Flüchtlinge im nordöstlichen Niedersachsen 1945–1948* (Hildesheim 1985).

Buscher, F., 'The Great Fear: The Catholic Church and the Anticipated Radicalization of Expellees and Refugees in Post-War Germany', *GH*, Vol. 21(2) (2003), pp. 204–24.

Buschke, H., 'Die Sozialistische Reichspartei im Raum Lüneburg 1949–1952', in B. Weisbrod (ed.), *Rechtsradikalismus in der politischen Kultur der Nachkriegszeit: Die verzögerte Normalisierung in Niedersachsen* (Hanover 1995), pp. 87–107.

Carey, J., 'Political Organization of the Refugees and Expellees in West Germany', *PSQ*, Vol. 66 (1951), pp. 191–215.

Carlin, W., 'Economic Reconstruction in Western Germany, 1945–55: The Displacement of "Vegetative Control"', in I. Turner (ed.), *Reconstruction in Post-War Germany: British Occupation Policy and the Western Zones*

1945–1955 (Oxford 1989), pp. 37–65.

Carstens, U., *Die Flüchtlingslager der Stadt Kiel: Sammelunterkünfte als desintegrierender Faktor der Flüchtlingspolitik* (Marburg 1992).

Christopeit, G., 'Die Herkunft und Verteilung der Evakuierten, Flüchtlinge und Vertriebenen in der Provinz Mark Brandenburg und ihr Verhältnis zu der einheimischen Bevölkerung', in M. Wille, J. Hoffmann and W. Meinicke (eds), *Sie hatten alles verloren: Flüchtlinge und Vertriebene in der sowjetischen Besatzungszone Deutschlands* (Wiesbaden 1993), pp. 86–109.

Connor, I., 'The Attitude of the Ecclesiastical and Political Authorities in Bavaria to the Refugee Problem 1945–50', PhD thesis, University of East Anglia, 1983.

Connor, I., 'The Bavarian Government and the Refugee Problem 1945–50', *EHQ*, Vol. 16(2) (April 1986), pp. 131–53.

Connor, I. 'The Refugees and the Currency Reform', in I. Turner (ed.), *Reconstruction in Post-War Germany: British Occupation Policy and the Western Zones 1945–1955* (Oxford 1989), pp. 301–24.

Connor, I., 'Flüchtlinge und die politischen Parteien in Bayern 1945–50', *Jahrbuch für deutsche und osteuropäische Volkskunde*, Vol. 38 (1995), pp. 133–68.

Connor, I., 'German Refugees and the Bonn Government's Resettlement Programme: The Role of the Trek Association in Schleswig-Holstein, 1951–3', *GH*, Vol. 18(3) (2000), pp. 337–61.

Connor, I., 'German Refugees and the SPD in Schleswig-Holstein, 1945–50', *EHQ*, Vol. 36(2) (2006), pp. 173–99.

Donth, S., *Vertriebene und Flüchtlinge in Sachsen 1945–1952: Die Politik der Sowjetischen Militäradministration und der SED* (Cologne 2000).

Dusik, B., 'Die Gablonzer Schmuckwarenindustrie', in F. Prinz (ed.), *Integration und Neubeginn: Dokumentation über die Leistungen des Freistaates Bayern und des Bundes zur Eingliederung der Wirtschaftsbetriebe der Vertriebenen und Flüchtlinge und deren Beitrag zur wirtschaftlichen Entwicklung des Landes*, Vol. 1 (Munich 1984), pp. 482–513.

Edding, F., *Die wirtschaftliche Eingliederung der Vertriebenen und Flüchtlinge in Schleswig-Holstein* (Berlin 1955).

Ellenrieder, S., 'Wohnverhältnisse von Flüchtlingen und Heimatvertriebenen in München in der Nachkriegszeit', *OA*, Vol. 120 (1996), pp. 317–90.

Enders, U., 'Die Kirchliche Hilfsstelle München', in F. Prinz (ed.), *Integration und Neubeginn: Dokumentation über die Leistungen des Freistaates Bayern und des Bundes zur Eingliederung der Wirtschaftsbetriebe der Vertriebenen und Flüchtlinge und deren Beitrag zur wirtschaftlichen Entwicklung des Landes*, Vol. 1 (Munich 1984), pp. 171–86.

Endres, R. (ed.), *Bayerns vierter Stamm: Die Integration der Flüchtlinge und Heimatvertriebenen nach 1945* (Cologne 1998).

Engelhardt, M. von, 'Bibliographieverläufe von Heimatvertriebenen des

Zweiten Weltkriegs', in Bayerisches Staatsministerium für Arbeit und Sozialordnung, Familie, Frauen und Gesellschaft (ed.), *Die Entwicklung Bayerns durch die Integration der Vertriebenen und Flüchtlinge. Forschungsstand 1995* (Munich 1995), pp. 49–77.

Engelhardt, M. von, *Lebensgeschichte und Gesellschaftsgeschichte: Biographieverläufe von Heimatvertriebenen des Zweiten Weltkriegs* (Munich 2001)

Erker, P., *Vom Heimatvertriebenen zum Neubürger: Sozialgeschichte der Flüchtlinge in einer agrarischen Region Mittelfrankens 1945–1955* (Wiesbaden 1988)

Erker P., 'Revolution des Dorfes? Ländliche Bevölkerung zwischen Flüchtlingszustrom und landwirtschaftlichem Strukturwandel', in M. Broszat, K.-D. Henke and H. Woller (eds), *Von Stalingrad zur Währungsreform: Zur Sozialgeschichte des Umbruchs in Deutschland* (Munich 1989), pp. 367–425.

Erker, P. (ed.), *Rechnung für Hitlers Krieg: Aspekte und Probleme des Lastenausgleichs* (Heidelberg 2004).

Exner, P., 'Integration oder Assimilation? Vertriebeneneingliederung und ländliche Gesellschaft – eine sozialgeschichtliche Mikrostudie am Beispiel westfälischer Landgemeinden', in D. Hoffmann and M. Schwartz (eds), *Geglückte Integration? Spezifika und Vergleichbarkeiten der Vertriebenen-Eingliederung in der SBZ/DDR* (Munich 1999), pp. 57–88.

Falter, J., 'Kontinuität und Neubeginn: Die Bundestagswahl 1949 zwischen Weimar und Bonn', *PV*, Vol. 22 (1981), pp. 236–63.

Falter, J. and C. Weins, 'Die Wahlen in der Sowjetisch Besetzten Zone von 1946: Eine wahlhistorische Analyse', in H. Mehringer, M. Schwartz and H. Wentker (eds), *Erobert oder befreit? Deutschland im internationalen Kräftefeld und die Sowjetische Besatzungszone (1945/46)* (Munich 1999), pp. 215–33.

Farquharson, J., *The Western Allies and the Politics of Food: Agrarian Management in Postwar Germany* (Leamington Spa 1985).

Farquharson, J., 'Land Reform in the British Zone, 1945–1947', *GH*, Vol. 6(1) (1988), pp. 35–56.

Farquharson, J., 'The British Occupation of Germany, 1945–46: A Badly Managed Disaster Area?', *GH*, Vol. 11(3) (1993), pp. 316–38.

Faulenbach, B., 'Die Vertreibung der Deutschen aus den Gebieten jenseits von Oder und Neiße: Zur wissenschaftlichen und öffentlichen Diskussion in Deutschland', *APZ*, B 51–52 (2002), pp. 44–54.

Frantzioch, M., *Die Vertriebenen: Hemmnisse, Antriebskräfte und Wege ihrer Integration in der Bundesrepublik Deutschland* (Berlin 1987).

Frantzioch-Immenkeppel, M., 'Die Vertriebenen in der Bundesrepublik Deutschland. Flucht, Vertreibung, Aufnahme und Integration', *APZ*, B 28 (1996), pp. 3–13.

Franzen, K.E., *Die Vertriebenen: Hitlers letzte Opfer: Mit einer Einführung*

von Hans Lemberg (Berlin and Munich 2001).
Friedrich, J., *Der Brand: Deutschland im Bombenkrieg 1940–1945* (Munich 2002).
Friesen, A. von, *Der lange Abschied: Psychische Spätfolgen für die 2. Generation deutscher Vertriebener* (Gießen 2000).
Führer, K.C., 'Managing Scarcity: The German Housing Shortage and the Controlled Economy 1914–1990', *GH*, Vol. 13(3) (1995), pp. 326–54.
Führer, K.C., *Mieter, Hausbesitzer, Staat und Wohnungsmarkt: Wohnungsmangel und Wohnungszwangswirtschaft in Deutschland 1914–1960* (Stuttgart 1995).
Fuhrmann, W., *Die Bayerische Lagerversorgung 1948–1951: Ein ernährungswirtschaftlicher Beitrag zur Versorgung von Gemeinschaftsverpflegungseinrichtungen und der Schulspeisung* (np, nd).
Glassheim, E, 'The Mechanics of Ethnic Cleansing: The Expulsion of Germans from Czechoslovakia, 1945–1947', in P. Ther and A. Siljak (eds), *Redrawing Nations: Ethnic Cleansing in East-Central Europe, 1944–1948* (Lanham, Boulder, New York and Oxford 2001), pp. 197–219.
Glensk, E., *Die Aufnahme und Eingliederung der Vertriebenen und Flüchtlinge in Hamburg 1945–1953* (Hamburg 1994).
Glensk, E., 'Großstädtischer Arbeitsmarkt und Vertriebenenintegration: Das Beispiel Hamburg', in D. Hoffmann, M. Krauss and M. Schwartz (eds), *Vertriebene in Deutschland: Interdisziplinäre Ergebnisse und Forschungsperspektiven* (Munich 2000), pp. 251–72.
Grass, G., *Im Krebsgang* (Göttingen 2002).
Grebing, H., *Flüchtlinge und Parteien in Niedersachsen: Eine Untersuchung der politischen Meinungs- und Willensbildungsprozesse während der ersten Nachkriegszeit 1945–1952/53* (Hanover 1990).
Grebing, H., 'Politischer Radikalismus und Parteiensystem: Die Flüchtlinge in der niedersächsischen Nachkriegspolitik', in B. Weisbrod (ed.), *Rechtsradikalismus in der politischen Kultur der Nachkriegszeit: Die verzögerte Modernisierung in Niedersachsen* (Hanover 1995), pp. 259–68.
Grieser, H., *Die ausgebliebene Radikalisierung: Zur Sozialgeschichte der Kieler Flüchtlingslager im Spannungsfeld von sozialdemokratischer Landespolitik und Stadtverwaltung 1945–1950* (Wiesbaden 1980).
Grosser, C., T. Grosser, R. Müller and S. Schraut, *Flüchtlingsfrage – das Zeitproblem: Amerikanische Besatzungspolitik, deutsche Verwaltung und die Flüchtlinge in Württemberg-Baden 1945–1949* (Mannheim 1993).
Grosser, T., 'Das Assimilationskonzept der amerikanischen Flüchtlingspolitik in der US-Zone nach 1945', in C. Grosser, T. Grosser, R. Müller and S. Schraut, *Flüchtlingsfrage – das Zeitproblem: Amerikanische Besatzungspolitik, deutsche Verwaltung und die Flüchtlinge in Württemberg-Baden 1945–1949* (Mannheim 1993), pp. 11–54.
Grosser, T., '*Wir brauchten sie nicht zu nehmen, sind aber froh gewesen,*

daß sie hier gewesen sind. Die Aufnahme der Heimatvertriebenen und SBZ-Flüchtlinge in Mannheim 1945–1960', in C. Grosser, T. Grosser, R. Müller and S. Schraut, *Flüchtlingsfrage – das Zeitproblem. Amerikanische Besatzungspolitik, deutsche Verwaltung und die Flüchtlinge in Württemberg-Baden 1945–1949* (Mannheim 1993), pp. 55–128.

Grosser, T., 'Von der freiwilligen Solidar- zur verordneten Konfliktgemeinschaft: Die Integration der Flüchtlinge und Vertriebenen in der deutschen Nachkriegsgesellschaft im Spiegel neuerer zeitgeschichtlicher Untersuchungen', in D. Hoffmann, M. Krauss and M. Schwartz (eds), *Vertriebene in Deutschland: Interdisziplinäre Ergebnisse und Forschungsperspektiven* (Munich 2000), pp. 65–85.

Grottendieck, M., 'Zwischen Integration und Abstoßung: Probleme der Eingliederung von Vertriebenen im münsterländischen Greven sowie von "antifaschistischen Umsiedlern" im mecklenburgischen Ludwigslust im Vergleich', in D. Hoffmann and M. Schwartz (eds), *Geglückte Integration? Spezifika und Vergleichbarkeiten der Vertriebenen-Eingliederung in der SBZ/DDR* (Munich 1999), pp. 247–71.

Grünbacher, A., 'The Chancellor's Forgotten Blunder: Konrad Adenauer's Foundation for Refugees and Expellees', *GP*, Vol. 13(3) (2004), pp. 481–98.

Haerendel, U., 'Die Politik der "Eingliederung" in den Westzonen und der Bundesrepublik Deutschland: Das Flüchtlingsproblem zwischen Grundsatzentscheidungen und Verwaltungspraxis', in D. Hoffmann, M. Krauss and M. Schwartz (eds), *Vertriebene in Deutschland: Interdisziplinäre Ergebnisse und Forschungsperspektiven* (Munich 2000), pp. 109–33.

Hajna, K.-H., *Die Landtagswahlen 1946 in der SBZ: eine Untersuchung der Begleitumstände der Wahl* (Frankfurt a. M. 2000).

Handl, J and C. Herrmann, 'Sozialstruktureller Wandel und Flüchtlingsintegration: Empirische Befunde zur beruflichen Integration der weiblichen Vertriebenen und Flüchtlinge des Zweiten Weltkrieges in Bayern', *ZfS*, Vol. 22(2) (1993), pp. 125–40.

Handl, J. and C. Herrmann, *Soziale und berufliche Umschichtung der Bevölkerung in Bayern nach 1945. Eine Sekundäranalyse der Mikrozensus-Zusatzerhebung von 1971* (Munich 1994).

Handl, J., 'War die schnelle Integration der Vertriebenen ein Mythos?', in R. Endres (ed.), *Bayerns vierter Stamm: Die Integration der Flüchtlinge und Heimatvertriebenen nach 1945* (Cologne 1998), pp. 183–214.

Hendriks, G., 'The Oder-Neiße Line Revisited: German Unification and Poland's Western Border', *Politics and Society in Germany, Austria and Switzerland*, Vol. 4(3) (1992), pp. 1–17.

Heuser, B., 'The *Historikerstreit:* Uniqueness and Comparability of the Holocaust', *GH*, Vol. 6(1) (1988), pp. 69–78.

Hirsch, H., 'Flucht und Vertreibung. Kollektive Erinnerung im Wandel', *APZ*, B 40–1 (2003), pp. 14–26.

Hirsch, H., *Schweres Gepäck: Flucht und Vertreibung als Lebensthema* (Hamburg 2004).

Hoffmann, D., 'Vertriebenenintegration durch Arbeitsmarktlenkung? Zur Beschäftigungspolitik der SBZ/DDR (1945–1950), in D. Hoffmann and M. Schwartz (eds), *Geglückte Integration? Spezifika und Vergleichbarkeiten der Vertriebenen-Eingliederung in der SBZ/DDR* (Munich 1999), pp. 173–92.

Hoffmann, D. and M. Schwartz (eds), *Geglückte Integration? Spezifika und Vergleichbarkeiten der Vertriebenen-Eingliederung in der SBZ/DDR* (Munich 1999).

Hoffmann, D., M. Krauss and M. Schwartz (eds), *Vertriebene in Deutschland: Interdisziplinäre Ergebnisse und Forschungsperspektiven* (Munich 2000).

Hohenstein, A., 'Aufnahme und Eingliederung von Flüchtlingen im Landkreis Dannenberg 1945–1948', in D. Brosius and A. Hohenstein, *Flüchtlinge im nordöstlichen Niedersachsen* (Hildesheim 1985), pp. 87–181.

Holz, M., *Evakuierte, Flüchtlinge und Vertriebene auf der Insel Rügen 1943–1961* (Cologne 2003).

Hübner, P., 'Industriearbeit als Faktor der Vertriebenenintegration in der SBZ/DDR' in D. Hoffmann, M. Krauss and M. Schwartz (eds), *Vertriebene in Deutschland: Interdisziplinäre Ergebnisse und Forschungsperspektiven* (Munich 2000), pp. 291–312.

Hughes, M., *Shouldering the Burdens of Defeat: West Germany and the Reconstruction of Social Justice* (Chapel Hill and London 1999).

Hughes, M., '"Through No Fault of Our Own": West Germans Remember Their War Losses', *GH*, Vol. 18(2) (2000), pp. 193–213.

Isaac, J., *Die Assimilierung der Flüchtlinge in Deutschland* (London 1948).

Jaenicke, W., *Vier Jahre Betreuung der Vertriebenen in Bayern 1945–1949: Ein Bericht über den Stand der bisherigen Eingliederung und über ungelöste Probleme, anläßlich des vierten Jahrestages der Errichtung der bayerischen Flüchtlingsverwaltung* (Munich 1950).

Jaworski, R., 'Die Sudetendeutschen als Minderheit in der Tschechoslowakei 1918–1938', in W. Benz (ed.), *Die Vertreibung der Deutschen aus dem Osten: Ursachen, Ereignisse, Folgen* (Frankfurt a. M. 1985), pp. 29–38.

Jessen-Klingenberg, M., '"In allem widerstrebt uns dieses Volk": Rassistische und fremdenfeindliche Urteile über die Heimatvertriebenen und Flüchtlinge in Schleswig-Holstein 1945–1946', in K. H. Pohl (ed.), *Regionalgeschichte heute: Das Flüchtlingsproblem in Schleswig-Holstein nach 1945* (Bielefeld 1997), pp. 81–95.

Kaltenborn, S., 'Wohn- und Lebensverhältnisse von Vertriebenen 1948 in Thüringen', in D. Hoffmann and M. Schwartz (eds), *Geglückte Integration? Spezifika und Vergleichbarkeiten der Vertriebenen-Eingliederung in der SBZ/DDR* (Munich 1999), pp. 273–87.

Kirchenkanzlei der Evangelischen Kirche in Deutschland (ed.), *Die Lage der*

Vertriebenen und das Verhältnis des deutschen Volkes zu seinen östlichen Nachbarn (Hanover 1965).

Kleinert, U., 'Die Flüchtlinge als Arbeitskräfte – zur Eingliederung der Flüchtlinge in Nordrhein-Westfalen nach 1945', in K. J. Bade (ed.), *Neue Heimat im Westen: Vertriebene, Flüchtlinge, Aussiedler* (Münster 1990), pp. 37–60.

Kleßmann, C., *Die doppelte Staatsgründung: Deutsche Geschichte 1945–1955* (Göttingen 1982).

Knopp, G., *Die große Flucht: Das Schicksal der Vertriebenen*, 3rd edn (Munich 2002).

Koller, R., *Das Flüchtlingsproblem in der Staatsverwaltung: Entwickelt am Beispiel der bayerischen Flüchtlingsbetreuung* (Tübingen 1949).

Krause, C., 'Flüchtlinge und Vertriebene in Rostock – Versuch einer Situationsbeschreibung für die Zeit vom Mai bis August 1945', in M. Wille, J. Hoffmann and W. Meinicke (eds), *Sie hatten alles verloren: Flüchtlinge und Vertriebene in der sowjetischen Besatzungszone Deutschlands* (Wiesbaden 1993), pp. 148–58.

Krauss, M., 'Die Integration Vertriebener am Beispiel Bayerns – Konflikte und Erfolge', in D. Hoffmann and M. Schwartz (eds), *Geglückte Integration? Spezifika und Vergleichbarkeiten der Vertriebenen-Eingliederung in der SBZ/DDR* (Munich 1999), pp. 47–56.

Krauss, M., 'Das "Wir" und das "Ihr": Ausgrenzung, Abgrenzung, Identitätsstiftung bei Einheimischen und Flüchtlingen nach 1945', in D. Hoffmann, M. Krauss and M. Schwartz (eds), *Vertriebene in Deutschland: Interdisziplinäre Ergebnisse und Forschungsperspektiven* (Munich 2000), pp. 27–39.

Krippner, A. and S. Wiechmann, 'Diskriminierung und Ausgrenzung bis ins Grab: Flüchtlinge auf dem Friedhof Eichhof', in T. Herrmann and K.H. Pohl (eds), *Flüchtlinge in Schleswig-Holstein nach 1945: Zwischen Ausgrenzung und Integration* (Bielefeld 1999), pp. 127–48.

Krug, M., 'Das Flüchtlingsproblem im Raum Hannover (Die Altkreise Burgdorf, Hannover, Neuburg a. Rbge. und Springe) 1945–1950', in M. Krug and K. Mundhenke, *Flüchtlinge im Raum Hannover und in der Stadt Hameln 1945–1952* (Hildesheim 1988), pp. 1–81.

Krug, M., and K. Mundhenke, *Flüchtlinge im Raum Hannover und in der Stadt Hameln 1945–1952* (Hildesheim 1988).

Kühne, A., *Entstehung, Aufbau und Funktion der Flüchtlingsverwaltung in Württemberg-Hohenzollern 1945–1952: Flüchtlingspolitik im Spannungsfeld deutscher und französischer Interessen* (Sigmaringen 1999).

Kühnl, R., R. Rilling and C. Sager, *Die NPD: Struktur, Ideologie und Funktion einer neofaschistischen Partei* (Frankfurt a. M. 1969).

Kurzweg, C., *Die Vertriebenenpolitik der Liberal-Demokratischen Partei Deutschlands: Das Beispiel Sachsen 1945–1950* (Hamburg 2004).

Lattimore, B. Jr., *The Assimilation of German Expellees into the West German Polity since 1945: A Case Study of Eutin, Schleswig-Holstein* (The Hague 1974).

Lee, S., 'CDU Refugee Policies and the Landesverband Oder/Neiße: Electoral Tool or Instrument of Integration?', *GP*, Vol. 8(1) (1999), pp. 131–49.

Lehmann, A., *Im Fremden ungewollt zuhaus: Flüchtlinge und Vertriebene in Westdeutschland 1945–1990*, 2nd edn (Munich 1993).

Lemberg, E. and F. Edding (eds), *Die Vertriebenen in Westdeutschland: Ihre Eingliederung und ihr Einfluß auf Gesellschaft, Wirtschaft, Politik und Geistesleben*, 3 vols (Kiel 1959).

Lemberg, E. and L. Krecker (eds), *Die Entstehung eines neuen Volkes aus Binnendeutschen und Ostvertriebenen: Untersuchungen zum Strukturwandel von Land und Leuten unter dem Einfluß des Vertriebenenzustroms* (Marburg 1950).

Levy, D., 'Integrating Ethnic Germans in West Germany: The Early Postwar Period', in D. Rock and S. Wolff (eds), *Coming Home to Germany? The Integration of Ethnic Germans from Central and Eastern Europe in the Federal Republic* (New York and Oxford 2002), pp. 19–37.

Lüttig, A., *Fremde im Dorf: Flüchtlingsintegration im westfälischen Wewelsburg 1945–1958* (Essen 1993).

Lüttinger, P., 'Der Mythos der schnellen Integration: Eine empirische Untersuchung zur Integration der Vertriebenen und Flüchtlinge in der Bundesrepublik Deutschland bis 1971', *ZfS*, Vol. 15(1) (1986), pp. 20–36.

Major, P., The *Death of the KPD: Communism and Anti-Communism in West Germany, 1945–1956* (Oxford 1997).

Malecki, H.J., *Die Heimatvertriebenen in Niedersachsen* (Hanover 1951).

Marshall, B., 'German Attitudes to British Military Government 1945–47', *JCH*, Vol. 15 (1980), pp. 655–84.

Martens, H., *Die Geschichte der Sozialdemokratischen Partei Deutschlands in Schleswig-Holstein 1945 bis 1959*, 2 vols (Malente 1998).

Martin, H.-W., '*... nicht spurlos aus der Geschichte verschwinden': Wenzel Jaksch und die Integration der sudetendeutschen Sozialdemokraten in die SPD nach dem II. Weltkrieg (1945–1949)* (Frankfurt a. M. 1996).

Mauch, B., 'Die bayerische FDP: Porträt einer Landespartei 1945–49', PhD thesis, University of Erlangen-Nuremberg, 1965.

McGowan, L., *The Radical Right in Germany 1870 to the Present* (London 2002).

Mehlhase, T., 'Die SED und die Vertriebenen: Versuche der politischen Einflußnahme und der "Umerziehung" in den ersten Nachkriegsjahren in Sachsen-Anhalt', in M. Wille, J. Hoffmann and W. Meinicke (eds), *Sie hatten alles verloren: Flüchtlinge und Vertriebene in der sowjetischen Besatzungszone Deutschlands* (Wiesbaden 1993), pp. 159–77.

Mehlhase, T., *Flüchtlinge und Vertriebene nach dem Zweiten Weltkrieg in Sachsen-Anhalt: Ihre Aufnahme und Bestrebungen zur Eingliederung in die Gesellschaft* (Münster 1999).

Meinicke, W., 'Die Bodenreform und die Vertriebenen in der SBZ und in den Anfangsjahren der DDR', in M. Wille, J. Hoffmann and W. Meinicke (eds), *Sie hatten alles verloren: Flüchtlinge und Vertriebene in der sowjetischen Besatzungszone Deutschlands* (Wiesbaden 1993), pp. 55–85.

Melendy, B., 'Expellees on Strike: Competing Victimization Discourses and the Dachau Refugee Camp Protest Movement, 1948–1949', *German Studies Review*, Vol. 28 (2005), pp. 107–25.

Melis, van D., '"Angabe nicht möglich" – Integration statt Entnazifizierung der Flüchtlinge in Mecklenburg-Vorpommern', in D. Hoffmann and M. Schwartz (eds), *Geglückte Integration? Spezifika und Vergleichbarkeiten der Vertriebenen-Eingliederung in der SBZ/DDR* (Munich 1999), pp. 161–70.

Menges, W., 'Wandel und Auflösung der Konfessionszonen', in E. Lemberg and F. Edding (eds), *Die Vertriebenen in Westdeutschland: Ihre Eingliederung und ihr Einfluß auf Gesellschaft, Wirtschaft, Politik und Geistesleben*, Vol. 3 (Kiel 1959), pp. 1–23.

Merritt, A.J. and R.L. (eds), Public *Opinion in Occupied Germany: The OMGUS Surveys 1945–1949* (Urbana, Chicago and London 1970).

Messerschmidt, R., *Aufnahme und Integration der Vertriebenen und Flüchtlinge in Hessen 1945–1950: Zur Geschichte der hessischen Flüchtlingsverwaltung* (Wiesbaden 1994).

Mintzel, A., *Die CSU: Anatomie einer konservativen Partei, 1945–72* (Opladen 1975).

Mintzel, A. and H. Oberreuter (eds), *Parteien in der Bundesrepublik Deutschland* (Opladen 1992).

Moeller, R. G., 'War Stories: The Search for a Usable Past in the Federal Republic of Germany', *AHR*, 101 (1996), pp. 1008–48.

Moeller, R. G., 'Sinking Ships, the Lost Heimat and Broken Taboos: Günther Grass and the Politics of Memory in Contemporary Germany', *Contemporary European History*, 12 (2003), pp. 147–81.

Müller, C.-J., *Praxis und Probleme des Lastenausgleichs in Mannheim 1949–1959* (Mannheim 1997).

Müller, R., 'Von den Schwierigkeiten einer Bergstraßengemeinde im Umgang mit den Heimatvertriebenen. Dossenheim 1945–1950', in C. Grosser, T. Grosser, R. Müller and S. Schraut, *Flüchtlingsfrage – das Zeitproblem:Amerikanische Besatzungspolitik, deutsche Verwaltung und die Flüchtlinge in Württemberg-Baden 1945–1949* (Mannheim 1993), pp. 197–223.

Mundhenke, K., 'Hameln: Eine Fallstudie zur Eingliederung von Flüchtlingen 1945–1952', in M. Krug and K. Mundhenke, *Flüchtlinge im Raum Hannover und in der Stadt Hameln 1945–1952* (Hildesheim 1988), pp. 83–206.

Nahm, P., ... *doch das Leben ging weiter: Skizzen zur Lage, Haltung und*

Leistung der Vertriebenen, Flüchtlinge und Eingessessen nach der Stunde Null (Cologne and Berlin 1971).

Naimark, N., *The Russians in Germany: A History of the Soviet Zone of Occupation, 1945–1949* (Cambridge, Mass. and London, 1995).

Naimark, N., *Fires of Hatred: Ethnic Cleansing in Twentieth-Century Europe*, 2nd edn (Cambridge, Mass. and London 2002).

Neumann, F., *Der Block der Heimatvertriebenen und Entrechteten 1950–1960: Ein Beitrag zur Geschichte und Struktur einer politischen Interessenpartei* (Meisenheim 1968).

Niethammer, L., *Entnazifizierung in Bayern: Säuberung und Rehabilitierung unter amerikanischer Besatzung* (Frankfurt a. M. 1972).

Niethammer, L. and A. von Plato, *"Wir kriegen jetzt andere Zeiten"* (Berlin 1985).

Oberpenning, H., *'Arbeit, Wohnung und eine neue Heimat …': Espelkamp – Geschichte einer Idee* (Essen 2002).

Ó Dochartaigh, P., *Germany since 1945* (Basingstoke 2004).

Overmans, R., 'Personelle Verluste der deutschen Bevölkerung durch Flucht und Vertreibung', *Dzieje Najnowsze*, Vol. 26(2) (1994), pp. 51–63.

Pape, P., 'Flüchtlinge und Vertriebene in der Provinz Mark Brandenburg', in M. Wille, J. Hoffmann and W. Meinicke (eds), *Sie hatten alles verloren: Flüchtlinge und Vertriebene in der sowjetischen Besatzungszone Deutschlands* (Wiesbaden 1993), pp. 110–32.

Parius, B., 'Flüchtlinge und Vertriebene in Osnabrück und im Osnabrücker Land', in K.J. Bade, H.-B. Meier and B. Parisius (eds), *Zeitzeugen im Interview: Flüchtlinge und Vertriebene im Raum Osnabrück nach 1945* (Osnabrück 1997), pp. 13–91.

Pfeil, E., *Der Flüchtling: Gestalt einer Zeitenwende* (Hamburg 1948).

Pfeil, E., *Fünf Jahre später: Die Eingliederung der Heimatvertriebenen in Bayern bis 1950* (Frankfurt a. M. 1951).

Plato A. von, 'Fremde Heimat: Zur Integration von Flüchtlingen und Einheimischen in die neue Zeit', in L. Niethammer and A. von Plato (eds), *"Wir kriegen jetzt andere Zeiten"* (Berlin 1985), pp. 172–219.

Plato, A. von, 'Vergangene Perspektiven? Schwerpunkte, Fragen und Probleme der Flüchtlingsforschung vor und nach der Wende', in D. Hoffmann, M. Krauss and M. Schwartz (eds), *Vertriebene in Deutschland: Interdisziplinäre Ergebnisse und Forschungsperspektiven* (Munich 2000), pp. 87–107.

Pohl, K.H. (ed.), *Regionalgeschichte heute: Das Flüchtlingsproblem in Schleswig-Holstein nach 1945* (Bielefeld 1997).

Prinz, F. (ed.), *Integration und Neubeginn: Dokumentation über die Leistungen des Freistaates Bayern und des Bundes zur Eingliederung der Wirtschaftsbetriebe der Vertriebenen und Flüchtlinge und deren Beitrag zur wirtschaftlichen Entwicklung des Landes*, 2 vols (Munich 1984).

Pscheidt, E., 'Die Ansiedlung der Graslitzer Musikinstrumentenhersteller auf dem Montan-Gelände in Kraiburg', in F. Prinz (ed.), *Integration und Neubeginn: Dokumentation über die Leistungen des Freistaates Bayern und des Bundes zur Eingliederung der Wirtschaftsbetriebe der Vertriebenen und Flüchtlinge und deren Beitrag zur wirtschaftlichen Entwicklung des Landes*, Vol. 1 (Munich 1984), pp. 560–96.

Pscheidt, E., 'Die Flüchtlingslager', in F. Prinz (ed.), *Integration und Neubeginn: Dokumentation über die Leistungen des Freistaates Bayern und des Bundes zur Eingliederung der Wirtschaftsbetriebe der Vertriebenen und Flüchtlinge und deren Beitrag zur wirtschaftlichen Entwicklung des Landes*, Vol. 1 (Munich 1984), pp. 197–270.

Püschel, E. *Die Hilfe der deutschen Caritas für Vertriebene und Flüchtlinge nach dem zweiten Weltkrieg (1945–1966)* (Freiburg im Breisgau 1972).

Rauscher, A. (ed.), *Kirche und Katholizismus 1945–1949* (Paderborn 1977).

Rautenberg, H.-W., 'Die Wahrnehmung von Flucht und Vertreibung in der deutschen Nachkriegsgeschichte bis heute', *APZ,* B 53 (1997), pp. 34–46.

Reichling, G., *Die Heimatvertriebenen im Spiegel der Statistik* (Berlin 1958).

Reichling, G., 'Flucht und Vertreibung der Deutschen: Statistische Grundlagen und terminologische Probleme', in R. Schulze, D. von der Brelie-Lewien and H. Grebing (eds), *Flüchtlinge und Vertriebene in der westdeutschen Nachkriegsgeschichte: Bilanzierung der Forschung und Perspektiven für die künftige Forschungsarbeit* (Hildesheim 1987), pp. 46–56.

Reichling, G. and F. H. Betz, *Die Heimatvertriebenen: Glied oder Außenseiter der deutschen Gesellschaft?* (Frankfurt a. M. 1949).

Rock, D. and S. Wolff (eds), *Coming Home to Germany? The Integration of Ethnic Germans from Central and Eastern Europe in the Federal Republic* (New York and Oxford 2002).

Roesler, J., 'The Black Market in Post-war Berlin and the Methods Used to Counteract it', *GH*, Vol. 7(1) (1989), pp. 92–107.

Roesler, J., 'The Refugee Problem in the Soviet Occupation Zone 1945–1949', *GDR Monitor*, No. 21 (Summer 1989), pp. 1–20.

Rogers, D. E., *Politics after Hitler: The Western Allies and the German Party System* (London 1995).

Roseman, M., 'The Uncontrolled Economy: Ruhr Coal Production, 1945–8', in I. Turner (ed.), *Reconstruction in Post-War Germany: British Occupation Policy and the Western Zones 1945–1955* (Oxford 1989), pp. 93–123.

Rothe, W., *Vertrieben und angekommen: Flüchtlinge und Umsiedler in Neubrandenburg: Dokumente und Berichte aus den Jahren 1945 bis 1948* (Neubrandenburg 1996).

Rudolph, H., *Evangelische Kirche und Vertriebene 1945 bis 1972*, 2 vols (Göttingen 1984).

Rusche, M., 'Die Eingliederung der Vertriebenen in Mecklenburg-Vorpommern, dargestellt unter besonderer Berücksichtigung der Wohnraumproblematik', in M. Wille, J. Hoffmann and W. Meinicke (eds), *Sie hatten alles verloren: Flüchtlinge und Vertriebene in der sowjetischen Besatzungszone Deutschlands* (Wiesbaden 1993), pp. 133–47.

Schäfer, T., *Die Schleswig-Holsteinische Gemeinschaft 1950–1958: Mit einem Beitrag zur Entstehung des 'Blocks der Heimatvertriebenen und Entrechteten'* (Neumünster 1987).

Schieder, T. (ed.), *Dokumentation der Vertreibung der Deutschen aus Ost- und Mitteleuropa*, 5 vols (Wolfenbüttel 1953–61).

Schier, S., *Die Aufnahme und Eingliederung von Flüchtlingen und Vertriebenen in der Hansestadt Lübeck: Eine sozialgeschichtliche Untersuchung für die Zeit nach dem Zweiten Weltkrieg bis zum Ende der 50er Jahre* (Lübeck 1982).

Schillinger, R., *Der Entscheidungsprozess beim Lastenausgleich 1945–1952* (St Katharinen 1985).

Schmidt, H., *Das Vereinsleben der Stadt Weinheim an der Bergstraße* (Weinheim 1963).

Schmidt, U., '"Drei- oder viermal im Leben neu anfangen zu müssen ..." – Beobachtungen zur ländlichen Vertriebenenintegration in mecklenburgischen "Bessarabier-Dörfern"', in D. Hoffmann and M. Schwartz (eds), *Geglückte Integration? Spezifika und Vergleichbarkeiten der Vertriebenen-Eingliederung in der SBZ/DDR* (Munich 1999), pp. 291–320.

Schoenberg, H. W., *Germans from the East: A Study of their Migration, Resettlement and Subsequent Group History since 1945* (The Hague 1970).

Schrammek, N., *Alltag und Selbstbild von Flüchtlingen und Vertriebenen in Sachsen 1945–1952* (Frankfurt a. M. 2004).

Schraut, S., *Flüchtlingsaufnahme in Württemberg-Baden 1945–1949: Amerikanische Besatzungsziele und demokratischer Wiederaufbau im Konflikt* (Munich 1995).

Schraut, S., 'Die westlichen Besatzungsmächte und die deutschen Flüchtlinge', in D. Hoffmann and M. Schwartz (eds), *Geglückte Integration? Spezifika und Vergleichbarkeiten der Vertriebenen-Eingliederung in der SBZ/DDR* (Munich 1999), pp. 33–46.

Schraut, S. and T. Grosser (eds), *Die Flüchtlingsfrage in der deutschen Nachkriegsgesellschaft* (Mannheim 1996).

Schreyer, K., *Bayern – ein Industriestaat: Die importierte Industrialisierung: Das wirtschaftliche Wachstum nach 1945 als Ordnungs- und Strukturproblem* (Munich and Vienna 1969).

Schulze, R., 'Growing Discontent: Relations between Native and Refugee Populations in a Rural District in Western Germany after the Second World War', *GH*, Vol. 7(3) (1989), pp. 332–49.

Schulze, R. (ed.), *Unruhige Zeiten: Erlebnisberichte aus dem Landkreis*

Celle 1945–1949 (Munich 1990).

Schulze, R., 'Zuwanderung und Modernisierung – Flüchtlinge und Vertriebene im ländlichen Raum', in K. J. Bade (ed.), *Neue Heimat im Westen. Vertriebene, Flüchtlinge, Aussiedler* (Münster 1990), pp. 81–105.

Schulze, R., 'Alte Heimat – neue Heimat – oder heimatlos dazwischen? Zur Frage der regionalen Identität deutscher Flüchtlinge und Vertriebener – Eine Skizze', *Nordostarchiv*, No. 6 (1997), pp. 759–87.

Schulze, R., 'The German Refugees and Expellees from the East and the Creation of a Western German Identity after World War II', in P. Ther and A. Siljak (eds), *Redrawing Nations: Ethnic Cleansing in East-Central Europe, 1944–1948* (Lanham, Boulder, New York and Oxford 2001), pp. 307–25.

Schulze, R., 'The Struggle of Past and Present in Individual Identities: The Case of German Refugees and Expellees from the East', in D. Rock and S. Wolff (eds), *Coming Home to Germany? The Integration of Ethnic Germans from Central and Eastern Europe in the Federal Republic* (New York and Oxford 2002), pp. 38–55.

Schulze, R., '"Wir leben ja nun hier". Flüchtlinge und Vertriebene in Niedersachsen – Erinnerung und Identität', in K. J. Bade and J. Oltmer (eds), *Zuwanderung und Integration in Niedersachsen seit dem Zweiten Weltkrieg* (Osnabrück 2002), pp. 69–100.

Schulze, R., R. Rohde and R. Voss (eds), *Zwischen Heimat und Zuhause: Deutsche Flüchtlinge und Vertriebene in (West-) Deutschland 1945–2000* (Osnabrück 2001).

Schwab, I., *"Neue Heimat – Neues Leben"? Flüchtlinge und Vertriebene in Leipzig 1945 bis zum Beginn der 50er Jahre* (Leipzig 1999).

Schwartz, M., 'Vertreibung und Vergangenheitspolitik: Ein Versuch über geteitte deutsche Nachkriegsidentitäten', *DA*, 30 (1997), pp. 177–95.

Schwartz, M., '"Ablenkungsmanöver der Reaktion": Der verhinderte Lastenausgleich in der SBZ/DDR', *DA*, 32 (1999), pp. 397–409.

Schwartz, M., '"Vom Umsiedler zum Staatsbürger". Totalitäres und Subversives in der Sprachpolitik der SBZ/DDR', in D. Hoffmann, M. Krauss and M. Schwartz (eds), *Vertriebene in Deutschland: Interdisziplinäre Ergebnisse und Forschungsperspektiven* (Munich 2000), pp. 135–66.

Schwartz, M., '"Zwangsheimat Deutschland": Vertriebene und Kernbevölkerung zwischen Gesellschaftskonflikt und Integrationspolitik', in K. Naumann (ed.), *Nachkrieg in Deutschland* (Hamburg 2001), pp. 114–48.

Schwartz, M., *Vertriebene und "Umsiedlerpolitik": Integrationskonflikte in den deutschen Nachkriegs-Gesellschaften und die Assimilationsstrategien in der SBZ/DDR 1945–1961* (Munich 2004).

Schwartz, M., 'Dürfen Vertriebene Opfer sein? Zeitgeschichtliche Überlegungen zu einem Problem deutscher und europäischer Identität', *DA*, 38 (2005), pp. 494–505.

Seggern, A. von, *'Großstadt wider Willen': Zur Geschichte der Aufnahme und Integration von Flüchtlingen und Vertriebenen in der Stadt Oldenburg nach 1944* (Münster 1997).

Seraphim, P.-H., *Die Heimatvertriebenen in der Sowjetzone* (Berlin 1954).

Skorvan, M., *Das Hilfswerk der Evangelischen Kirche und seine Flüchtlingsarbeit in Hessen 1945–1955* (Wiesbaden 1995).

Spiegel-Schmidt, F., 'Religiöse Wandlungen und Probleme im evangelischen Bereich', in E. Lemberg and F. Edding (eds), *Die Vertriebenen in Westdeutschland: Ihre Eingliederung und ihr Einfluß auf Gesellschaft, Wirtschaft, Politik und Geistesleben*, Vol. 3 (Kiel 1959), pp. 24–91.

Steinert, J.-D., *Vertriebenenverbände in Nordrhein-Westfalen 1945–1954* (Düsseldorf 1986).

Steinert, J.-D., 'Organisierte Flüchtlingsinteressen und parlamentarische Demokratie: Westdeutschland 1945–1949', in K.J. Bade (ed.), *Neue Heimat im Westen: Vertriebene, Flüchtlinge, Aussiedler* (Münster 1990), pp. 61–80.

Stickler, M., *'Ostdeutsch heißt Gesamtdeutsch': Organisation, Selbstverständnis und heimatpolitische Zielsetzungen der deutschen Vertriebenenverbände 1949–1972* (Düsseldorf 2004).

Strothmann, D., '"Schlesien bleibt unser": Vertriebenenpolitiker und das Rad der Geschichte', in W. Benz (ed.), *Die Vertreibung der Deutschen aus dem Osten: Ursachen, Ereignisse, Folgen* (Frankfurt a. M. 1985), pp. 209–18.

Stüber, G., *Der Kampf gegen den Hunger 1945–1950: Die Ernährungslage in der britischen Zone Deutschlands, inbesondere in Schleswig-Holstein und Hamburg* (Neumünster 1984).

Tätigkeitsbericht des Hauptausschusses der Flüchtlinge und Ausgewiesenen in Bayern, 1947 (Munich 1947).

Tauber, K., *Beyond Eagle and Swastika: German Nationalism since 1945* (Middletown, Conn. 1967).

Theisen, A., 'Die Vertreibung der Deutschen – Ein unbewältigtes Kapitel europäischer Zeitgeschichte', *APZ*, B 7–8 (1995), pp. 20–33.

Ther, P., 'The Integration of Expellees in Germany and Poland after World War II: A Historical Reassessment', *SR*, Vol. 55(4) (1996), pp. 779–805.

Ther, P., *Deutsche und polnische Vertriebene: Gesellschaft und Vertriebenenpolitik in der SBZ/DDR und in Polen 1945–1956* (Göttingen 1998).

Ther, P., 'A Century of Forced Migration: The Origins and Consequences of "Ethnic Cleansing"', in P. Ther and A. Siljak (eds), *Redrawing Nations: Ethnic Cleansing in East-Central Europe, 1944–1948* (Lanham, Boulder, New York and Oxford 2001), pp. 43–72.

Ther, P., 'Expellee Policy in the Soviet-occupied Zone and the GDR: 1945–1953', in D. Rock and S. Wolff (eds), *Coming Home to Germany? The Integration of Ethnic Germans from Central and Eastern Europe in the Federal Republic* (New York and Oxford 2002), pp. 56–76.

Ther, P. and A. Siljak (eds), *Redrawing Nations: Ethnic Cleansing in East-Central Europe, 1944–1948* (Lanham, Boulder, New York and Oxford 2001).

Thränhardt, D., *Wahlen und politische Strukturen in Bayern 1848–1953* (Düsseldorf 1973).

Tormin, W., *Die Geschichte der SPD in Hamburg 1945 bis 1950* (Hamburg 1994).

Trittel, G., *Die Bodenreform in der Britischen Zone 1945–1949* (Stuttgart 1975).

Trittel, G., 'Von der "Verwaltung des Mangels" zur "Verhinderung der Neuordnung": Ein Überblick über die Hauptprobleme der Wirtschaftspolitik in der Britischen Zone 1945–1949', in C. Scharf and H.-J. Schröder (eds), *Die Deutschlandpolitik Grossbritanniens und die Britische Zone 1945–1949* (Wiesbaden 1979).

Trittel, G., 'Die *Sozialistische Reichspartei* als Niedersächsische Regionalpartei', in B. Weisbrod (ed.), *Rechtsradikalismus in der politischen Kultur der Nachkriegszeit: Die verzögerte Normalisierung in Niedersachsen* (Hanover 1995), pp. 67–85.

Turner, I., 'British Occupation Policy and its Effects on the Town of Wolfsburg and the Volkswagenwerk 1945–1949', PhD thesis, University of Manchester, 1984.

Turner I. (ed.), *Reconstruction in Post-War Germany: British Occupation Policy and the Western Zones 1945–1955* (Oxford 1989).

Unger, I., *Die Bayernpartei: Geschichte und Struktur 1945–1957* (Stuttgart 1979).

Varain, H.J., *Parteien und Verbände: Eine Studie über ihren Ausbau, ihre Verflechtung und ihr Wirken in Schleswig-Holstein 1945–1958* (Cologne 1964).

Viewegh, T., 'Die Plassenburg – ein Vorzeigelager?', in R. Endres (ed.), *Bayerns vierter Stamm: Die Integration der Flüchtlinge und Heimatvertriebenen nach 1945* (Cologne 1998), pp. 21–53.

Wachs, P.-C., *Der Fall Theodor Oberländer (1905–1998): Ein Lehrstück deutscher Geschichte* (Frankfurt a. M. 2000).

Waldmann, P., 'Die Eingliederung der ostdeutschen Vertriebenen in die westdeutsche Gesellschaft', in J. Becker, T. Stammen and P. Waldmann (eds), *Vorgeschichte der Bundesrepublik Deutschland: Zwischen Kapitulation und Grundgesetz* (Munich 1979).

Weiher U., *Flüchtlingssituation und Flüchtlingspolitik: Untersuchungen zur Eingliederung der Flüchtlinge in Bremen 1945–1961* (Bremen 1998).

Weisbrod, B. (ed.), *Rechtsradikalismus in der politischen Kultur der Nachkriegszeit: Die verzögerte Normalisierung in Niedersachsen* (Hanover 1995).

Wennemann, A., 'Flüchtlinge und Vertriebene in Niedersachsen: Vergangenheitsorientierung und Strukturwandel', in K. J. Bade (ed.), *Fremde im Land: Zuwanderung und Eingliederung im Raum Niedersachsen seit dem Zweiten Weltkrieg* (Osnabrück 1997), pp. 77–124.

Wiesemann, F., 'Erzwungene Heimat: Flüchtlinge in Nordrhein-Westfalen', in G. Brunn (ed.), *Neuland: Nordrhein-Westfalen und seine Anfänge nach 1945/46* (Essen 1986), pp. 163–73.

Wille, M., *Die Vertriebenen in der SBZ/DDR: Dokumente*, 3 vols (Wiesbaden 1996–2003).

Wille, M., 'Die Vertriebenen und das politisch-staatliche System der SBZ/DDR', in D. Hoffmann, M. Krauss and M. Schwartz (eds), *Vertriebene in Deutschland: Interdisziplinäre Ergebnisse und Forschungsperspektiven* (Munich 2000), pp. 203–17.

Wille, M., 'Compelling the Assimilation of Expellees in the Soviet Zone of Occupation and the GDR', in P. Ther and A. Siljak (eds), *Redrawing Nations: Ethnic Cleansing in East-Central Europe, 1944–1948* (Lanham, Boulder, New York and Oxford 2001), pp. 263–83.

Wille, M., J. Hoffmann and W. Meinicke (eds), *Sie hatten alles verloren: Flüchtlinge und Vertriebene in der sowjetischen Besatzungszone Deutschlands* (Wiesbaden 1993).

Winkler, Y.R., *Flüchtlingsorganisationen in Hessen 1945–1954: BHE – Flüchtlingsverbände – Landsmannschaften* (Wiesbaden 1998).

Wolff, S., 'Introduction. From Colonists to Emigrants: Explaining the "Return-Migration" of Ethnic Germans from Central and Eastern Europe', in D. Rock and S. Wolff (eds), *Coming Home to Germany? The Integration of Ethnic Germans from Central and Eastern Europe in the Federal Republic* (New York and Oxford 2002), pp. 1–15.

Woller, H., *Die Loritz-Partei: Geschichte, Struktur und Politik der Wirtschaftlichen Aufbau-Vereinigung (WAV) 1945–1955* (Stuttgart 1982).

Woller, H., *Gesellschaft und Politik in der amerikanischen Besatzungszone: Die Region Ansbach und Fürth* (Munich 1986).

Zayas, A. de, *Nemesis at Potsdam: The Expulsion of the Germans from the East*, 3rd edn (London 1989).

Ziegler, W. (ed.), *Die Vertriebenen vor der Vertreibung: Die Heimatländer der deutschen Vertriebenen im 19. und 20. Jahrhundert: Strukturen, Entwicklungen, Erfahrung*, 2 vols (Munich 1999).

Ziemer, G., *Deutscher Exodus: Vertreibung und Eingliederung von 15 Millionen Ostdeutschen* (Stuttgart 1973).

Index

Note: 'n.' after a page reference indicates the number of a note on that page. Page numbers in *italic* refer to illustrations.